THE TEXANS

What They Are—And Why

THE TEXANS

What They Are—And Why

By DAVID NEVIN

BONANZA BOOKS · NEW YORK

For Luciana,
Who put a turtle on my desk

ACKNOWLEDGMENTS

Grateful acknowledgment is made to the following for permission to use the material described below:

Mrs. Zora Sterling of Corpus Christi, for quotations from *Trails and Trials of a Texas Ranger,* by her husband, the late William Warren Sterling, former Adjutant General of Texas, copyright 1959 by William Warren Sterling.

Little, Brown and Company and Robert J. Kleberg, Jr., of the King Ranch, for quotations from *The King Ranch,* by Tom Lea, copyright 1957 by the King Ranch.

University of Texas Press and Mrs. Terrell Maverick Webb, for quotations from *The Texas Rangers,* by Dr. Walter Prescott Webb, copyright 1935 by Walter Prescott Webb and 1965 by Terrell Maverick Webb.

The Texas Observer Co., Ltd., for quotations from *The Texas Observer,* issues in 1958 and 1965.

Time, Inc., for a quotation from *Fortune,* November, 1961.

Tree Publishing Co., Inc., and Champion Music, Inc., both of Nashville, Tennessee, for quotations from "Walk Out Backwards," by Bill Anderson, Copyright 1960 by Tree Publishing Co., Inc., and Champion Music, Inc.

The source of all quotations is clearly marked in the body of the work.

FOREWORD

I am a Texan and I have lived much of my life in Texas. I learned my craft on Texas newspapers. Now that I must live and work away from Texas, I find my perceptions and understandings oddly heightened when I go home to visit. So this book has been in latent process through much of my life and all of the people who helped me learn and grow have helped this book, and to them I owe gratitude and respect.

Many people have helped me quite directly and have taken part in the material in this book, as their places in its pages testify, and to them I am grateful. There are a few more who must be mentioned specifically. There are my parents, Col. Stanley McLeod Nevin, U.S.A. Rtd., and Mrs. Mary Reinhardt Nevin, who took me to Texas in a wicker basket when I was two weeks old and who, each in his way, instilled in me a permanent affection for the written word. There is Joel Westbrook, now of Waco, from whom, over many years, I learned things of value about Texas and about living. There is Holland McCombs, now of Dallas, with whom I sat through a long, cool, quiet afternoon in the coffee shop of the Menger Hotel in San Antonio and talked out the ideas that were to become the basic theme of this book. There is David Witts of Dallas, who appears importantly herein but who in addition has given me rare insights into the root Texas; my son, David Z. Nevin, who described an incident in the desert; David Roberts of San Antonio, who generously shared his reportage; Henderson Shuffler of Austin, whose humor combined with his sensitive historical grasp helped me put the present into perspective; Trammell Crow of Dallas, a humanist by nature and a businessman by choice, who helped me relate business in Texas to the whole of Texas life; Joe Alford of Dallas, who made the oil business in Texas real and understandable; George Fuermann of Houston, for a certain view of his city; Don Jackson of New York, for the use of his unpublished manuscript on Lee Harvey Oswald; Richard Balmos of San Antonio, for the story, told so many years ago, of Matilda Friend, and Dr. E. S. James of Denton, for permission to draw on his splendid sermon.

Finally, of all the people who helped, the most important was my wife, Luciana Colla Nevin, a Texan who first came from Italy, who pondered every word and every thought herein, who was involved day by day and step by step in the thinking, analyzing, agonizing, and rewriting, and who thus shared fully in the pain and the pleasure of its creation.

D.N.

Byram, Connecticut
April, 1968

THE TEXANS

What They Are—And Why

CHAPTER

I

1

The pilot was a country boy from West Texas, big and broad and very hard, with hands like rocks and mean little eyes in a wide, flat-planed face that was marked by the sun. He would be bad in a fight because he would kick you after you went down; he wore cowboy boots with heavy heels and he would call it stomping and he would enjoy it. He had seen dude ranchers before, out of the city and bound for their places in the desert, seen them come and go, seen some of them leave a trail of unpaid bills.

"I don't take no credit cards," he said. "I don't take no checks." He stood at the counter at the Midland airport, his voice as flat as his face. His new twin-engine aircraft stood outside, sleek in the brilliant sunshine.

David Witts got angry. He is a roundish man, husky and dark, and the blood came up in his face with a curious blackening. "What do you take?" he asked. "Would cash do?" The charge was $160. Witts dropped a hundred and a fifty and a ten on the counter. The pilot picked them up and led the way outside. He acted as if nothing had happened.

Witts and his partner, Carroll Shelby, had come out from Dallas and were going on to their Terlingua Ranch. Everyone got in and the pilot fired his engines and put his aircraft down the runway and into the air. His big country hands were easy on the controls. Shelby was riding beside him and after a while they began to talk and then Witts leaned forward and joined them. Witts and Shelby had been wartime pilots and they talked airplanes. They were smiling easily. Everyone acted as if nothing had happened and perhaps nothing had. It was cool at altitude and the plane was comfortable.

Below, the land looked hard and dangerous. It was a dry hardpan, baked brown, with clumps of sage and tumbleweed and here and there a dust devil spinning into the sky. The ranch lay 200 miles ahead, in the open desert along the Mexican Border, tucked into that great curve of the Rio Grande that is known as the Big Bend. The ranch is called the Terlingua for a little ghost town of that name which lies on its lands and it covers 220,000 acres of country that is as wild and raw as any in the nation.

Both Witts and Shelby grew up bone poor in Texas during the 1930s and for both the image of real success is to own a ranch. This is true of many boys who grew up in the Texas country and admired the rancher with his shiny boots and his pearl buttons and the harsh crack of command in his voice, and it goes far beyond the equally valid fact that ranches are the best tax shelter in America today and nearly mandatory for a man who is making a great deal of money in a short time. Witts, a man of great tension leavened with good humor, operates a thriving law firm in Dallas. As soon as he began making money, he started buying land on a series of shoestrings. The Terlingua was his third spread and by far the biggest and most important, and for a time before he got on top of it and the pressure began to ease, it stretched the shoestring taut as rawhide. Shelby is a lean man, just off-handsome, with a wide, engaging smile. Driving in striped farmer's overalls, he grew famous in international automobile racing not only for winning but for his casual and somehow elegant air. For years he dreamed of making a U.S. competition car and this led to the sleek bomb he called the Cobra and thence to a multi-

2

million-dollar manufacturing plant in Los Angeles. Beneath his easy manner and his Texas accent and grammar, he is a razored businessman. But his emotional image of success still is land. Witts handled portions of Shelby's legal business and one day in an airport over a drink they fell to talking about land and land hunger. "Hell," said Witts after a while, "why don't you take half my Terlingua spread?"

Shelby calculated less than a minute. "Okay," he said, "done." They shook hands on a deal that involved about a million dollars apiece. Their accountants would work out the fine adjustments later. They ordered another drink to celebrate Shelby's entry into the cattle-ranching business and began to plan their joint future.

Beneath the plane, the empty land slipped by. Much of the United States is checkerboarded, man-marked with the plow. But this land was untouched—hunted over, perhaps, grazed over, fought over, but never broken. It is poor on its surface and rich in its depths: the plane passed over an old oilfield, derricks long dismantled but the pumps still busy. It was like a ghost city, straight roads running neatly to each cleared pump site, all laid out in orderly rows. It was so big that one end faded into the aft horizon before the plane cleared the other end, and in that stretch there was not a single person. Nothing moved but the walking beams of the pumps, rocking steadily like a thousand iron donkeys gravely feeding.

The land began to rise into hills that were preparing to become mountains. There were mounds and then small volcanic peaks thrust from the ground in perfect cones. The mesas appeared, their tops flat, their cliffsides sheer, whole pastures thrust hundreds of feet into the air all at once. The draws were deep gashes in the ground, for the rain in this country, when it finally comes, is as violent as the heat and the wind and, in its way, the emptiness. They were hacked twenty, thirty, forty feet deep with sheer sides that powder and slide when they're dry and slick and slide when they're wet, and it is death to be trapped in one when the water comes down. Only a fool pauses long in a draw.

The glare coated the land in a sunshot mist. It looked a place for goats, perhaps, or prairie dogs or coyotes or even wolves, but not for men. The plane passed into real mountains, flying at 8,600 feet in bumpy air, shuddering and slipping over the bare rock ridges that stood close below. It passed Cathedral Peak for which the Cathedral Ranch is named, crossed Doubtful Canyon, so named, they say, because if you get lost, it's doubtful you'll get out, spanned the famous 0 2 Ranch which is operated by Lykes Brothers, the steamship company, and runs down flush to the Terlingua. Then the plane crossed into the Terlingua itself with miles of ground yet to go and the men began searching the valleys for sight of the ranchhouse and the dirt landing strip.

Now the ground was sere brown to dull red to orange, fired by centuries of sun until it looked like the inside of a kiln. It was made up of countless planes and angles, draws and cliffs and ridges and mesas and flats, and through it all wound a most improbable creek, its sandy bed stained dark by the winding damp. The land was etched and worked by the wind, dirty, dry, cruel, unyielding, dangerous. An untrained man placed here alone probably would die. There is an odd excitement about this fact, for only the plane, itself flimsy and easily downed, stands between man and an ultimate testing of his resources. Except in the finality of death, civilized man rarely perceives an ultimate; here it is thrust upon him and it is as if the bindings of civilization and thus of restraint are loosening.

In the plane, the men were eager and excited. They come here rarely, but nevertheless, they were coming home. A water tank passed below, bright as an emerald in the brown-burnt dirt, a windmill turning beside it. "That tank's on our ranch, Carroll," Witts said. "I put in that mill. More water than when we saw it last." Off to the side was a hill uncannily shaped like a woman's breast, nipple rampant. Shelby winked. "Squaw Tit Mountain," he said.

Up ahead, in a jagged blue bank thrown across the plane's path lay the Chisos Mountains, standing almost 8,000 feet, beautiful and dark and wild. They are the heart of the Big

Bend National Park, along the north border of which the ranch lies. The ranchhouse and the strip appeared below and the pilot put his aircraft sharply over and down and roared directly over the house, his propellers pitched to rasp against the silent desert. The house was a plain stone structure with a metal roof, a windmill standing nearby, animal pens and a big corral in which several horses milled uneasily at the plane's noise. A man came out of the house and got in a green car and drove toward the strip.

The plane made another pass over the dirt runway and a herd of goats ran in every direction, hardy, skinny little animals with border collies yelping and snapping behind them. The pilot watched the puffs of dirt their sharp hoofs threw up and read the wind direction.

The strip ran deceptively uphill. The pilot came in hot and high and used up half the runway before he touched down at better than 100 mph. The roll-out was very fast and up ahead boulders and big cactus plants marked the end of the runway. In a firm, hard voice, Shelby said, "Use your brakes," and the pilot, knuckles suddenly white, jammed those boots against the brake pedals and the plane slowed, bucking on its long tricycle gear. It turned flush at the end of the strip and rolled back to the point where the old green car had stopped.

A heavy man with a round, kindly face got out. He was wearing glasses and he had a sweat-stained hat with a big brim shoved on the back of his bald head, so that a fringe of gray hair showed. He wore scuffed boots and khakis and a heavy leather belt with a huge buckle won at some forgotten rodeo these many years ago, and his big belly hung precariously over that belt. This was Harold Wynne, sixty-two years old, the ranch foreman, a genial but natively tough man who carried easily the responsibility for the daily operation of nearly a quarter-million acres of land.

Shelby thrust open the plane's door and stretched. The air was cooling and it felt good to be down with the motors stilled. He grinned at Wynne.

"How're you, you old fart?" he said.

Wynne smiled. "Hello, Carroll," he said rather gravely. He looked pleased, as if he had been complimented, and in the terms of the place, he probably had.

It was startlingly dry and the men's feet made puffs of dust and the wind blew them away. The ground was rocky and hard and nearly white. Now the mountains seemed to tower all around. The Chisos were blue in the distance and the setting sun caught the minerals in those close by and showed red and tawny and sometimes black and gradually the shadows grew deep. The scattered goats wandered back through the knee-high greasewood, hardy creatures with pot bellies who could forage on the slopes of hell. This was a cattle ranch and no one was proud of goats, but desert ranchers cannot be choosers.

A cowboy named Boots, his face burned dark as an Indian's, began loading the men's gear into a pickup truck. The pilot, his little eyes expressionless, shook hands all around as if everyone had become business associates and perhaps even friends and then he got into his plane. It went down the runway quickly and jumped into the cooling air. It swung north over the hills, glinting in the evening sun, abandoning the raw country and returning to the slick city where it belonged, and on the ground its noise died away and left the country sounds and a certain loneliness.

The ranchhouse was stone, built by men for men, solid but tasteless. Audra Wynne, Harold's wife, a gentlewoman with a sweet smile, perhaps more quiet than usual in the presence of the owners, met them at the door. As the dark fell down outside she brought them to her table, sagging in the way of the country—potatoes and corn and green beans and tomatoes and lettuce and *cabrito* and venison and beef and milk and tea and coffee and biscuits and honey and rich white gravy and apple pie and toothpicks.

There was whisky on the deal table in the big room and after dinner the men went there to drink and talk. Witts, however, took vodka in canned grapefruit juice and Wynne, a little distrustfully, joined him. Wynne has lived in this country all his life, ranching and riding its empty hills as a peace officer.

6

He likes to talk, as do most men in a lonely country, for there is little other entertainment and stories are important; they need not be true, but they should be interesting.

". . . there was eleven of us and now they're all dead but me; the Mesicans had raided us and we decided to hit 'em back. We rode into Mexico at dawn, waded the river, and by noon we was pretty deep in and we heard a thunder up ahead and there came forty outlaws riding us down. It was Canderio Vasquez' bunch and I figured there'd be a massacre *dee*-luxe. Well . . .

". . . so I come up on his blind side and I jabbed him in the ribs with a forty-five and his Adam's apple jumped up and down like the clapper on a bell . . .

". . . when we used to pack hunt in the Chisos, years before it all become a national park, there was this fellow who'd finish his dinner in a hurry and come over to our campfire and mooch some of ours. One night we mixed up a big stew of scraps for the dogs and had it ready when he got there. He asked for a plate and we give it to him and about the time he'd finished, the owner of the dogs walks up and looks in the pot and says, 'Now who the hell's been in them guts and lungs and such I was boiling for the dogs?' and the fellow who'd eaten the plate got up and puked in the greasewood and he never mooched no more dinners . . ."

Shelby laughed and laughed. He poured himself another drink and put his feet on the table. "By God," he said, "it's good to be on your own place. What we need around here is a little music."

Wynne said, "That cowboy, Boots, he plays a mean guitar."

"Hell, send for him," Shelby said. "Let's have some music."

"He lives a good piece, in an old house on the other side of the ranch. I'll have to send a hand for him. And he might be gone to bed by now."

Shelby hesitated, but Witts, a curiously set look on his dark face, said, "He works for us? Get him over here."

Boots came in carrying a cheap guitar. He was a small man, about thirty, body lean and hard, clean-shaven, wearing scrubbed and faded jeans. Boots had earned his living with that guitar, playing at country dances around West Texas, and then he had started his own little band and played one-night stands all up through New Mexico and beyond and the pressure and the travel and the honkytonk ways caught him and he started drinking whisky and now he was cowboying, eighty miles from the nearest town and his fingers were stiff with rope and reins.

But he had a drink and another and he picked away at the guitar and he began to warm a little. Shelby swings from Los Angeles to Paris and points between in the international racing crowd, but he has not lost his taste for the old country music and his foot kept gentle time. Boots' voice grew as he remembered words and tunes and presently it came full, a sort of falsetto whine riffled with anguish, and he sang, "I've Got A Hangover Heart From Your Kisses Last Night." It was corny, but it expressed the simple emotions by which people live—and in the desert country, where human contact is infinitely more precious, this little man with his mournful slender face and his sad eyes and his songs of broken love seemed entirely valid.

"Get after it, Boots," Wynne said loudly. He poured another drink, more vodka and less juice, and his face was beginning to flush. He slapped his leg and grinned.

Boots bent his head and riffled the strings. " 'I'd rather live a life of lies and fantasy than face the truth and realize you're leaving me . . . so walk out backwards if you must go and please don't wave goodbye—just wave one last hello . . . just walk out backwards and I'll think you're walking in . . .' " * The men roared with laughter and it was impossible to tell from Boots' face what he was thinking. "My God," Wynne shouted, "he's my *segundo!* He works like a dog all day and plays like that at night." And then he shouted, "Get after it, Boots, get after it. Or I'll fire your ass tomorrow!"

But David Witts had stopped drinking. He looked uneasy and irritated. Time was wasting and hands were drinking and

* From "Walk Out Backwards" by Bill Anderson, copyright © 1960, by Tree Publishing Company, Inc., and Champion Music, Inc.

he didn't like either. Shelby didn't care, but then, Witts runs the ranch. He bought his first ranch seven years earlier, a lovely little place of about 1,000 acres in the rolling Hill Country near Lyndon Johnson's beloved LBJ Ranch. He only put $1,000 down and he bought a herd for nothing down. He bought a pair of gaudy orange boots to wear with one pantleg tucked inside. Now those boots were taking on an honest look, scuffed, their orange glow dulling; now he runs, all told, more than half a million acres in three widely separated ranches of which the Terlingua is the most important. He operates it all from his law office, a handsome corner room in a downtown Dallas office building, and only rarely is he actually able to visit the ranch. Out on the ground itself, however, Harold Wynne has no difficulty at all in perceiving who really runs the Terlingua. "David," he says simply, "doesn't really understand."

By his own definition, Witts is a scrambler. He is one of those men of prodigious excess energy; to walk with him is to dogtrot and he attacks elevator buttons with an angry jab. He has been scrambling ever since he finished World War II with everything he owned tucked into a B-4 bag, went through law school with honors, opened a practice and started dabbling in business and then in land. But nothing had prepared him for the magnitude of the Terlingua. The ranch stood then at about 140,000 acres at about $10 an acre and he saw no possibility that he could swing it. But the idea amused him and he began to push and maneuver and bang and whipsaw and although the asking price held firm, the down payment began to shrink and the terms to expand and when it was all done, the ranch cost David Witts $20,000 in cash money—and he borrowed that from the bank. He agreed to pay $25,000 a year for three years and then $100,000 a year to the finish. "That three years gave me room to move," he said, "and that's all a scrambler needs." Now he had a vast stretch of land on which there had been no active ranching in so many years that the very signs of man were sinking back into the desert. There were hundreds of miles of fence to string, miles of road to cut, wells to be drilled, tools and buildings and, of course, stock to buy. Witts bought a thousand head of cattle at $150 each, ten per cent down and ninety from the bank, because banks will lend on walking stock and they won't on fences and windmills. He put Harold Wynne on the ground and he began ranching the Terlingua.

If Wynne has no doubts as to who makes the Terlingua work, neither does Witts, sitting in his office in Dallas and maneuvering to meet the huge payments of interest, principal and improvements. He whipped the Terlingua by himself, set it up and got it moving, made it work and prosper, and now it is part of him. When Shelby came in, the battle already was won and it simply meant things could go faster with more capital. They bought another 80,000 acres that bordered the main ranch, drilled more wells, strung more fence.

There in the ranchhouse that night, as Boots sang on to the desert's loneliness, Witts keyed down slowly, relaxing, thinking about the Terlingua. "This is an empire," he said. "It was cheap enough to buy and big enough to work. It's got grass. I've found water all over it. If I can get irrigation wells, I've got 40,000 acres of bottomland never cut by a plow that soil testers say is as good as the Imperial Valley in California. The winter weather is just like Palm Springs and we've got a complete ghost town we can turn into a resort. There are old mercury mines there and a company wants to reopen them. They've found sulfur on adjoining property and we've probably got some too. Probably got oil. Got a little bit of gold. Got the world's biggest supply of candelaria wax [a wax of great purity used in industry and taken from a small plant that looks like marijuana and grows in the desert]. And when I get a stand of Johnson grass going, I can run five thousand head of cattle." He sat up straight, his eyes snapping with enthusiasm, his dark face flushed. "Man, this is an absolute empire—and the mortgage is down to hardly more than a million."

2

By daylight, it had the look of empire. The air at dawn was sharp as crystal. Harold Wynne came out of the ranchhouse and got into his blue four-wheel-drive pickup truck. Its engine made an alien sound amidst the wind sound and the animal sound of the ranch. He drove out of the yard, past the corral and the pens, the truck rattling over the cattle-guards. The road, which he had cut from the desert soil with an old yellow bulldozer, wound away from the buildings and into the hills. The truck climbed and rattled and spat stones from under its tires. At a high spot Wynne stopped and got down to survey the land.

The sun climbed and bled away the gentle morning colors. It stood in a sky washed nearly white with glare. The glare spread over the whitish, alkali land and in the shadow under the five-inch brim of his straw hat, Wynne's eyes sank deeper into their sockets. The wind droned hot across hundreds of miles of dry land with nothing to slow it or break its way. Its noise, the feel of it in the ears and the eyes, the relentless pressure of it is always on this land. The sky above Wynne was huge and open and he could see to every horizon. The air was so dry and light and clear that even peaks that were blue in the distance seemed at once near and yet endlessly far. In all the distance that Wynne could see, nothing moved except a single steer on a far slope and the restless flutter of the grease-wood in the wind. A man Wynne knows, who has surveyed much of this country, summed it up one day: "There's places up here where you can see the whole world."

Wynne's boots were already dusty. The ground was hard but powdery dry and shot with little stones. The grass grew brittle as straw in bluish clumps the size of two fists with bare ground from a foot to a yard all around. Stem for stem, this is some of the most nutritious grass in the world, but there aren't many stems. Greasewood grows everywhere, bright to the eye and sour to the spirit, a bushy little plant of the evergreen family that avidly takes what moisture and strength the land has and gives nothing in return. Sometimes it is called the creosote plant and it drips a venomous fluid onto the ground; it is so bitter that no animal, not even goats or deer, will eat it. But when it rains in the desert a sharp, pungent, rather dry odor comes from the wet greasewood. It is a clean and bracing smell and it excites the desert people, perhaps because it bespeaks itself of rainwater, which is always a delight in the desert.

There are cactus plants of endless variety, but the real measure of this country is the tasajillo—a small, bushlike cactus with two-inch thorns. These thorns have a loose brownish husk that makes them look blunt and innocuous, but inside that husk is a graceful needle with some of the spring and sharpness of surgical steel. When a man rides into it, it will drive through his boot clear to the bone and it will carry its husk with it. It will slip out as easily as a needle—but it will leave that husk deep in the wound to fester and pain for months.

And the sun comes down like flame. It sears and shrivels the plants until, like the needles of cactus, they can cast no shade. It browns the rocks and heats the air and weathers the men who live here. They wear ventilated hats with wide brims and long-sleeved shirts but the sun cuts through to the flesh. Their sweat pours out but it dries before they can feel it and the evaporation produces an illusory coolness. So there is an element of dry-eyed comfort as the body fluids drain away and, for those who are unwary, certain sunstroke approaches.

The blue truck went on, soaring on pastures that sloped up to meet the sky, shuddering down into ragged draws with the thorns of the cat claw shrieking on its sides. Once it flushed a band of whip-legged little deer; they flashed out of sight, floating in graceful bounds with their white danger flags flying. An armadillo walked in the truck's path, believing himself impervious in his prehistoric armor, and Wynne, not wishing to shatter that illusion, slowed carefully. Empty as it looks, the land is full of wildlife. The deer compete with the cattle for grass. Mountain lions come up from Mexico to hunt and coyote and fox still run in the brush. The wolves are gone and the great mountain sheep are hunted out and the eagles that can spiral out of sight into the sky are going. But big black-winged hawks still seek mice and rock squirrels and prairie dogs, and the scavenging vultures still ride the swirling thermals with their curious telescopic eyes focused on whatever moves below. There are no mosquitoes and few flies, but scorpions wait under rocks with a two-inch stinger that will swell a man's hand as big as a ham and can kill a child. Black tarantulas with thick furry legs move steadily across this land, sometimes alone, sometimes by the hundreds of thousands until the land itself seems to blacken and shimmer.

The truck stopped at a windmill that stood beside a round concrete water tank and Wynne got out. The mill turned steadily in the driving wind and though it was small, up close its galvanized steel blades made a loud whirring noise and the whole machine gave a surprising sense of power. The tank, five feet high and twenty across, was half full of water. A bright red snake about four feet long lay motionless in the water, head and tail hanging down toward the bottom in the attitude of death with only his bloated mid-section afloat. He had come out of the desert in search of the water that even a snake must have, and managed in some impossible way to mount the sheer sides of the tank and had fallen in. Then, of course, there was no way out and finally the snake had begun to succumb to the vast irony of drowning in the middle of the desert. Wynne found a long stick and hooked it under the inert body—and at the touch, the little head jerked out of the water and weaved, looking for the enemy, its little tongue darting out. It was dying, but it was still prepared to fight. With a sudden lifting motion, Wynne flung it twenty feet from the tank. It landed with a wet *thwack* and lay there motionless, the ground around it wetted by its fall.

"I drilled this well," Wynne said. "I drilled 28 wells since we started ranching this spread [in 1962] and I never hit a dry hole yet. David Witts said he wanted wells for water for the cattle to drink—you can't raise stock without any water at all— and he sent the drilling contractor out from Alpine. Drilling contractor says, 'Well, Harold, where you want me to drill?'

"I cut me a branch from a greasewood bush and held it in both hands and went to divinin'. Never done that before, but I heard it worked, and it did. Pretty soon that branch turned down hard and I said drill right here. He did and he hit water at 170 feet. There'd never been no water in this country. Nobody ever thought to drill wells—it was too dry and ugly-looking. Another day a geologist was out here with David and he got to looking scientifically and picked out a spot for a well. The contractor got down to two, three hundred feet and didn't hit, so I cut me a greasewood branch and walked around and about a hundred yards from the rig I found a strong water indication. So I told him to move that rig over and he did and he hit water at 160 feet."

Divining successfully for water fascinated Wynne. It was like discovering a new power. Now, over a proven water supply, he demonstrated proudly. He stripped a greasewood plant down to a fork and held it sprung up in reverse between his two hands in such a way that the natural spring of the wood made it want to come down. Then he walked across the land, an odd, big-bellied figure in boots and khakis and a wide-brimmed hat with the branch flared up in front of him, and after a while, it turned down sharply. He put it in the hands of a visitor who walked the same path and at the same place felt the branch twist down. It had stood until then against its natural inclination, and then it twisted irresistibly down.

"Water, that's what done it. You walked over a water vein and it twisted right out of your hand. It would have done that if you hadn't known there was water there. That's how I found all the wells," Wynne said.

He walked back to the tank. The snake was gone. There was no mark of his passage on the hard ground. He had revived and slipped away and the air had dried the water drops and it was as if he had never been. "Well, I'll be damned," Wynne said mildly.

He had come to inspect the cattle. They are lean, rangy animals with springy legs, spotted and brindled in every color and more than half-wild. When it is time to move them to another pasture where the grass has improved, Boots and the other hands saddle up and ride after them. A single pasture in this country may cover 10,000 acres and the cattle spread all over it in their search for grass. The men wear heavy chaps to guard against the thorns. They circle the pasture's edges to get the herd moving, hurrahing gently lest the bulls decide to stand and fight. Sometimes the mavericks balk. A big steer can turn in an instant and hurtle away and then the cowboy stages a frantic race. If he loses, the steer shoots up a canyon and the cowboy must go after him and engage in a hot little fencing match as he tries to get around him and drive him back to the herd. The cowboy carries a canteen to ward off heatstroke but rarely bothers with food, and for the whole day, galloping, shouting, breathing the dust of a thousand hoofs, he drives the cattle for miles to the new pasture. He calls it "chousing" them, and Wynne watches this closely and with displeasure. The more they are choused instead of gently induced to walk along the more pounds they drop and Wynne is in the business of raising pounds of beef.

When the blue truck stopped, the cattle had begun moving hopefully toward it, for in times of extreme drought Wynne sometimes forks hay from the back of this truck for supplemental feed, and this is not the sort of thing that cattle forget. They were Mexican scrub steers, spotted in every color and knock-kneed, a far cry from the splendid blooded Herefords, square blocked, their hair a bright curly red, that Witts keeps on the other ranches. Wynne had bought 600 steers in Mexico, average weight 375 pounds. He would sell them soon at more than 500 pounds, and at 25 cents or more a pound, he would clear more than $20,000 for this herd. The daily weight of the ranch rests squarely on Wynne. He buys and sells the cattle. If they sicken, he treats them. He locates the wells, guides the fencing (in the first four years he installed 225 miles of fencing at $600 a mile), decides when and how much to feed the cattle. He builds the herd through careful selection, supervises the ranch purchases and watches its supplies, hires its new hands and disciplines its old hands. It is up to him, every day, to make the Terlingua go.

He fired the truck's engine and the cattle turned away in

disappointment. The truck rolled on, through the next pasture and the next and the next. It passed a shipping pen and came upon what had been the headquarters of a small working ranch before it was absorbed into the Terlingua. The pens and the barn stood empty. The rude cabin was partly collapsed. There was no sign of life and the truck did not stop.

There is a peculiar sense of aloneness on the ranch. In all the winding miles he drove, Wynne did not see another human being. He did not meet a vehicle. When he stopped the truck, he left it squarely in the middle of the road; no one would be coming. That assurance of aloneness was exhilarating, as if in the absence of the direct pressure of the rest of humanity— pressure almost always upon us—a man could expand and grow bigger and stronger. And then the truck topped a final ridge and there below lay a highway, an asphalt strip with a line down the center, Texas Route 118 from Alpine to the Big Bend National Park. The truck wound down the last hill, went through the last gate and onto the sudden smoothness, and everything was changed. That stripe in the center meant civilization, the rules of society which say that things must be orderly in order to be possible. Then the magic of the open land was gone. There were no cars in sight, but on such a road, man is not alone.

Wynne was not, however, off the ranch. The state highway bisects the ranch, but the land on either side is the Terlingua's and up ahead lay the town of Terlingua, which the ranch owns in its entirety. Presently a dirt road forked from the highway beside an incongruous sign urging tourists to visit Terlingua and Wynne turned off and followed it in.

Terlingua is a ghost town. For half a century its mercury mines supported some five hundred people. The mines flooded in 1940 and were closed and the people moved away. The streets on which they lived are still plain, lined by mounds of adobe crumbling back into the desert from which it came. The sun glares white on the alkali soil and there is no shade nor even a saving touch of green and soon the eyes begin to ache. Except for the wind, there is no sound or motion among these houses where once there was so much life, where in defiance of the desert children were born and old men died and couples made love in the night, and there is a feeling of death—or perhaps it is just a denial of life—which is eerie and disturbing. Or maybe it is just that the desert won.

The mine shafts are still open under their collapsed wooden frameworks and a pebble dropped in falls in long silence before it announces with a faint splash that the water is still there. The mine offices are open, too, the records littering the floor. There are letters and grocery orders and tally sheets and canceled checks dating back to the 1890s, the ink fading but the paper still fresh in the dry air. There is a shell of a movie house and a tiny jail with a metal roof in which prisoners must have had their sins baked out long before the courts could act, and overlooking it all on a hill is a house that once was handsome and strong, with a breeze-swept gallery from which a man could look beyond the Rio Grande, into the hills of Mexico.

There is only one whole building left, the Terlingua Inn. Carl Hearn rents it from the ranch, operates it and lives in it. It has a single big public room with a bar at one side and a juke box on the other and upon entering it there is an immediate sense of coolness and comfort. It is the only public place for miles, and it lures beguiled tourists and thirsty men in search of beer and both stay for lunch and the extraordinary cornbread that Hearn makes in black skillets and serves with every meal.

Wynne, in effect the landlord, stopped his truck in front of the inn. He walked in, put a quarter on the bar, took the beer that Hearn opened and stood talking sociably. Hearn fitted the desert. His face was a mottled red and his voice was low and slow. He might have lived his whole life in Terlingua. In fact, however, he had been there only about a year. He was a driller of oil wells by trade and had worked on drilling rigs all over the world. It sounded exotic and fascinating, but the reality of it was simple loneliness. The only person in the world whose company he really wanted was his wife, Bobbie, and working overseas meant leaving her for months and even years.

"I was so lonely," he said, "I just sort of hurt all over. I was always looking for some way I could come home and stay. I came back from Venezuela in 1958 with $31,000, most money I ever did have. I went up to Odessa and got in the spudnut [doughnuts made of potato flour] business and one year later I was broke and on my way to a drilling rig in Dhofar, Arabia.

"I remember I come to town and got me my cookers and my mixers and I got a building and paid the lease and bought a couple little Volkswagen trucks for deliveries and got my counters and my stools and all the things I needed to sell the spudnuts, and when I got it all done, the banker said to me one day, 'You know, a man's a damn fool to go into the spudnut business here. This ain't a spudnut town. This is a beer town!' So I says to the banker, 'I sure wish you'd told me that 'fore I got in the spudnut business!'"

Someone asked Hearn why he had picked spudnuts, meaning, of course, why hadn't he invested in something he understood. He looked completely guileless. "Well," he said, "I wanted something where I could stay home and be with my dear little wife." He stood by the table as Wynne ate, glad for the chance to talk. "You know, on my twenty-second wedding anniversary I was in Dhofar, Arabia, 750 miles out in the desert from Aden, and I'd been there for eight months on a rig. I woke up at three in the morning on my wedding anniversary and I wrote my little wife a letter and I still remember it." He leaned on the table and in a soft, singsong voice he recited the entire letter, which was in the form of doggerel and not very good doggerel at that. But its need and its anguish were real and its loneliness matched the loneliness of the desert outside; when he had spun out the whole long poem there was silence and he stood there with a beatific smile, remembering, and then he said, "You want another beer, Harold?"

As Wynne was leaving, his hat pulled down against the white glare outside, he paused at the counter. He picked up a lifeless-looking plant, one of several for sale. It was a dull brown, fernlike, perhaps of the evergreen family, a tightly curled clump the size of a fist that once had lived in the desert. "This looks dead, doesn't it?" Wynne said. "But it ain't. It's just hibernating. Put that in water and it'll turn bright green." Hearn produced a saucer of water and Wynne floated the plant. Immediately it drew water up and began to uncurl and soon a flush of green appeared and crept down its leaves. "After a while the whole thing will get green and pretty as can be," Wynne said. "We call it the resurrection plant."

3

The little black bull with no horns bowed his neck. His shoulder muscles ridged. Tension came in the air and a hundred cows stopped their cropping and watched. He snorted. A somewhat larger red bull with mean, stubby horns approached him meaningfully from one side. Wynne said, "That black bull is tough. Even with the horns bred off him, he can take the red bull." The red bull paused, glaring. The little black bull, anger coming up hot as the desert wind, swung ponderously to face him and in an instant the red bull thought it all over and changed his mind. He snorted hastily to establish his courage and then he backed carefully away and the black bull relaxed and the cows began to feed.

The Terlingua Ranch lies in Precinct Four, Brewster County, Texas, and while it may be trite to say it, the fact is that Precinct Four of Brewster County, Texas, is bigger than the entire state of Rhode Island.

It has less than one hundred registered voters. These voters were individually important to Wynne because at this time he was running for county commissioner from Precinct Four. Every Texas county has four precincts, and the four commissioners, with the county judge, govern the county. Wynne, with the new-found dignity of operating the biggest ranch in the county, was challenging the incumbent of fourteen years, a man who had spent considerable effort in cultivating the voters.

Wynne had been a ranchman all his life, but he had been many other things, too. He had been a deputy sheriff and a special ranger and a manhunter; before there were paved roads in this country, before there was a Big Bend National Park, he had ridden these lonely hills for weeks at a time in search of men who lived on stolen cattle. In those days he had developed an acerbic tongue, a quickness with his fists, a skill with the gun, and he had made enemies. Now he was out cultivating friends and politicking in the special way of this country. He already had given two barbecues, with spicy roast goat and a steer from the Terlingua and tubs of beer and an old friend, now a special agent for the Texas Liquor Control Board, who had come down with his shotgun and kept everybody friendly. Wynne hadn't made any speech; that might seem pushy; he had just mingled with the crowd and told stories and solicited their votes.

Politicking is a very low-key affair in this country. These are a lonely and individualistic people. They do not think of themselves as a massed electorate and would resent being treated as one. They prize their vote and they expect to be solicited properly. There are, after all, few enough opportunities for visiting. Wynne traveled the entire precinct in the blue pickup and when he found a little group of people he would stop and get out and tip his hat to the ladies and shake hands with the men and talk a little. They would talk about the weather and the dryness and the price of cattle; about a deer someone had shot, a horse someone had traded, a woman someone had married. And Wynne would say, "I guess you've heard I'm running for commissioner . . . I'd sure appreciate your vote." Pain would strike their faces that he would even mention it: Why, Harold, of course . . .

Courtesy is endemic here, perhaps because the penalty for discourtesy can be so violent. Of course, just to see a human face in a lonely land is a pleasure that gentles anyone's voice. But it also is true that a desert man's domain is land and animals over which he exercises absolute authority, and that becomes his habit. He is not used to being crowded and he is proud and quick to resentment. As it once did everywhere in Texas, trouble out here leads readily to fists and even gunfire.

As the blue truck rolled on, someone asked Wynne if he

thought the people with whom he had just visited really would vote for him. "Well," he said hopefully, "they said they would." Only natural optimists survive in politics. Night had fallen on the candidate's rounds and up ahead the lights of the store at Study Butte shone in the dark. Study Butte appears on maps as a tiny town, but it seems to consist of no more than a weathered frame store building set back from the highway and a cluster of sagging houses. No lights showed in the houses; a single bulb naked in the store pierced the night and as the truck turned in a dog began to howl.

"We'll have a beer," Wynne said. He cleared his throat. "I don't drink much. I remember the night David and Carroll were down and we had Boots in singing—why, I got downright drunk that night. I was right embarrassed the next day. That stuff David was putting in the juice—vodka, was it?—must have been pretty strong. It sure snuck right up on me."

Actually, Wynne is a handy drinker, as his arrest record amply demonstrates over a couple of pages: "Drunk, Drunk & Disorderly, Drunk & Affray, Drunk & Assault," spread over the years and over the state, the documentation of a man who could put away a dozen bottles of beer at a sitting and feel called upon, from time to time, to defend his honor. Yet in a sense the vodka had crept up on him, because Wynne drinks as a countryman: drinking is not a social matter, done at home; it is a celebration, when a man goes to town after a long dry spell, knocks back his dozen bottles of beer in a tavern and kicks up his heels.

The truck rattled and shook in the ruts that led to the Study Butte store. It was a desperate building with none of the presence of the Terlingua Inn, its unpainted sides ground gray in decades of sun and wind, its floors splintered and scarred. It was a grocery, general store and bar. In one corner a filthy monkey huddled pitifully in a cage. In the opposite corner two men and a woman, approximately as unattractive as the monkey, sat at a table with the pattern of their drinking recorded in rows of empty beer bottles. The storekeeper greeted Wynne, and one of the men at the table teetered his chair back on its rear legs and called, "Harold, I hear you're running." He was a big man, taller and heavier than Wynne and somewhat younger. He wore scuffed boots and dirty khakis and a sweat-soaked hat on the back of his head. A lock of heavy hair fell down to his eyes and his face was spongy. He was perhaps half-drunk.

"That's right," Wynne said.

The woman said in a shrill voice, "Why, I believe I won't vote for either one. T'other is a friend of mine, you know that, but I couldn't vote against Harold."

The man had both hands on the table. He was grinning in a way that was arrogant and insolent and Wynne turned fully to face him. "Well, goddammit," he said, "I'm going to vote for Harold. He's the best damned man around!" He paused, slyly. "Only man better'n Harold, by God, is me!"

Wynne stood in the middle of the store and his neck seemed to bow slightly. There was a sudden tension in the room, a silence that seemed to ring, and the woman's eyes were bright. The moment came and went. The other man spoke for the first time, his voice soft and friendly. "We're with you, Harold . . ."

The campaign roughened in its closing days. Wynne's arrest record was widely discussed. It seemed more serious at this particular time than it had before or would later. Rumors were started against him. A pamphleteer attacked him in print. But Wynne remained hopeful, his image of himself unimpaired, and so he was unprepared for the disaster of the election. When the votes were counted, his opponent had eighty-two votes. Wynne had eight.

It was a smashing blow, but Wynne did not permit it to crush him. "I am surrounded by liars and thieves," he wrote David Witts, and he continued to go to the Terlingua Inn and drink a companionable bottle of beer and show his face. He remained friendly enough, but it no longer was necessary to cultivate voters and that certainly had a bearing on what happened at Carl Hearn's big Fourth of July barbecue.

Wynne took a brace of goats to the Terlingua Inn, and he and Hearn barbecued them in a lather of savory sauce, and people in dusty boots and wash-faded jeans came from miles around to celebrate. When the *cabrito* was gone, everyone began drinking beer in earnest and the jukebox wailed with the anguished tunes of lonely people in lonely places and the dancing started. Wynne himself swung first this lady and then that about the room, his big boots thumping, and soon the whole building was shaking. And he laughed and hurrahed his friends and drank a dozen bottles of beer.

One of the guests was a heavily muscled man who was very drunk. He was somewhat younger and a good sixty pounds heavier than Wynne. Hearn tried to persuade him to be quiet, but he wandered about the room colliding with people and tables. Wynne sat at the bar watching and when the man approached him, Wynne said in a suddenly sharp voice, "He's trying to get you to do what's right. Now you settle down or I'll beat your ass. And you know I can do it, don't you?"

Surprisingly, the man nodded and staggered across the room to the front door and onto the veranda. A group of his friends stopped him and Wynne could hear them cursing. He walked out onto the broad porch and in the group gathered there was a man who had said things before the election which Wynne thought inexcusable. He was a slender, gray-looking man, perhaps a few years younger than Wynne but also somewhat lighter. Now he looked at Wynne and dislike flamed in his face. "What are you doing out here, you son of a bitch?" he said.

"You shouldn't have said that," Wynne said, and hit him in the face. The man flew off the veranda and sprawled in the gravel on his shoulders and Wynne ran down the steps. The man rolled over and came up and Wynne hit him again and knocked him down. Blood streaked down his face. Someone turned on the lights of a truck so that everyone could see. A crowd gathered on the veranda.

The man got up and made for Wynne in a rush and Wynne caught his shirt front in his left hand and hit him in the mouth with his right in one snapping motion and the man went down on his face. Blood glistened on the gravel. He pushed himself up, poised a moment and lunged. Wynne heard anger in the crowd's muttering from the veranda and he knew it was time to finish it. The man took a wild punch at Wynne's head and Wynne stepped to his left and drew the man in close and put his whole body behind a right-hand punch. The man's head snapped back. Blood sprayed red in the truck's headlights. The man's boots cleared the ground and he landed on his back like a grain sack and his body dug a furrow in the gravel. Wynne waited a moment to see if he would move and when he didn't, Wynne went back inside the Terlingua Inn with his hand aching and sat at the bar and had another beer and he kept saying, "A man shouldn't come and eat my goat meat and then talk to me that way."

4

This is open, empty country. Wynne can stand on a mountain-top on his own land and in a certain direction, the farthest peak he can see, bluing in the distance, is still on the ranch. There are hundreds of miles of fence to ride and countless canyons where the cattle can hide and there are bear and deer and mountain lion and coyote and fox and in all this reach of land he will not see another man except for his own cowboys. He stops his truck in the middle of the road; he leaves the keys in the ignition. He is alone—and should he see a stranger, it probably means trouble.

The ranch is the biggest spread in Brewster County, and the ranchhouse is seventeen miles from the highway. Only recently did electricity come that distance and still more recently a telephone. It is a full eighty miles from the county seat at Alpine, where a sheriff and a deputy headquarter, and in all that empty eighty miles, even today, there is no real law but what a man can provide for himself.

Sitting at supper on the Terlingua, David Witts wore clothes and boots that were scuffed, but on his wrist was the small, flat watch reminiscent of his rich corner office in Dallas and his silk suits. He listened to Wynne talking about the not so very long ago days when life was cheap and Mexicans' lives were even cheaper.

"You know," he said, "the layer of civilization is pretty thin on all of us. I found that out in the war—it isn't hard to kill when you believe your cause is right and it's the custom of the time. It wasn't hard to drop bombs.

"Out in this country, your city notions peel away. Out here you take care of yourself and of your land. No one else will— no one else can. We've only had a telephone a few weeks. Now I suppose we could call—but as a practical matter, we couldn't expect help till sometime the next day. And anyway, in this kind of country you can't operate a ranch this size by calling for help all the time."

He fell silent at his table, remembering the difficulty of getting the ranch and then of keeping it, of reclaiming it from the desert and improving it, of meeting its financial demands. The blood came up to blacken his face and in an entirely different tone of voice, he said, "I'll tell you this—anyone coming on my land can look to get killed."

When Witts bought the Terlingua in 1962 and asked Wynne to take charge, it had not been operated as a working ranch for years. Its fences were down or had never been built. It had few roads and they were impassable. Its buildings were collapsed. Even its boundaries were indistinct. Before Wynne agreed to take it he rode every acre on horseback, camping at night in the open, cooking his meals on a fire and sleeping in a bedroll he carried lashed behind his saddle.

He looked at everything and calculated—the fencing, the roads to be cut, the wells and the buildings that would be needed. When he was finished he went back to Alpine and called Witts in Dallas and agreed to take over. Then he rounded up a fencing crew and building supplies and a bulldozer with which to open the roads. But before he did anything else, he had one paramount task.

Because the ranch had not been operated or fenced in so many years, men all through that country had fallen into the habit of using it as open range, grazing their herds on its land, freely hunting its deer. Wynne drove for miles, notifying everyone he could locate that real ranching was starting on the Terlingua again and that it no longer would be open range. "I'll respect everyone's pastures," he kept saying, "and I want them to respect mine." Eventually, of course, he was challenged. In a desert store with a dozen men listening, a big, rawboned man in sweat-marked khakis said evenly, "By God, Harold, I reckon I'll ride where I please."

A flinty look came over Wynne's normally rather benign face. "Now you listen to me," he said, and everyone did. "I used to be a right good shot, I expect some of you remember that, but I've gotten to be mighty pore these days, mighty pore. Now, any man comes in my pastures, I'm gonna shoot his horse out from under him. But I'm such a pore shot that I'm liable to miss the horse and hit him. Might just shoot him. You understand what I mean?"

They understood. They knew Wynne would ride the Terlingua with a .30 caliber carbine butt-up in an oiled saddle boot and they knew he would shoot. And they knew that when he did the community would judge him right, and so they stayed off his land. It is basic to the frontier that a man protects his land and his cattle with gunfire if necessary. The frontier is still close in Texas and occasionally, in places of real isolation, it still exists.

CHAPTER

II

It was a handsome office, done in the rich royal blue of expensive rugs and drapes and the muted gold of good wood furniture. It lay in a corner of the ninth floor of the Southwest Tower in the city of Houston, a full six hundred miles from the lonely country of the Terlingua Ranch and much further still on the spectrum of difference. The handsome sign outside the office door and facing the elevator bank said The Pennzoil Company; inside, the men who run this modest but thriving oil company, the handsome and rather debonair Brothers Liedtke, Hugh and Bill, who had started their careers sixteen years earlier as beginning lawyers, were at the end of months of secret planning. In small, innocuous lots, from brokers all over the country, they had been purchasing stock in United Gas Corporation, a powerful company roughly nine times the size of Pennzoil. Already they held 275,000 shares, with just under $10,000,000 invested. That, however, was only the beginning, because now they intended to take over United Gas. It was a move of startling audacity. They rechecked their plans and their forecasts, smiled and nodded and decided: they would go all the way.

In the balmy winter sunshine outside, the towers of Houston

reared above their ninth-floor suite of offices. Houston is the sixth biggest city in the nation. It is by far the fastest growing city in America except for Dallas, which edges it by a mere percentage point. It is the nation's third seaport. It calls itself the world capital of the oil and gas business. Its buildings leap up at the sky in pellmell competition, each soon to be eclipsed by another. It is a comfortable city, with pleasant restaurants and clubs. Its Warwick Hotel, with marble, carved wood, statuary, rugs, tapestries lifted intact from failing European castles, is genuinely elegant and comfortable as well, all done in surprisingly good taste. Outside the Warwick are leaping fountains, which, though some sophisticated Houstonians shake their heads, do grace the city. Across the street in a grove of lovely liveoaks is Houston's exciting Museum of Modern Art. A half-century-old symphony orchestra is merely one of the residents of a new forty-million-dollar complex of buildings devoted to the arts. Another is the J. S. Bach Society, which despite the esoteric nature of its programs usually fills the house. The Alley Theater is one of the best off-Broadway groups in the nation and lands big foundation grants. The Texas Medical Center with its cancer hospital and its artificial heart research is one of the nation's great medical groups. The most esoteric of all man's scientific endeavors, manned space flight, originates here and there are two major league teams and one of the world's more unusual stadiums. Houston is, in short, a genuine city—not merely a collection of people living together for this reason or that, or simply a center point for lines of commerce and communication, but a city with a life and a spirit of its own. In fact, Houston is the new Texas.

As such it is a natural setting for that group of youngish, tough, sophisticated and moneyed swingers who rather set the tone for Texas today and of whom the Brothers Liedtke are valid if somewhat new members. In a sense, at least, this group is the new aristocracy of Texas, grounded in business and finance rather than land. There never has been an aristocracy grounded in intellect in Texas, if there was one anywhere in the country, and there is little room in the Texas power structure for writers, professors, artists or others without money and a stake in business. President Johnson recognized this very early in his political career, which is the real significance of his acquisition of wealth, a significance Eastern writers tend to misunderstand. To be fully a power in Texas takes money and there are few exceptions. Now, to be clear about it, this new swinging aristocracy and the old-line moneyed power structure of Texas intermingle and coexist and sometimes duplicate but they are not one and the same and some of the most powerful men in Texas are hardly swingers. Aristocracy and power, however, need not be the same; and it is a characteristic of this new aristocracy that while it requires money because it requires a style of living that is expensive, money nevertheless is not the criterion for acceptance. Rather, the criterion is manner and attitude.

The money which powers this group is new money, rarely more than second-generation money, but the group's approach to it is modest and calm. They have made outmoded and unfashionable the gaucheries that once marked Texas; the time is over for the importing of 50,000 camellias to decorate the wedding lawn, of Harold Byrd's brassy parties after the Texas-Oklahoma football game every October, of entire trains taken to Hollywood for capers with film figures.

They are a handsome people, then, this new aristocracy. Grace David, who draws her money from oil and for pleasure operates a pretty little bookshop in Houston dealing only in rare volumes, cries breathlessly, "Oh, they're just the funnest of the fun people!" Her phraseology hardly fits her dignified books, but it does rather fit the group itself. They are fun to be with. They have fun themselves. In fact, the thing that makes them not only acceptable but even sought after in New York and San Francisco and all over Europe is that they live not just well but vigorously, potently, with élan and spirit.

They often are physically good-looking people. The men carry themselves lightly and well. They are tailored to advantage and they tend to be lean, hard, clear-eyed. They are likely to have dropped golf and polo for handball and tennis, fashionable games that require less time. Most of them have pools at home and use them regularly. They are tanned winter and summer because they follow the sun. They enjoy good food and good whisky, but rarely to excess. Their women can be superb, slender and studiously finished, the end product of the best of the hairdresser's and the cosmetician's arts, wearing the gowns of the great designers and the jewels of the great houses. They demonstrate a certain suppleness of personality, an easy ranging from graciousness to friendliness. Their counterparts in the East might find some of them too much—too fine a gown too casually worn, too many jewels, too easy a personality—but this, of course, is finding fault with the place and the time, with the proximity of these people to their own frontier.

They enjoy comfort. Their homes are handsome and well appointed, though only occasionally lavish. Often they maintain a ranch, partly because a certain orientation to the land remains, partly because it is a mark of prestige, partly for the tax write-off. Their ranch places tend to be comfortable too, with pools, air-conditioning, hunting cars and landing strips for their airplanes. Most of them maintain airplanes and they are turning to small jets; Bill Liedtke once remarked, perhaps not entirely in jest, that upon arriving at an affair, he felt faintly abashed to see Pennzoil's old DC-3, itself a considerable airplane, surrounded by the sleek jets.

Whether by their own aircraft or the commercial jet-liners, they travel constantly. Trips to Europe are casual. They fish in the Bahamas, shoot in Ireland and Africa, ski in Switzerland and in Vail, Colorado (a resort practically made with Texas money), and sun in Acapulco. They put together a pipeline deal in Australia, come back by way of Saudi Arabia, stop at Venice for the galleries and in Spain for some hunting, and on their way home, pause in New York for a party, the theater, and a conference with the bankers.

These are city people. The roots of Texas power grow surely from the land, but power today is in the cities. These men live in the cities, work in offices, fly from one city to another, exercise on the city's courts, play in the city's salons; going to the country, even to their own property in the country, is an outing.

Their cachet, oddly enough, is a limited form of culture. They have the money and they take the time to develop active interests. Most of them are well educated, often in the East, and a few have developed active intellectual pursuits: archeology, history, oceanography, languages. Culture in general is weak in Texas, though there are strong theater and music groups, and several excellent art museums. It is in the private collection of art, however, that the group shines, and it is almost a sure admission to its midst to be a serious collector. Many of its members come to collecting for its prestige or its investment value, but almost everyone, in the end, learns to enjoy what they collect because they are collecting beauty and beauty has its own passion. So in time they become skilled, they specialize in certain areas that affect them more powerfully, they haunt the galleries in New York and Europe. Some send agents overseas to purchase for them; sometimes a dozen or two dozen will combine to commission an agent who searches for finds in their particular areas. Some simply decorate their homes and their offices; for a few collecting becomes a way of life and their homes take on the tone of private museums, with great painting and sculpture mingling with the work of new young artists who may be great tomorrow. They are people of high intelligence and great capacities, and they become first knowledgeable and then intense and finally fascinated with the subject and begin assembling important collections.

They can be gay, these people with their taste for culture and travel and the pleasures of the world, for *jalapeñas* and *mariachis* and *fiesta*, but in sum, they are serious people. They are concerned. They are good parents rearing good children. They pump money into charities and private schools that interest them. They develop and run clean nonpartisan city governments and they are active in state and national politics.

Their seriousness, in fact, points up their most important collective flaw, which is the complete seriousness with which they regard themselves. This may grow from their very newness, which reduces perspective and in turn makes humor unappreciated and perhaps even threatening. They have almost no capacity to laugh at themselves. The expression of an ironical view of their society produces only cold stares. To be less than totally approving and totally serious about their basic excellence and intrinsic rightness somehow constitutes an attack, and they gird themselves to repel such attacks as they would bandits approaching their money. The result is a rigidity of attitude that denies the ranging freedom of real thought. It denies intellectuality. And the fact is that although there are genuinely fine minds among them and even occasional intellectual brilliance, they are not an intellectual people. Even their cultural interests focus primarily on the arts of the senses and not of the mind.

A society of closed intellect generates a rather one-dimensional and not very forgiving view of its fellow men. The people of the new aristocracy work hard for their towns and their charities, but one cannot help the feeling that they do so more as a matter of *noblesse oblige* (and because it is good for business) than out of affection for the clay of mankind. They are political conservatives, oriented to the needs of business, and if they are not really rightwing in the hard terms of, say, the Birch Society, neither do they have much sympathy for those people at the opposite end of the financial spectrum from themselves or much patience with the efforts of those people to improve things. Texas is not a socially enlightened state and it is this new aristocracy, by virtue of intelligence, education, culture, and position, that could change that. But, despite the efforts of some individuals, collectively it does not do so.

Challenging its social conscience raises the question of its size. Is this group truly significant, or is it merely a handful of colorful, swinging, somewhat self-centered people? Inclusion in such a group is arbitrary, of course; the names of obvious members spring to mind, but listing them is pointless because there are no real leaders. It really is just a group of people who to a greater or lesser extent, depending on the individual, live along these patterns. The core group, limited for no other reason than the real wealth the ultimate extension of such living requires, probably is only a few hundred. But peripheral people, who share some phases of the life and the attitude, may well run into the thousands. For one of the basic points of Texas is that no artificial barriers are imposed on what a man is capable of doing by himself.

The new aristocracy, then, is a wide-open society that leaves everything to the individual. Mere money alone is not enough, but money only ten minutes old is quite acceptable provided its owner has life and charm, a sense of propriety and responsibility to the community and its charities, at least some feeling for culture or a willingness to acquire feeling and a certain openness of spirit. As Holland McCombs, who is one of the great long-term observers of the Southwest, has said, "Five to ten per cent are horse's asses who slip in, of course, and not a bad ratio at that, but the rest are genuinely solid people."

And the other criterion is that they must work hard, for their community, their projects, and even their country perhaps, but most certainly and most importantly for themselves. Because wealth here is new it tends to be concentrated so that individuals often have vastly more money at their command than what would be considered real wealth in the East. But they do not relax and live on it; the life of either the playboy or the coupon clipper is frowned on; there are a few of these, otherwise entirely acceptable, but somehow they do not seem to survive at the top levels. For these are a hard, active people. They are the new Texans, the counterpart of the people who broke the land, and they are breaking new fields in business and commerce and building, and they are entirely serious about it. The old tool was the gun and the horse, the rope and the plow and the branding iron. The new tool is capital and the guts to use it. Capital came to Texas in the form of huge pools of oil and oil made everything possible. The people use capital not so much for manipulation and advantage as for building, growing, booming off in many directions. Nor is it even that they have so much money but rather that they have learned how to get money and how to use it, how to shove all the chips into the pot with a steady hand and a clear eye and go for showdown in the toughest game left in America today. That, in simple terms, is what Bill and Hugh Liedtke did that afternoon in the Pennzoil offices on the ninth floor of the Southwest Tower in Houston when they finally made their move.

That was in November of 1965. Both men were in their early forties, originally children of frontier oil but now well conditioned by the East and the new sophistication. They were born and reared in Tulsa, one of the great oil centers, where their father was divisional counsel for Gulf Oil. That has a staid, corporate sound today, but in the 1920s the oil business everywhere was young and wild and men made fortunes this year and busted out the next. Out of this exciting ambience, the two young men went back to the staid, solid Ivy League for training at Amherst in Massachusetts. Both served as naval lieutenants, junior grade, in the Pacific during World War II and, according to a story they tell, they met briefly on Saipan and agreed then to go into business when the war was done. As it was for a great many other young men of the time, Texas was a natural starting place. They took law degrees at the University of Texas; Hugh, the older, finished first and earned a graduate degree from the Harvard Business School while Bill finished at Texas. And then they opened a law practice in Midland, Texas.

Midland already was a boomtown. With its slightly larger sister city, Odessa, it lies near the center of the Permian Basin, a great circular pattern of oil fields some 250 miles across. This is West Texas desert country, dusty, brown, crackling dry—but deep under the barren surface, it is wet and black with oil. No single field in the Basin compares with the great East Texas Field that changed the entire nature of oil in America, but altogether, the Basin supplies more than a tenth of the nation's oil production. This was cattle country originally, and Midland and Odessa were rutted little towns. A visionary erected a twelve-story office building in Midland and, then went broke while everyone snickered and called it "the batroost" because it was so consistently empty. As field after field came in all around and the pipelines were laid to bring the oil and gas out efficiently, Odessa was a little nearer to the action and so drew the blue-collar workers and the yards that handled pipe and pumps and heavy drilling rigs. But Midland had that office building, and since oilmen have a near-paranoiac need to cluster so they can watch each other and deal together, Midland became the business and the banking center. Odessa grew up rough and bawdy—a beer town, as the banker told Carl Hearn on the eve of his spudnut venture. By comparison, Midland had clean fingernails and office pallor, but it also had the money and the control. More buildings began to go up beside the old veteran. Suburbs of handsome homes appeared. Eastern development money poured in and with it came bright young Ivy Leaguers, war veterans, men who had proved their own capacities in combat and were unwilling to wait on the old-fashioned patterns of slow seniority in the East. They were looking for action, for a booming place where their only limits would be their own capacities, and they found it in Midland. They saw no reason, however, to give up the amenities they had known at home. An excellent theater group began to grow, started by a man with a pioneering streak of his own and an affection for the desert climate. A symphony orchestra took shape. A luxurious tennis club—a social step above, surely, the old country or golf club—took shape with special screens to block the constant driving wind. The population went from 9,000 in 1940 to 21,000 in 1950 to 60,000 in the late 1950s. At one point Midland had more millionaires per capita and more office space per capita than any other city in the world.

It was in this hustling world, at the beginning of the postwar boom, that the Liedtke brothers opened their law firm. It was not very successful. Bill has said since, "We spent most of our time getting divorces for our friends' maids and not getting paid for it." But almost immediately they switched to oil. New fields were opening in Scurry County and they began dealing in leases as agents for friends of their father's in Tulsa. Soon they were in it on their own, buying, selling, trading, leasing, drilling and eventually acquiring production property. It was risky, tenuous, infinitely exciting, rich with rewards for those who were brave and lucky, ready with disaster for those who weren't.

Liedtke & Liedtke grew and grew. Midland was growing too, and one of the men leading the pack was another Ivy Leaguer, George Bush, son of Senator Prescott Bush, Democrat of Connecticut. In 1953, the Liedtke brothers and Bush (who now himself is a Republican Congressman from Houston) formed Zapata Petroleum Corp. They capitalized it at one million dollars; the Liedtkes raised half of that in Tulsa and Bush raised the other half in New York. Liedtke has been quoted as saying the stock "was worth seven cents a share" at that time. They had planned to spend their capital in several oil fields, but then the Jameson field broke in Coke County and they plunged. They finished their dealing with 125 producing wells—and their stock boomed up to twenty-three dollars a share.

Flushed with success, they opened Zapata Offshore Drilling Co. with heavy investments in drilling rigs that would bore for oil in a hundred feet of water and more. Here—if you had the capital to go after it—was the last great oil frontier in the United States. In the Gulf of Mexico, the continental shelf extends out from shore at gradually greater depths for hundreds of miles before it falls into deep ocean, and theoretically there is reachable oil under all that shelf. Zapata's first rig was the Scorpion, costing three and a half million dollars; in a lovely fancy flight, they named their second, equally valuable, the Vinegarroon, after a West Texas variety of scorpion. In 1954, the Liedtke-Bush companies had $500,000 gross revenues and $180,000 net revenue; three years later, income was $6,700,000 and net revenue was $600,000. Things were coming along.

Eventually they separated; Bush took the offshore portion and moved to Houston, and the Liedtkes operated Zapata. By

1960 they were in a cooperative drilling program with the South Penn Co., a Pennsylvania firm that marketed the retail oil called Pennzoil and was one of the original Rockefeller companies that made up the old Standard Oil Company until the Supreme Court ordered it dismantled. South Penn was a bigger firm than Zapata, but its management was old and tired and Zapata's was young and fresh. South Penn offered Hugh Liedtke its presidency. Instead, after preliminary moves, the two firms merged in 1963 with the two Liedtke brothers in control. They renamed it the Pennzoil Co. and moved it to Houston. In Pittsburgh it had been a staid and careful company; in Houston it ran like a dynamo, for Hugh Liedtke was the man, as an observer later said, "who knew how to make it walk." He had a surplus of cash. He purchased 150,000 shares of Texas Gulf Sulphur at eighteen dollars a share as an investment and after that company's fortuitous strike of zinc, copper, and silver at Timmins, Ontario, sold out at forty-eight dollars for a profit after taxes of almost $3.4 million. He acquired a pipeline to add to those Pennzoil already operated. He repurchased 170,000 shares of Pennzoil for about ten million dollars to firm the company's position. For another ten million dollars he purchased the outstanding third of a California subsidiary. He tried to merge with Kendall Oil (the Securities and Exchange Commission blocked him) and did acquire Wolf's Head Oil, as one of a total of eight mergers or acquisitions Pennzoil made in this hyperactive period. Liedtke closed 7,400 "unproductive wells" and streamlined the operation, and by 1965 Pennzoil's profits had doubled and its stock had split two for one.

And it was fun, too. The Liedtkes had opened their handsome offices in Houston, ordered comfortable homes from excellent architects, flown their DC-3 all about the country, become intimates of powerful politicians, fished in the Bahamas, played in the mountains, indulged in tennis and theater and parties and pleasure. And all that year of 1965, they were preparing for the next move.

United Gas Corporation of Shreveport, Louisiana, was a big,

old-line producer and distributor of oil and gas. It had huge assets and great potential, but over the years it had grown lethargic. It had not developed much of its reserves. It had gas transmission lines from Pensacola to the Mexican Border but it was losing customers. Its officers had become social powers in Shreveport, a small and provincial city, and they obviously were comfortable and complacent. They owned a pitifully small amount of stock in their own company, 14,560 shares in total, and they seemed to regard their position more as a trust than as a call for aggressive management. As a result, profits were steady but on a plateau at a time when other utility companies were highly profitable. United Gas stock had reflected this situation: it had been at thirty-five dollars for months, and had not been over thirty-nine dollars in four years. Stockholders were generally disgusted.

And all the while, the Liedtke brothers, lean and hungry, were looking for something for Pennzoil to swallow. Eventually they fixed on United Gas. It was, as *The New York Times* noted after the fight was well engaged, somewhat like a mouse trying to swallow an elephant. United Gas was about nine times the size of Pennzoil. There are other figures, however, that bring the situation into better perspective. United Gas income for the previous year was only five times that of Pennzoil—and its earnings were only slightly more than twice those of Pennzoil.

So the Liedtkes decided to take United Gas and as a vehicle they chose a method that is becoming increasingly popular, the cash tender offer. It is simple, clean, direct. An offer is made to buy a company's stock at well above the market price provided a sufficient number of shares are tendered to the buyer. A sufficient number is whatever the buyer needs to take control. The old proxy battle, in which the newcomer tried to persuade the stockholders that he could improve the company if they let him vote their stock, was messy, expensive and uncertain. Theoretically, at least, the tender offer is quick and clean: by the deadline, enough stock is offered or it isn't and the buyer succeeds or fails. The Liedtkes intended to make a tender offer for United Gas stock.

The drawback, of course, was money. There were 12,868,982 shares of United Gas stock outstanding, held by some 55,000 owners, the largest of whom was the trust department of the Chase Manhattan Bank with 600,000 shares. To take effective control, Pennzoil would have to get at least ten per cent of the stock; that meant a minimum of fifty million dollars—and that was more than half the total value of Pennzoil itself.

On May 13, 1965, the Liedtke brothers issued orders to a handful of brokers over the country to buy United Gas stock in small parcels and hold it for an unnamed purchaser. This was the first in a series of crucial moves. The need for secrecy was paramount. If they bought heavily, they would drive up the price and, even worse, they would alert United Gas management and its stockholders to the possibility of some sort of action which in turn would have—or could have—provoked countermeasures.

Only the brothers themselves, their financial vice president and strategist, J. H. Young, and perhaps an attorney or two knew their plans at this point. The name United Gas was not mentioned in conversation; it was referred to, Young is reported to have said much later, as Company X. The Liedtkes are not very pompous men; surely, even with an eight-hundred-million-dollar company riding in the balance, they grinned a little self-consciously over that. Nevertheless, they checked their wastebaskets for fear a casual note in the wrong hands would give them away. And finally, by October 17, without creating a ripple in the United Gas price structure or a tremor of disquiet in its somnolent executives, Pennzoil held 275,000 shares worth nearly ten million dollars.

Now they were ready. They were preparing to make a tender offer for a minimum of one million shares of United Gas stock at a price of forty-one dollars a share—or six dollars over its current market price. The premium, of course, was designed to attract stockholders irritated and discouraged by United's long inactivity. The Liedtkes went to New York, still in the deepest sort of secrecy, and began to set things up. The old-line financial firm of White, Weld & Co. agreed to underwrite the project, which meant, in a sense, that it would stand behind that million-share offer. They went to the prestige-laden law firm of Simpson, Thatcher & Bartlett, which covers two floors of a big building at 120 Broadway in lower Manhattan. They walked down the wide and stately corridors with their rugs and paintings and excellent furniture, walked through the genteel silence in which more than a hundred lawyers work, men who will never see their names on the letterhead, and went to the office of Whitney North Seymour, Sr., senior partner, and sat under his Spy cartoons and looked out his wide windows to the matchless view of New York Harbor with great ships steaming in, and arranged with him to serve as chief counsel for the venture. They went to the towers of the Chase Manhattan Bank and arranged to borrow the forty-one million dollars they would need on short-term financing, to be replaced with longer-term arrangements when the dust settled. The Mellon National Bank and Trust Company in Pittsburgh agreed to serve as depository for the stock offer.

On the morning of November 22, Pennzoil published its offer. The news stunned United Gas. Ed Parkes, its president, learned of it only when a broker read it on the Dow Jones ticker and called him. He was widely quoted as saying that morning, "I wouldn't know what to tell my mother right now if she asked me whether to take the offer." One week later, however, he sent individual letters to each of the 55,000 stockholders expressing dismay at the tender offer and suspicion of Pennzoil's intentions. He assured them that their officers did not plan to sell their own stock, such as it was. When it learned of the letter, Pennzoil relaxed; its single worry, that some United stockholders might not hear of the tender offer, had been solved by United's management.

The million shares were promptly offered. They flowed into the Mellon Bank in a constant stream, there to be held until the play was over. United Gas went into U.S. District Court in New York to ask for an injunction that would have blocked Pennzoil's acquiring more than ten per cent of United's stock. Grave and dignified, Whitney North Seymour came down from his towers and told Judge Frederick Van Pelt Bryan that United's move was "nothing but an attempt by the present management of United to avoid a change" in management.

While the maneuvering went on, the stock poured in. It reached two million shares offered, then three million shares. Now the ante in this game had climbed to one hundred twenty million dollars and it was still growing. Suddenly it all got very serious. There was constant communication between Pennzoil in Houston, White, Weld & Co. in Manhattan, and the Chase Manhattan Bank. Of course, Pennzoil was not actually obligated to purchase more than the original one million shares it had sought—but Seymour told the court that Pennzoil had arranged bank loans for the purchase of at least three million shares and possibly more. Judge Bryan refused to grant the injunction and United Gas appealed to the Second Circuit Court of Appeals.

The only question before the stockholder is should he sell, and no one fully knows what motivates him. Perhaps the publicity moved him, perhaps he feared the future or perhaps he was just weary and willing to take his profit and go. Whatever the reason, the stock continued to pour in. The figure went to four million, five million and beyond. It leveled out finally at 5,159,033 shares, five times what Pennzoil had bargained for, which, with the 275,000 shares it already owned, would give it 42 per cent of United Gas and, of course, absolute control.

But the cost of taking that stock would be more than twice what Pennzoil itself was worth. It would mean borrowing on a monumental scale. It would mean, in short, that a pair of Texas buckoes who only sixteen years before had been getting divorces for their friends' maids would be borrowing more than a fifth of a billion dollars. They thought it over for a while; so, they said, let's do it.

And it wasn't so hard, in a sense. Chase Manhattan faltered briefly and then rallied. It provided the basic cover for the loan as it formed a lay-off syndicate that is reported to have included some twenty banks, including at least one in Texas. On December 22, just in time for Christmas, the appeals court rejected United Gas's plea and Pennzoil asked the Mellon Bank to go ahead with the formal purchase. Every share tendered was taken. The final loans to cover the payments came to $214,975,000.

And it is not that it was such a big deal, though it was. It was not even Texas money they used, because everyone knows that the real money and the real moneymen are in the East and they always have been and maybe they always will be. So the point of real interest here is not so much that they were able to get the money as that it seemed perfectly natural to them to try. For they are children of oil and oil has boomed and boomed, and over the years in Texas, it has come to make all things seem possible.

CHAPTER

When Harold Wynne thoughtfully drops a handful of extra
.30 caliber cartridges into his pocket before he gets in his blue
pickup truck and starts across the Terlingua Ranch; when Bill
Liedtke looks at his brother and grins and says, Yeah, let's
borrow a fifth of a billion dollars, why not?, they stand almost
as caricatures of what makes the state of Texas unique, certainly in the United States and perhaps in the whole world.
I suspect there has never been anything quite like Texas, and
even if this is not widely recognized or understood, all the
same it may account for the fascination Texas obviously has
for the rest of the country.

Basic America, it seems to me, is made up of two most
powerful drives. The first is this country's proximity and relationship to its own frontier. The second is its great wealth or
accumulation of capital. The proximity to its frontier gives
America its thrust and drive and hardness and daring. Its
wealth built the new technology that is reshaping the world—
the overpowering bigness, the massed scientific knowledge,
the ever-expanding organization, marketing techniques un-
equaled anywhere in the world, the increasing investment per
worker, all depending on the mass and the weight of its capi-

tal. Taken together, these are the qualities that have made the United States the most powerful nation the world has ever known.

I believe that Texas can be taken as a microcosm of the greatness of America.

And so saying, I hasten to qualify, for by no means am I saying that Texas is the greatest part of this nation. Nor do I say that Texas represents the best of this nation, for I do not believe that it does. Given the pioneering drive and the capital power on which the many facets of this country rest, the best of what we are might be our collective capacity for intellectual excellence and international conscience. And I would judge that in Texas these are among the least evident of capacities. This is fitting to my thesis, for intellectuality and altruism are luxuries possible in a society that has passed beyond the hard core of its beginning. As a microcosm of this nation's power, Texas remains basic, direct, hard, still firmly fastened in its beginnings, not great itself but only at the core of greatness. Still, it is well to remember that its size makes Texas not just another state but actually an entire region with all of a region's impact on the whole.

I am saying, then, that Texas is exciting because of two qualities which make it an epitome of the American experience. I believe that this epitome does not quite exist anywhere else in America and therefore is unique. The two qualities are, first, Texas' genuine proximity to its own frontier and, second, the conditioning and the polishing given this frontier outlook by the sudden and dramatic discovery of huge pools of capital in the form of oil.

The time is within living memory when in most parts of Texas a man looked to himself and if necessary to his own handgun for his basic protection. Even within the last decade, killing a man who threatened one's life seemed reasonable enough both to the man who was threatened and to the jury which later examined him. A mere half-century ago there was incredible violence along the Mexican Border and men habitually went armed against bandits. Outlaw and Indian fights were intimate childhood lore for men still hale and strong today. Because much of its land was poor and dry, Texas did not fill rapidly with settlers and thus quickly achieve a stable society. Long after most of the rest of the nation was well established, there were wild and lonely sections of Texas. Some of those sections are wild and lonely today. The men who lived on such land necessarily were independent. They acted on their own best judgment for their own best interests and they took care of themselves. Out in the Big Bend country, where the law is eighty miles away, Harold Wynne still does that. Of course parts of Texas are getting crowded and of course the old attitude is slowly fading—but I believe that, nevertheless, the attitude of the pioneer is basic to the mind of Texas today. And it conditions what Texas is and how Texas acts and perhaps most important, it sets the tone for what Texas does.

In the midst of all this, the oil blew in. Its huge pools underlay nearly every county in the state and it was instant wealth and in time it became capital. It was a gift of the earth, never before suspected, and men who had always been poor were suddenly rich and it was easy. Not everyone had money, of course—Texas is low on the per capita income scale and always has been—but everyone knew someone who had hit and a whole contagious atmosphere of excitement and action began to develop. Texans used their money; they made it work and they made more of it or they busted and someone else began to use it. Thus it came about that great pools of fluid capital formed; and although the average man was not necessarily flush, it did mean that there was money in the community and it was available. Things were happening and there was always a sense of action.

At its simplest—and despite what I have said, Texas is not a simple state and does not yield fully to simple answers—these two factors of the frontier and the sudden gift of oil from the ground must be taken together. The frontier provides the spirit and the willingness to act and the capital pools provide the capacity to act and the two interwork upon each other and each leaves the other stronger. Capital used with the frontier outlook takes on an imaginative and creative power far beyond its normal use in a more settled financial society. And powered by huge capital, the frontier outlook takes on scope and strength and motion far beyond its own innate possibilities.

That, I believe, is the key. Most of the western states share, to some extent, Texas' frontier heritage but they lack that sudden infusion of capital. And for all of the Texas oil, the real money in this country lies in the East. But it is tied in the hands of an old, comfortable, cautious society where it is carefully protected but rarely exercised to its full power and impact.

For what we are describing in Texas is an attitude. It grows from the frontier and it grows from the availability of great sums of money and that is what makes Texas a booming place. It does not mean that Texas as a state is rich or that Texans as individuals are rich, for neither is true; but it does mean that this is a place where all things are possible, where the man with a dream, if he works hard enough and dreams well enough, can make it come true. That is what makes the coup of the Liedtke brothers not only possible but even probable, for though their money came from Wall Street, their attitude and their decision grew in Texas. And finally, it is not the oil or the money or the buildings or the growth that makes Texas exciting. It is the attitude.

CHAPTER

1

Now that I live in the East, I feel the excitement of Texas more than ever when the airplane door opens and I see the great sweep of the sky with its horizons buried in the dimming distance. This unlimited sky is characteristic of the plains, of course, but it symbolizes for me the sense that you can go so far so freely and so openly—the sense, in other words, of opportunity. This is illusory too: most Texans don't want wide opportunity, don't seek it and certainly don't find it.

But opportunity is here and the man who wants to seize it may, which further conditions the Texas mind. This is a state which regards itself with a unity and pride unknown anywhere else in America except, perhaps, in New York City itself. Part of this attitude of affectionate self-regard grows from the vicarious sense of community accomplishment, of belonging to a somehow superior entity. Superiority is in the eye of the beholder; nevertheless, there are a number of things worth examining that have their bearing on the development of the Texas mind.

There is the state's incredible size. It is only a state by an accident of politics, for it certainly is regional in nature. It stretches nearly a thousand miles from east to west and changes gradually from swamplands to desert mountains. From its southern tip, a tropical fruit country washed by the Gulf of Mexico, it runs for nearly a thousand miles north into the high plains country that marks Colorado and western Kansas. This plain element of size alone helps develop the attitude of pride and optimism and latent power; it is as if Texans see their state as a great beast which they tamed and made their own.

Yet mere mileage is the poorest of denominators of size. The real measure of the extent and the impact of Texas and, indeed, of its very meaning lies in its multiples. It has multiples of nearly everything, of climate, terrain, cities and even cultures which when worked together in fine mosaic form the complexity of the whole.

It has, for instance, not merely one or two or a few, but seven complete and separate river systems (as well as three border rivers and one that traverses the Panhandle). Each has its own elaborate watershed with its system of tributaries and drainage and each delineates a specific segment of the state before it drains off to the sea.

It is the only state in the nation with three separate and roughly equal major cities, each totally unlike the other. Most states have one major city; a few have two. Houston, caught at last in the mainstream of American industrial development, now is pulling ahead of Dallas and San Antonio, but for years they were roughly equal in size and importance though not at all alike in nature. San Antonio is an old city, even by terms a Bostonian might choose, and it maintains an air of elegance, culture, gentility, and graceful living. A nonindustrial military center, it turns back easily to those not-so-distant days when the military officer corps were automatically the socially elite, and it retains a Latin sense of courtesy that sets it apart from the rest of the state. Dallas is an icy business center, with some of the passionate acquisitiveness of Manhattan and some of the banality of the Midwest. Its energy is overwhelming and dollar-oriented and it produces a handsome if somewhat humorless way of living. Houston is a sprawling, energetic, careless place, neither pretty nor tidy but warmly pleasant. Industrially based, it is growing in staggering leaps, but with an almost casual attitude toward its own importance. Each of these three cities is individual, independent of the others, strong in its own right and sharply different. Yet each of them, in its way, orients directly to the image of power and pride that makes Texas—and in their size and individuality, each adds to that image.

Texas is hardly beautiful taken over-all, but there is much beauty in its individual parts. Their diversity is extraordinary, and the violent change in terrain and even climate serves to make the state all the more a vast and prideful region than a political subdivision. In Newton County, on the Louisiana border, an average fifty-six inches of rain falls every year. Swamp water stands waist deep in places, furrowed by a swimming snake, marked by giant cypress trees garlanded with Spanish moss. Driving near here one night in a violent rainstorm on a highway laid through a swamp, I saw a tiny alligator, plainly a baby, struggling across the road and I slowed and waited for him to pass. And at the other end of the state, nearly a thousand miles away, Hudspeth County draws less than eight inches of rain. The altitude averages near four thousand feet and the air is so dry that neither heat nor cold is uncomfortable. Nearby are mountains that startle people who believe that all of Texas is flat.

The Guadalupe Mountains rise to well over eight thousand feet in spots and, though not so precipitous, are actually higher than the jagged Chisos, which overlook the Terlingua Ranch. Driving near this country on a blazing day years ago I encountered a migration of the desert's ugliest (though not at all its most deadly) inhabitants—black tarantulas. They were big creatures with a leg span of several inches, and thousands upon thousands of them were moving south for reasons I never learned. They were crossing the highway, crawling steadily, each a few feet from the next, and as far as I could see, they darkened the road. The car hurtled along, crushing the black bodies with loud noises, and entirely obliviously, the survivors continued their even trek. Far to the north I could see them coming; to the south, going. As much as anything I ever saw, this vast migration of tarantulas suggested the magnitude, the harshness, the deserted openness of this country.

There is a section of East Texas along the Louisiana border and north of the swamp country where the rainfall is still heavy and the mosquitoes seem big as sparrows and not nearly so pleasant. You drive for miles through great pine forests, and when you stop they are quiet in the way of forest lands, with the whispering sound of wind in the tops and the floor a slippery layer of shining needles. It is called the piney woods and this, with a small section of the western mountains, is the only place in the state where pines grow readily (except for an odd and vagrant patch in central Texas called "the lost pines" as if they had strayed from home). The soil is red clay, moist and soft, and the harsh gashes the road-builders leave are quickly softened by forest ferns.

Only a bit farther west the air gets drier and the hold of the pines begins to relax. Postoak and blackjack and elm and hickory and black walnut trees creep in and there are little farms with cleared cattle pastures. Farther on toward the central part of the state the soil is black and strong and the little farms begin to give way to what once were plantations and which left this section of Texas with the overtones of arrogance and racism that are part of the plantation legacy. This farming belt in the center of the state runs down from Oklahoma to the Gulf, where it spreads out in a coastal plain that is flat and rich and produces huge crops of cotton and grain sorghum.

Much of South Texas—nearly everything below San Antonio—is called the brush country for the endless miles of bushy mesquite trees and cedar clumps that cover it. Once this was grassland, in the day of the buffalo, with streams that ran sweet and clear. But heavy grazing destroyed the grass and the noxious bushes crept in and covered it. There are valiant and sometime successful efforts to eradicate them, and some day this may all be grassland again. But today it remains covered with spindly mesquite trees no more than ten feet high with grass growing only in isolated spears. Webb County, in the heart of the brush country, with Laredo its county seat, gets only slightly more rain than Brewster County, and except for the false green of the mesquite (which compares to the grease-wood in Brewster) it is almost as sere. This is an area of great ranches. The magnificent King Ranch stands at nearly three quarters of a million contiguous acres. Dolph Briscoe, Jr., son of one of the great ranching names of Texas, operates a total of more than a million acres in ranches spread generally across this area and into Mexico. I remember one cool fall day on Briscoe's Catarina Ranch when the pearburner was working. This powerful flamethrower, operated from a tank on the back of a pickup truck, burned the needles off that round and fibrous-leafed cactus known in the ranch country as prickly pear. The cattle delight in it when its needles are stripped, and on this day a good fifty head were lined up behind the truck in a long string, moving as it moved, contentedly eating the freshly burned and still smoking cactus leaves. They simply were having a hot lunch.

Yet if you drive south through this largely barren country for a good 150 miles (passing right through the King Ranch and past a neat sign that in ominous understatement says, "Warning—no gasoline or water for the next 56 miles.") you come to the lower Rio Grande Valley and startling contrast. For suddenly you are in a comparatively arid but genuine tropical garden. It is on the approximate latitude of Miami, the air is soft and balmy, the growth is lush. Its basic industry is citrus, particularly a sweet red grapefruit developed here that grows well nowhere else. The groves are lovely in the season, row upon row of small trees with waxy dark green leaves, the fruit shining in red and yellow dots, offset against a creamy brown soil. The grove borders are often marked with lines of towering royal palms, standing a hundred feet tall with their majestic fronds clumped at the top, marching in orderly rows clear across the vast horizon. Papayas and bananas and lime trees grow readily in people's yards and bougainvillea climbs their houses with clumps of brilliant blossoms. Despite the relative dryness there are little oxbow lakes everywhere, called *resacas*, that mark the ancient bed of the Rio Grande in its final turns as it joined the sea. Usually the Valley remains warm over the winter and it fills with elderly winter tourists from throughout the Midwest and even Canada. I recall walking with a friend years ago in Brownsville from the newspaper where we worked to a tiny *pandería* that sold us *pan dulce*, a marvelous cinnamon-dusted bread, on a day when a norther had abruptly dropped the temperature from the middle eighties to perhaps the high sixties. Shivering, my friend, a Valley native, suddenly cried with real passion, "Oh, *damn* this cold!"

Fort Worth likes to call itself the place at which the West begins, and perhaps this is true. But for me, the West has always started at San Antonio and it always will. The western part of Texas is a long, gradual tilt that rises from sea level to more than 4,000 feet without a perceptible slope. It begins with a long thrust of rolling highlands reaching north and west from San Antonio. The immediate portion is a sort of miniature badlands, rocky, hilly, filled with gullies and draws, lined in cedar and liveoak, with occasional waterfalls and springs and winding, deep-shadowed rivers, which Texans call the Hill Country. In the heart of this area is Lyndon Johnson's alternate White House, the LBJ Ranch, which is bringing visitors to the Hill Country from all over the world. But Texans have always prized it for its genuine beauty, which explains the outrageous per acre price they are willing to pay for it. That price, in fact, permits an average return on the investment of little more than one per cent, a triumph of land passion over judgment.

If you head west from the Hill Country, you will cross land that becomes steadily drier, higher, more arid and less productive. It is grazing land in which the clumps of strong grass grow steadily farther apart and cactus becomes ever more common. Eventually you will strike the Rio Grande and work your way on out to El Paso, and you will find that the common denominator of all this land is its hardness. The highways run straight as string for endless miles and when you stop at a roadside park you can hear the cars coming when they are still miles away, a faint roaring over the wind that gradually increases until the car passes with a scream at a steady eighty miles an hour and fades into the distance and the sound is gone. And then there is a scratching at your feet and a rock squirrel no bigger than a mouse flicks his tail at you and runs across the road. Eventually, moving westward, you will strike the buttes and mesas that are so much a part of the world in which Harold Wynne lives, and on beyond that, the upper valley of the Rio Grande, just out of El Paso, where irrigation produces handsome crops and a filling station owner said to me a little pensively one day, "I'd like to see it rain. It hasn't rained in two years. I mean right around here close, there hasn't been no rain in two years."

If you swing northwesterly from the Hill Country, the terrain changes still again. You pass out of the quick and pretty little hills, into a more rolling and somewhat barren sheep and goat area, into the near-desert of the Permian Basin around Midland and Odessa and on to the Panhandle, which the people who live there call the high plains. This is table flat land that once was cattle country and now is one of the largest stretches of irrigated farming land in the world. Everything is big scale. Men till thousand of acres with machines, develop machines to fit the plants and then refine the plants better to fit the machines, bore holes hundreds of feet into water veins and attach pumps that can throw a foot-thick stream of water night and day. They raise bumper crops of grain sorghum, vegetables, and cotton, and the gins operate night and day during the season. The wind is steady here, a constant roaring in the ears, because there is nothing to break it for hundreds of miles. The sky is light and perhaps more than any other place in Texas, here the horizons seem so incredibly distant as simply to disappear. Can there be limits in a country like this? Mountain men are comfortable in the close protection of hill and rock always at their back—but once a man has been a plainsman, there is no going back, for the sight of that far horizon, that open, empty land on every side, means freedom.

These multiples of terrain, the range from swamp to desert mountain, from citrus grove to the high plains, have tremendous effect on the mind of the Texan, for they remind him always of the difference and thus of the size and the power of the entity of which he is a part. Yet of all the multiples which mark the Texas mind, the most important and the one that makes the greatest difference is the combining of cultures. For there are three basic cultures come together in Texas, and while plainly they do interact upon each other, yet to a surprising degree they remain separate and distinct and prideful.

I have always liked the western part of the state best. There is that open quality, a sense of distance and a hardness, as if here a man, in his outlook and his attitude, is more independent. People here tend to be a little friendlier, probably because there are fewer of them and always have been and thus the appearance of a stranger's face is more likely to mean a pleasure than a problem. These are the broad and open reaches where the cowboy began.

The cowboy has become an authentic American folk hero; indeed, he has become *the* American folk hero. Now he is showing signs of becoming the folk hero of the world. There are fast-draw clubs in Tokyo, for instance; the members wear jeans and buckskin jackets and Stetson hats and boots from El Paso and in oiled holsters on their hips they carry Colt .45 single-action pistols, commonly known as thumbbusters. Only the fold of eyelid over the cowboy's black eyes and the triangular face mark him as something different from what you might encounter out beyond Amarillo. On the other side of the world, in that citadel of sophistication, Paris itself, there are similar clubs. All over Europe, jeans are advertised; they are widely popular with the youngsters.

The Western film spread the image, of course, but its appeal goes to the roots of man's trouble with the industrial society he has created which now conditions every moment of his day, every facet of his life. The cowboy does not interest people in the underdeveloped, still rural parts of the world; they have their own. But in the crowded, industrialized nations, the cowboy is coming to stand for the free spirit of man, operating at a time and in a place in which he could condition the world around him instead of being conditioned by it.

Nowhere is this truer than in Texas itself, which is now seventy-five per cent urbanized and operating in a culture which depends more and more on industrialization, which is to say massed society instead of the individual. Yet as a matter of historical fact, the cowboy began in Texas. For here the first of the great ranches began, the first systematizing of the beef industry. Two new concepts developed immediately before and after the Civil War—mass production of beef for food instead of just for hides, and the moving of great herds of live animals on the hoof. It was out of this pattern that for the first time in history men stopped being herders of cows and that hell-for-leather fellow, that handler of wild and rangy cattle in mass, the American cowboy, was born. This is of great importance to the Texas mind. For even as the Texan venerates the image, he feels that he is a legitimate part of it and it quickens his senses and gives him a feeling of action and free horizons. This is partly pride, but it also is partly kinship to the idea of man without limits beyond those which nature imposes.

More important, however, than the free spirit of the cowboy was the slow development of the Western ethic, which was a land ethic, in fact, or one which for its viability depended on the free land of the frontier, land always available to those who were tough enough to take it and to hold it. This Western ethic, in which a man relied on himself because he was operating out beyond, where both the benefits and the strictures of society were growing thin, is probably the dominant cultural pattern in Texas today.

There are many aspects of this, as we will see later, but the ones that concern us here are the propensity for privilege and for violence which accompany as natural corollaries the idea of self-reliance. In this land of the West, in a time now almost gone but yet not quite, a man not only could do as he pleased, but to survive, must do as he pleased. Nor could he expect to have his way, the way that he believed was best, at least for him, without being ready to fight for it. He fought the Indians who held the land, he fought his fellows who came with him to take it, he fought the land itself. And when it was over, either he lost, or he won the right to do largely as he pleased. That same sense of violence and privilege runs through Texans today and is seen directly on every side; it also, indirectly, contributes to the sense of opportunity and excitement that still burns in Texas.

East Texas, on the other hand, is a direct extension of the Old South and it faithfully reflects the Southern culture. It lies generally east of a line drawn north and south from Dallas, and though in area it is less than a quarter of the state, in population it is probably more than half. Its religion is basically fundamentalist and its people are more moralistic about matters of sex and the use of alcohol than about their treatment of their brothers. In the summer the climate is desperately hot and heavy, but it cools in the evening and the odor of honeysuckle floats in the air. It is largely farm and plantation country, just as the Old South spawned powerful plantations on its rich land and little dirt farms on its poor land. The agricultural patterns of Texas are reversing themselves today; western cattle lands are becoming cotton farms irrigated with deep well water, while the exhausted cotton land of the east is being turned into small, grassy cattle pastures. But the relationship to the Old South remains plain. The people talk in a soft, slurred accent, muddier than the drawl of the western plains. There is a big oppressed Negro population and the white East Texan treats it approximately as his counterpart in Mississippi does. For this, as much as Mississippi, was slave country, and it produced the same attitudes and excesses that slavery anywhere does, and particularly the cruel and virulent form that developed in America.

Oddly enough, a case can be made that those two dominant characteristics growing from the Western ethic—a sense of violence and of privilege—grew also, though in a less open and honest way, from the Southern heritage of the East Texan. The strain of violence in the South can probably be traced to the strain of privilege that runs equally strong and certainly grows directly from the institution of slavery. Slavery produced a people inferior by legal definition, and then emancipation removed the protection that ownership and commercial value once had afforded them. The white man saw himself as privileged by the color of his skin; certain work was "nigger work" and automatically beneath him; as a superior being, he turned naturally to violence to support his own concept of himself, violence against Negroes, of course, but being a prideful fellow laden with the conceit of privilege, against as well those fellow whites who failed to appreciate sufficiently the value he had assigned himself.

Without belaboring the point, it can be said fairly that this sense of privilege and violence threads through Southern history, and that as East Texas is a product of the South rather than the West, so East Texas shares these threads.

The third great culture is Latin, rolling up from the south. Texas shares 889 miles of border with Mexico; originally she was part of Mexico; she fought her first war against Mexico; her ties are long and binding. Mexico always was a class country, and if she now is allowing a middle class slowly to emerge, she has until now consisted of a tiny elite and a massed peonage. Some of this peonage has lived quietly in Texas for generations, mostly in the southern part of the state, continuing its traditions of language, attitude and servitude. Though some of its members, more in every generation, break away, this peonage has come to constitute an oppressed minority in South Texas, at least in economic terms.

There is a curious ambivalence in the relations of the Latin and the Anglo-American, the Mexican and the Texan. They develop passionate hatreds and deep disgust for each other—but they assume each other's habits and language and food and even affectations. They are becoming one whether they like it or not.

Sometimes the two cultures abut upon each other. I recall standing on Franklin Mountain in El Paso with Tom Lea, whose books as well as his paintings demonstrate his knowledge and his passion for this country. He was looking with a painter's eye and in the brilliant light that makes El Paso like only a handful of other places in the entire world, we could see both sides of the Rio Grande clearly. I know of no other place in which two such distinct cultures come together in cities which have nearly a million total population and are separated only by a river.

"Look there," Lea said, pointing down a residential street in Juarez. "Notice the sharp definition of the street. The Latin builds his house flush to the street and you see a solid masonry line drawn as with a ruler. He prizes his patch of green, too, but it is a private thing, not for show but for the spirit. Inside those houses, you'll find the patio with the patch of grass, flowering plants, perhaps a fountain." He turned, to point back across his own El Paso. "Now look down that street. It's fuzzy-edged, irregular; its edges are the people's yards, each a little different, with the houses sitting back from the street in an irregular line. The Texan turns outward. He builds his house like the rest of America, in a compact unit, with a lawn in front designed at least as much for other people to see as for his own pleasure. I guess it's too violent a change from our own patterns to absorb—after all, my house has a lawn in front too—but the Latin way really seems the better of the two."

But just the same, in a way that the Negro, torn from his native culture and thrust at once into a new country an ocean away, has never been able to manage, the Latin has put his imprint on Texas. That imprint swings down the border, particularly in the southern part of the state. The cities are bilingual, the population and voting rolls heavily Latin, and most of the officials are Latin. Nor should it be thought that Texas' discrimination against Latins ever cut clear across the spectrum. It is more that Mexico's old class attitudes were faithfully reflected in Texas: at the social heights in San Antonio there were always Latin families who looked down on all Anglo-Americans and dealt only with the most socially elite.

In general, the Texan is more fond of things Latin than he is of Latins. He likes to visit Mexico. He likes Mexican food, if in a somewhat anglicized version. Spanish words creep into his vocabulary. If the cowboy is a powerful symbol, so is the Mexican *charro*, that colorful horseman with the great sombrero and the silver-studded saddle.

And in the end, the Latin temperament fits very nicely with the Texan's. For the Latin tends to be happy, gay, bright, flamboyant, optimistic. He also carries a strain of violence, a preoccupation with the matter of being a full man, which he calls *machismo*, a pride that borders on arrogance and on folly—and because he has all these things, he has a sense of privilege, a sense that his mere existence establishes his privilege. His courtesy precludes the sort of casual roughness that comes naturally to many Texans and his acquiescence in his lowly over-all state in Texas seems to suggest a passivity which is not accurate. He is a man of spirit, handy with the women, clever with the guitar and a terror with the blade.

And change is coming on Texas now. The peons—Latins and Negroes—are rising. They are part of the world-wide rise of the brown-skinned peoples and there seems no question of their future. When they have completed that thrust, Texas will be the better, for their peonage and the arrogance of enforced class distinctions are one of the state's greatest failures. But in the meantime, there is a curious, though probably quite natural little by-product: a new, direct, aggressive attitude. The emancipated Latins' voices often are louder and more harsh. They speak as rapidly as people from the Bronx and they are almost purposely rude and direct in a country that still prizes indirection (which once was a Latin characteristic) and a soft voice. They are throwing off the old and for them, the old includes the soft voice and the courteous manner.

These multiples of culture, even more than those of climate and terrain and cities and distance, mark this state and its people. Of course they blend into and shape everyone who lives here, and yet to a surprising extent, I think these three cultures also maintain a sort of separateness, so that every Texan sees in them diversity and variety that makes his state and thus him different, that feeds his sense of pride of place, his optimism and his own latent power of accomplishment.

59

Yet for all the multi-facets that condition the Texas mind, for all the size and the diversity, there is still one more quality that overrides every other and leaves its permanent mark on the state and its attitudes. That quality is the inherent hardness of the land itself.

Only rarely is Texas soil really rich and productive. Usually it is weak and poor and often shot with stones. Some of it is mucky clay that defies most seed. Some was drained early of minerals by unrelenting cotton production. Some, where the grass was weakened, yields to a noxious tide of brush. Much of it is dry, sandy and stony, deeply carved by the erosion of floods and the constant driving wind, a harsh country surfaced in a dry crust that is literally hard to the foot and to the grass seed.

Texas always was and is today a big hardscrabble land that had to be broken and held by the pure strength of man. It was on that strength always that it was made to produce and prosper; never on the bounty of its own natural endowments. And that sense of strength which the land demands comes down today and conditions these people.

So it is not odd that from the start, the men drawn to Texas were fighting men. The first invaders were the Plains Indians who followed the buffalo down into what now is the West Texas grass country, the Apaches, the Comanches, the Kiowas, fighters who drove out the less warlike tribes that were there before them and who, when the time came, turned joyfully enough to fight the invading white man. What undid the Plains Indian was that he had no sense of place. The men who came to Texas to take the land were equal fighters with better arms who were well endowed with a concept of place, of property, of individual ownership, deeds, titles, land grants, and, consequently, a willingness to fight specifically. The Indian was always willing to fight, but his natural view of the land was general and impersonal and so could not stand against the specific intent of the white man to make *this* tract, this particular tract for which he now was fighting, his own.

Though the Spanish formed permanent missions in San Antonio in the early 1700s, they did little to colonize or extend physical control over the land they called *Tejas*. The first Anglo-Saxon settlers to come to Texas in an organized colony, led by Stephen F. Austin in 1821, were peaceful and quite legally formed. But Texas quickly became a natural haven for hot-blooded men—especially those in a bit of trouble at home—and the inherent violence in the situation is obvious from the fact that the Texas Revolution in 1836 came a mere fifteen years after the formation of that first colony. An extraordinary number of the men pouring into Texas came from Tennessee, which even today is considered a sort of spiritual home and originating force of Texas. They came from all over the then expanding United States, with the preponderance from the South. If a man was a wild young cock, full of spirit and fight, whose escapades were making things hot at home, he began to think of Texas. The Mexican government, which gained its independence from Spain by revolution in 1821, the year of that first colony, at this point encouraged immigration to Texas. All over the South, Texas was the new frontier, the place at which opportunity beckoned; land was free for the taking and what's more, a man could have a hell of a lot of fun. This attitude included everything from the lothario who had been caught in attention to another man's wife to the man who had killed in a duel of honor to the plain cutthroat—and it is not surprising that in places, it was considered rudeness to the point of insult to inquire of a man's antecedents.

There was a heavy migration directly from Europe, too: they came from all over the continent, but from Germany in such numbers that German is still spoken in parts of Texas today and there are whole areas where English emerges with a strong accent. These Europeans were often people fleeing combinations of starvation and political or religious oppression at home. Texas, with its bountiful land, pleasant climate and almost complete absence of any governmental control (the new Mexican government eight hundred hard miles away in Mexico City was constantly falling and being re-formed in a grisly succession of coups), seemed an absolute paradise. These were people with the spirit to resist oppression at home and the courage to come to a wild new country, and if upon arriving they found a willingness to fight in demand, they would not be laggards.

And indeed, the climate was swiftly heating. The Texas view of the Revolution, firmly graven in every Texan's mind and quite possibly accurate, is that Mexico provoked it and Texas settled it. It certainly is true that the dictator, Santa Anna, consolidating at last Mexico's own revolutionary government, was horrified to find such an Anglo-Saxon influx pouring into his northern areas. He dropped the old encouragement to the settlers, tried to turn off the flow and imposed various harsh conditions on those already there. Given the type of people who had been drawn to Texas already, trouble was sure to develop. And that fact, in turn, drew still more quickly the kind of man who simply liked to fight. Texans still love the story of the Tennessee lad who packed up in the middle 1830s and told his maw, "I'm going to Texas to fight for my rights."

He and his brethren did indeed fight in the brief but storied Texas Revolution. There was the bloody gallantry of the affair at the Alamo, where 187 men *elected* to die rather than retreat. Historians tend to give it low marks for usefulness, but it was magnificent. The war climaxed, as every Texas schoolboy knows, on the plains of San Jacinto. Sam Houston, an authentic American genius, fell back and back until in time Santa Anna's forces were strung clear across the state. And then at four o'clock on an April afternoon the Texans attacked at just the moment the unfortunate Mexican general was in his silken tent engaged in bedding a mulatto slave girl named Emily Morgan, owned by one Mr. Morgan of Morgan's Point, which is now part of the city of Houston. The little lady, as well she might, since Santa Anna was forthwith defeated and the Revolution won, has gone down in Texas history and song. My redoubtable friend Henderson Shuffler, who, among many other things, runs the Texana division of the great library which the University of Texas has built, has established to his satisfaction and mine that the song "The Yellow Rose of Texas," an air which politics gave a certain national currency, was written about this same Emily Morgan. The pretty little Yellow Rose is none other than that "high yaller gal" herself. Those whom this may startle should reflect on the times and recall that that lovely ballad "The Streets of Laredo" in an early version was a lament sung by a syphilitic cowboy as he lay dying of the consequences of love.

In fact, such things did mark the time and the place. It was hard, demanding country, but there was an element of gaiety, excitement, even fun. In addition to plain fighting men, Texas drew a class of men who might be called talented adventurers, men of brains, proven ability, organizational talent and a taste for the new and exciting. These were the men who soon were carving out plantations on the best land in East Texas and sending out such streams of cotton that long before the Civil War, Texas was a factor on the world cotton market. These men were of the same breed who later drew huge sums of money from England and Scotland for investment in cattle lands which the Indians happened to hold at the time—deals that on their face had elements of pure fraud and might in the end have gone down as such but for the extraordinary temper of the times and of the people. Years later, remembering those days, a man who was there said, "We made it on rawhide and guts." But they did make it.

They were hard fighters. The Ranger battalion that scouted for General Zachary Taylor at Monterrey in the Mexican War of 1846 was so murderous that it shocked the more civilized Army men. When a Ranger was killed, his friends on at least one occasion wiped out a whole village in retaliation. In the period after the Civil War when the state government resumed control, the Texas Rangers were re-formed, a battalion to fight Indians and another to fight the Mexican bandits who regularly swam the Rio Grande (in those pre-irrigation days one swam it instead of stepping over it, as frequently is possible today). When both these fronts were quieted, the battalions turned on the desperadoes who made it worth a man's life to travel unescorted, issued a book on wanted men known as the "bounty hunter's bible" and began exercising their lariats from the limbs of oak trees.

These were legendary fighters, professionals, naturals. But the fighting man who shaped the state, whose attitude is still reflected in the sense of resolution and vitality and independence that infuses it today, was much more basic. He was simply the man—and the woman—who moved onto the land, took it, held it, broke it to his use. The land itself was hard and unyielding. The pure labor that he poured into it to force it to return him a living was incredible. He weathered its droughts, its floods, its sandstorms, its driving wind that ground away the topsoil. And usually, sooner or later, he had to fight for it.

There were many deadly little fights, most of them unrecorded. One that has always struck me as at the root structure of Texas took place in a snowstorm in the lovely Llano Valley barely a century ago, in February, 1867. John Friend, a former cavalryman with a Civil War wound, had settled his family in a tiny community called Legion Valley, which no longer exists. It nestled in rocky country all covered with cedar and liveoak in a spot which today would be about twenty-five miles due north of President Johnson's ranch.

Friend had a son, Lee, who was eight, and a new wife, a pretty girl named Matilda, a minister's daughter then only nineteen and in the ninth month of her first pregnancy. A carpenter by trade, Friend built a stout cabin and then decided to go the twenty miles to Fredericksburg to buy sawed boards for its floor. The community seemed safe enough and the other men accompanied him. They left eight persons in Legion Valley—Matilda Friend, two married women with new babies, an unmarried girl and two children. When a raiding party of nineteen Comanche warriors riding far south of their usual fighting grounds reached the community it was obvious from the sudden frenzy that the men were gone.

Everyone ran into Friend's stout new cabin and Matilda dropped the door bar in place. She took down her husband's

.58 caliber Springfield muzzle loader from the pegs over the fireplace and laid it across her ironing board, aimed at the door. It was four feet, eight inches long, with a heavy octagonal barrel itself forty inches long, and she could hardly lift it. An Indian crashed against the door. Another began pulling at the upright pickets of which the house was built. A stake gave way and an arm reached in. Matilda shifted the heavy piece to the left to fire, but before she could do so the door burst open and a brave snatched it from her hands.

An arrow fired through the picket pierced her left arm, the barb out one side, the feathered shaft out the other. With her other hand she caught up her heavy smoothing iron and crashed it down on the Indian's head. He fell in a heap. She reached for a chair to hit him again and he rolled away, fitted an arrow and fired it into her side. It struck a rib, glanced around the breast bone and came out the other side. A third arrow struck her full in the breast and lodged there. She sagged back upon a bed, her head resting against the bed post.

The brave coiled a length of her long yellow hair in one hand and began scalping her with the other. She seized his knife and he shoved the blade completely through her hand. He sliced her scalp again and she tried to take the knife and he hit her three times in the head with the knife handle and knocked her unconscious. Then he finished scalping her, ripping away a piece of scalp about the size of a silver dollar.

She regained consciousness. She was lying on the packed dirt floor of her cabin and she could hear the cries of the women and children outside as they were loaded on horses and taken away. Then an Indian came back into the cabin. Perhaps to see if she was dead, perhaps merely to recover his arrow, he jerked hard at the shaft that had gone through her chest. It would not pull free and he let it go.

Matilda Friend kept her eyes shut and made no sound.

When the Indians rode away with their captives, she sat up and bound a cloth around her bleeding head. She took the point of the arrow piercing her chest and tried to wrench it through. She could feel the wood scraping the bone, but the arrow would not move and the pain was so violent that she stopped. She was alone with three arrows in her body, a serious hand wound and a piece of her scalp torn away. The neighbor nearest the little community lived a mile and a half away. She decided to go to his house.

She set out on the rocky, snowy path, stumbling and crawling and now and then falling and driving the arrows farther into her body. When she fell she scooped snow into her mouth, but it did not stop her thirst. It took her about three hours to reach the cabin. The people there took her in, removed the arrows, bound her wounds, slaked her thirst and placed her on a pallet. The next day she was blind but still alive.

Three weeks later she gave birth to a healthy, perfectly formed little girl whom she named Bell. Seven weeks later her vision returned. The bodies of everyone taken by the Indians except the two children were found not far from the cabin. Both the children eventually were recovered from the Indians, though Friend's son sickened and soon died. Matilda Friend had five more healthy daughters, reared them, saw them marry and helped them rear their own children. But until the day she died, in 1909, forty-two years later, the scalped place on top of her head never healed. It continued to ooze and each day she put a fresh dressing on it.

3

Never mind, for the moment, the seventy-five per cent urbanization of Texas today, the miles of neat, sterile "ranch-style" cottages that fill the urban neighborhoods six to an acre, the silvery cities that soar from the empty plains. The growth and muscle of Texas—and her future—lie in her cities, but the roots of her attitudes are still firmly fixed in the land. And so the fact that Texas is a hardscrabble land and always has been, that over the years it has demanded fighters to break and to hold it, is crucial to the state's character today.

Of all the things that fix the trouble or the ease that man will have with his land, weather is the most capricious and the most important. Even its subtle variations can make the difference between prosperity and disaster, and this is particularly true in Texas because the nature of the weather is such that much of the land is constantly on the edge of disaster anyway. But the city man lives under this same weather, and in a very real way this tends to relate him to the land, to bring together the urban sense with the rural, because Texas weather is such that everyone is aware of it.

There is a peculiar violence in this weather; I do not mean its famous heat or its occasional cold, which are only uncomfortable, but rather its propensity for tornadoes and hurricanes and killing droughts and winds that shave away the topsoil and deluges that flood the desert. And it is this that made Texas a hardscrabble land; more than the hardness and the poverty of the soil, the rocks, the dust, the ubiquitous mesquite or even the physical fighting once necessary, it was the weather that made life in Texas harsh.

I believe that the patterns and rhythms of weather have a profound psychic effect on the people who live under it. So I think it is not entirely coincidental that there is a sense of excitement, size and violence in both the people and the weather of Texas.

In West Texas each valley has a draw, which is not a creek, not even a dried creek, since it has no natural source, but is simply a runoff course for sudden rainwater. It is wide with a flat sandy bottom free of driftwood and normal debris and a peculiarly clean look as if it has been scoured. In fact, it is scoured each time there is a sudden rain on its watershed. Then the water leaps down it, a foot deep, five feet, fifteen. The howling water carries a great cargo of gravel and stones that scourge the draw. In a few hours, the water is gone. The next morning the sun burns and almost immediately it is dry and white and you can kick up dust puffs in its middle.

In a county with an average annual rainfall of twelve inches, a rancher can get his full allotment overnight. He is quite likely to get his rain not in slow, life-giving patters over the growing period, but in a few violent surges measured in inches.

Then, of course, the dry, hard ground throws off the water, refuses to absorb and store it against future need and use, sends it hurtling down into the gullies and on to the draws and to the rivers and finally to the sea, of no use to any man. The water comes with such force that it erodes new paths and leaves the hills marked and torn. It forms veritable streams in its rush to the draws, hurtling over land that was dry that morning, and it catches the cattle and bowls them off their feet and rolls them bawling toward the draw until they drown; and their bodies fetch up eighty miles away when the water falls. And then it may not rain again for a year. Sometimes this sheets a whole area with violent water. Sometimes it is confined to the watershed of a single gully and it drenches the ground and drowns the stock while on ranches all around the cattle bawl and waste in the dryness and refuse to eat and grow.

This pattern of sudden downpour is not limited to the dry west, though the west suffers more because the bare soil is less equipped with grass and timber to absorb and use the water and so the runoff is faster and more deadly. I know of a rancher in South Texas who built an earthen dam about a thousand feet long at the confluence of two small draws to create a pond—or, as Texans call it, a tank—with which to water his stock. Two years of rainfall, he felt, should about fill it. Within a week a rainstorm broke over his watershed, though it did not touch the surrounding ranches. The next morning, glittering in the bright sunlight, he found a full pond, perhaps three hundred acres, lapping peacefully at the top of the dam.

Nor are the cities exempt. San Antonio, which is so dry that mosquitoes are unusual, floods every spring. In the spring of 1966, rain clouds hung over Dallas for two days. The rain thundered down, creeks and draws filled, and eight persons were drowned. The eight deaths were sad but not startling: despite the state's dryness, sudden high water is common and drownings are frequent.

In a slower, quieter way, drought too is violent. There is a theory in Texas that drought comes in seven-year cycles and certainly the drought of 1950–1957 was murderous. The condition sneaks upon the land. The first year is just drier than usual. The second is still drier and there is real damage. In the next, men on marginal and not so marginal pastures can say with some precision that if there is no rain this year, they will fail. And their neighbors can say that if there is none the next year or the next, they too will fail.

Cattle herds are culled down as the grass dies and of course the price of cattle falls and falls. Dryland farmers put seed in the ground but nothing comes up save, perhaps, a sickly sprout that quickly browns. Ranchers begin feeding their basic herds with hay trucked clear down from the mountain farms of Colorado. The mesquite and liveoak trees, already twisted in their tortuous search for water, stop growing, though they do not die. All the plants look wilted. A fine film of dust covers everything, for there is no rain to wash it off. The humidity point of the air falls and falls and men's skin begins to crack and women age perceptibly. What grass there is seems dry and lifeless. The wildflower crop fails. The water table falls and wells begin to go dry.

The sun burns down out of a sky washed white and men and livestock together turn cranky and mean. Ranchers who face mortgage payments go under, for their ranches no longer are producing but their costs are even higher. The big, well-established spreads can survive, but they go deeply in the red. The agricultural economy slows down, equipment dealers go bankrupt, small agricultural towns suffer, bankers stretch themselves thin, ministers pray as regularly for rain as for salvation, and all through the drought country, lines of resignation are engraved permanently on men's faces.

When the grass is dead and gone, the bare land is prey to the constant wind. Men stand in their fields and watch their topsoil, which is the lifeblood of their land, soar into the sky in blackening clouds. Topsoil never comes back and it takes centuries to produce and it is a cruel thing to watch the wind blow one's livelihood away.

When the drought finally breaks, it is like a multitude of blessings showered on the land. The rain clouds roll up from the sea and empty themselves, but not necessarily with the usual violence. Sometimes they hang long over the land, seeping a gentle mist that falls everywhere and washes the plants and soaks slowly into the ground. Then the springtime turns green. Grass grows by the side of the road. The new mesquite leaves are a delicate, feathery green. The liveoak leaves gleam and the tree trunks are dark with rainwater. The wildflowers that have lain dormant come back and the fields are bright and gay, rich with whites and pinks and oranges and blues, the phlox and primrose and Indian blanket and Indian paintbrush and sometimes whole magnificent fields sheeted with the bluebonnets that Texans love, millions of tiny blossoms, dozens to a stem, each shaped precisely like the bonnet that the pioneer woman wore as her westward wagon crushed them under wheel. The fields turn green and the cattle begin to fatten, and they move around peacefully and easily. Men walk loosely, relaxed, filled again with hope and plans, and in the towns as well as the country the tension ebbs.

The wind is a fact of Texas life. In the high plains country, where it is always dry and where there are neither trees nor mountains to break the wind for hundreds of miles, the tumbleweed bounds along the highways and piles up in drifts along the fences. Dust storms tower thousands of feet into the air. They begin as a dirty smudge on the horizon, and at their greatest intensity they cut the visibility to a few score feet and the sky blackens until noonlight seems like dusk. The dust particles move at great velocity, forcing themselves into the tightest building and leaving little piles of dirt on the sills. Sometimes they scour an automobile of paint or pit its windshield until the glass is only translucent. But even when the air is clear and there is no dust, the wind blows; it makes a steady roaring in a man's ears and it leaches the moisture from his skin and after a while it can be maddening.

In the winter the cold rides this same wind in from the north. Texas cold comes from the Arctic Circle, down through Canada, across the Rocky Mountains and into the state with stunning speed. Cold fronts have moved southward at 25 mph and more. It is a startling experience. On a warm pleasant day one is walking along when suddenly from a new quarter—the northern quarter—a distinctly chill wind strikes. There is nothing gradual about it. The wind is new cold, and quite urgent. Within a few minutes there is a definite drop in temperature. Within an hour the temperature may fall twenty degrees or more; within a few hours, it may fall as much as fifty degrees. Then it will be cold, perhaps bitterly so, for a few days, with a gradual warming trend until again the air turns balmy. And then, in a moment, there will be that chilling breath from the north and the sudden and violent cycle of cold will begin again. This is the pattern all winter; this is how cold comes to Texas.

But except in the extreme north, the cold is modest; at the other end of the scale, however, it is different. The heat comes down in clouds, the moist, heavy heat of the South in the eastern part of the state—not so different from the heat of Mississippi—and the dry heat of the West. I have never found either intolerable, though once I went to Presidio in May, which is the time of the year when it regularly logs temperatures of 120 degrees and more and appears in newspapers all over America as the hottest recorded place in the United States. It is a tiny, nearly forgotten town lying in a bowl of small mountains (which accounts for the extremes of its heat) on the Mexican Border not far from the Terlingua Ranch and the Big Bend National Park. Most of the buildings are adobe with thick walls and the sun has burned everything a sort of soothing brown. It was so dry that the heat was not so much uncomfortable as it was numbing. The people detested their reputation for heat. To a man they assured me that Presidio was more comfortable than any of dozens of cities they mentioned, including Washington and New York. I remember a border patrolman, a man nearly forty, whose duty was to apprehend Mexican wetbacks, as they are called, aliens illegally crossing the Rio Grande, looking me right in the eye and assuring me he had chased one seven miles through the brush at a run and caught him and had suffered no ill effects. "One time I was up on top of yonder mountain"—pointing—"in my jeep and I saw a wet down at the bottom, and I ran all the way down that mountain and caught him and ran him back up to the jeep. It didn't bother me." Perhaps not. I, however, left after two days with a mild case of sunstroke and was sick for two weeks.

But these are small matters, heat and northers and dust storms and even flash floods. Texas regularly is battered by the two most powerful types of storms that strike North America. Out of the heat and the swirling air currents that roll off the plains come the tornadoes that lance out of the clouds and trace a deadly line across the earth, narrow and erratic and utterly unpredictable. Like a white-hot needle, their impact is concentrated on a tiny space; within that space little remains intact. Hurricanes roll across the Gulf of Mexico from their spawning grounds in the Caribbean and strike the coast of Texas with immense power that is spread evenly and implacably for miles. But sometimes, with vast cruelty, the two strike together. I remember flying over a ruined section of Galveston after Hurricane Carla struck in 1961. The hurricane winds had ripped off roofs and shattered buildings. Flooding seas had rolled through the streets, turning buildings askew. And there, plain from the air, clearly marked amidst the general devastation, was an erratic path of total devastation where a tornado had dipped out of the hurricane clouds and whipped Galveston with its tail.

Of all the disastrous weather I have covered in Texas, two storms summed up the ferocity, the suddenness and the sense of inherent violence that runs through its weather and is reflected in its people. One was a tornado that picked a murderous path through the city of Dallas. The other was a flash flood on the watershed of the Rio Grande that left thousands of people dead; no accurate count was ever possible.

The tornado began in the simplicity of two air currents that met at 10,000 feet directly over the city of Dallas, as chance would have it, and began to act upon each other. There was a tide of cool, dry air rolling east from the Rocky Mountains, and there was a movement of warm, moist air from the Gulf of Mexico. The latter was slightly lower, which was at the heart of the trouble to come, and again was a matter of chance. At the point of their juncture, the cool air above began to condense the warm air below and a little cloud formed and became a thunderhead and began to grow. It was a bit after three o'clock on the afternoon of April 2, 1957, and the thunderhead was still just a minor cloud and the sun slanted in beneath it and glittered against the shiny city below.

The basis of a great deal of weather is that elementary equation of physics, that warm air is light and tends to rise and cold air is heavy and tends to fall. The two air currents, each encountering the sharply different temperature of the other, tended to leave the suspension in which they had traveled and move, the one up, the other down. But since they were of roughly equal force, they blocked each other and in doing so became highly unstable, tumbling violently at their point of mixture. The condensation continued, building the thunderhead to 20,000 feet of increasing turbulence. It climbed to thirty, forty, fifty thousand and on, blackening steadily with streaks of dangerous sallow green.

To the people on the ground below, the air was merely growing oppressive. It was hotter than usual and heavier and now the whole sky was blackening and any fool could see that a little weather was in the making and wouldn't the rain be pleasant to ease this heat? The great thunderhead trembled in the sky, needing only a trigger to set it in motion. That trigger came from the west, riding the wave of cool, dry air. Born on a snowy mountainside, it was a distinctly colder jolt of air, imperceptible on the ground but nevertheless a genuine if small cold front. It was heavy, held in uneasy suspension, ready to fall. When it struck the moist, hot air below, it was heavy enough to fall right through. And the hot air it displaced, of course, shot right up through the hole it had left behind.

That was the breech. Now the hot air had a way to the heights and it formed itself into an orderly column a hundred yards wide and poured upwards. As it climbed into lighter air, it expanded and cooled until it was spread at the top and narrow at the bottom, in the shape of a funnel. As it cooled, the energy in its heat was transformed into motion and the speed with which it rose increased rapidly. And this was cumulative. The faster the air rose the more heat it gave off and the more motion it assumed. Soon it was a stunning gale of more than 150 mph—going straight up.

The heavy cloud sagged down until the city's buildings seemed to rip it and suddenly it poured out its rain. In precisely five minutes, a fraction under a half-inch of rain fell on Dallas, and then the rain stopped and a strange, dead calm fell over the city. The air seemed heavy as water. Overhead, that vertical column of air was gaining speed. It hit 200 mph, 210, 220. Black and greasy, it boiled past 65,000 feet—and it was still only about a hundred yards wide at its base. When its vertical speed hit 250 mph, it no longer could ignore the earth's rotation. Just as the water in a washbasin spins as it hurtles down the narrow column of the drain, that narrow column of violent air caught the sense of the earth's motion and began to turn, slowly at first and then with the speed inherent in its great power.

Then it was a tornado. The spin started at the top and whipped down the column of air and blew the bottom out of the cloud and against the ground and focused its great power in that tiny tip, and now the tornado began its deadly walk, wandering and skipping, leaping and touching, across the city of Dallas. Its winds were counterclockwise at more than 450 mph.

The weather bureau knew, of course, the potential of those roiling air currents, and had issued tornado warnings. But such warnings are frequent in Texas and not filled with meaning, for a tornado is like a bullet, deadly when it strikes but cutting a narrow path. And yet, like a bullet during combat, one never quite knows on tornado days when and where it's coming . . .

It struck nearly in the face of a deputy sheriff named C. C. Johnson who was driving in South Dallas. He saw buildings shudder and separate into sticks and pieces and he radioed in the first report. He squealed his car down narrow side streets and closed with the funnel. Hanging just behind it, he tracked its course across the city. His reports, fed over the city's radio stations, saved countless lives. Yet a great many people, some of whom saved themselves and some of whom didn't, simply saw it coming.

Willie Weaver was 55, a big, smiling man with an easy manner who had greased cars in a single filling station for twenty-five years. He liked his work and took it seriously and his reputation for probity was such that he could walk into the bank and borrow a thousand dollars on his signature whenever he chose. He was at the station that mad afternoon and everyone there saw the tornado at once. Instinctively they began to run for a golf course four blocks away where a deep drainage ditch would give them cover. But the ties of duty tightened on Weaver. He looked back; the station had been left unlocked; he stopped. He was neither articulate nor thoughtful, but he loved that station and now, with its door swinging open, it looked so vulnerable. He turned and trotted back and a youngster who admired him turned with him and against the growing noise of the storm, Weaver tried to explain his feelings. They reached the building just as the tornado struck. A flying oil can felled the youngster without hurting him seriously and Weaver ran into his grease room and knelt beside the grease rack, curled like a fetus. The building rattled and shook. The whole roof lifted off at once and light flooded the grease room and then the crumpled ceiling dropped in a shower of sheared timber and steel and concrete. As if by a miracle, not a piece of debris touched Weaver. But an edge of the terrible vacuum built inside the funnel by the centrifugal force of the spinning wind passed over him and snatched the air from his lungs and collapsed them like wet pillowcases and he died in a few minutes without a mark on his body.

The tornado mowed on at a steady, grinding 25 mph in a fairly straight line. Howard Roberts, a big, blunt-fingered machinist, had spent the afternoon sifting fertilizer onto his lawn. He watched the rain soak it in, then dressed his two-year-old daughter, Denise, his big fingers fumbling with the little buttons, and led her to the car parked in front. They were going shopping. He heard the roar of the tornado, hesitated, then threw the child down and dropped on top of her and seized a sapling at its base. The storm shook him like a rag, tore him from the tree, ripped off his shoes and his shirt and broke his back. It flung his daughter through the air and she hit the curb on the opposite side of the street and broke both her legs. But father and daughter lived.

Tom Davisson, a lean, flat-cheeked man with straight black hair and rimless glasses who in twenty-two years of exceedingly hard work had built his oil distributorship into a flourishing business, stepped out of his warehouse when a customer drove into his yard. He saw the roof fly off an iron and boiler works a bare two blocks away; and as the customer, an elderly farmer, became hysterical, Davisson seized him by the arm and dragged him toward a 1,900-gallon oil pressure tank lying empty on its side. It was built of five-eighths-inch steel and weighed 8,000 pounds. It was as good as a bomb shelter. They went head-first through the two-foot manhole at the end with perhaps five seconds to spare. Davisson could hear his building being torn apart; sheet metal from its roof rained shrapnel-like against the tank. A few minutes later Davisson stepped out and watched the funnel grind away and then turned and walked into the ruins of twenty-two years of hard work.

For just under an hour the tornado skipped and jabbed and maimed and missed its way across the crowded city. A woman lay on the floor and watched it lift her roof, walls and furniture and leave her unhurt. A few doors away a house collapsed and killed three of the four children playing in a bedroom. The path of devastation ran for twenty-one miles. There were ten persons dead, 198 injured—and so firmly was the violence of the storm implanted in the mind of a child who was there that for months a roll of thunder sent him into hysteria.

The great flood came in country that was always dusty and

dry and now was four years into a killing drought. On a Saturday morning in June, 1954, after unbroken months of a sunstruck sky, heavy clouds began to form over the watershed of the Pecos and the Devils Rivers, which together drain a huge section of West Texas into the Rio Grande. Both run southwest and both have cut deep canyons where they enter the master river of the border country, but for most of the year the water in both merely trickles.

Presently it began to rain. It fell first in little windlashed whippets, a pattering here and there that spotted the dust and formed separate little balls of mud. Then it fell more steadily and the ground was wet and the areas it had missed at first gradually became soaked and soon the rainfall was nearly steady for a hundred miles or so, across the watersheds of both rivers and beyond. Thus it rained for an hour, two hours, three, into the afternoon. Sometimes it slowed and here and there it paused for a minute or two and then began to fall again. There is a hunger for the presence of water in the desert and it does not grow from thirst; there is a yearning for the change and the drama of dark skies and the dust-settling purification of water washing down from above. When rain comes to the desert, men feel relaxed. The normal abrasions wear away and there is a sense of genuine, simple pleasure in watching it fall and listening to it splash. The sheep and the cattle feel this too. They stand in the rain and drink from the running rivulets and when they call to each other their voices have a low, contented sound.

The rain fell through the afternoon and into the night and toward the morning. Rain gauges that measured a few inches filled and were emptied and began to fill again. The range animals felt the ground soften beneath their feet and began drifting toward higher ground. Water ran from the bottom of every gully now and the draws that usually were dry carried small rivers of water. It was raining at dawn on Sunday and it continued all day. But the gentle character of the rain was gone; great sheets of water thundered down and a man walking in it felt a sensation of drowning. It cut a hundred new passages on every hillside, stripped away topsoil by the inches, tugged at the very foundations of buildings. Now the cattle were bawling in alarm. As night fell on Sunday its intensity increased. Sometime that night a rain gauge on an isolated ranch reached twenty-six inches. By dawn the little town of Pandale near the Pecos River, where fourteen families lived, had registered thirty inches of rainfall—and nine of those inches had fallen in one violent hour.

Imagine, then, a two-foot blanket of solid water laid over hundreds of square miles of land in less than two days. Grass and forest land has the capacity to absorb a great deal of water and restore it to the water table. But desert land, tight, hard-caked, unbroken by growing root systems, throws off the water after the first quick penetration of the dust on its surface. The volume of water that thundered down every gully and draw was astounding. Water rose so swiftly that entire herds were trapped and carried down to drown. Ranch houses and buildings were lifted intact and hurtled into the streams to shatter into kindling on the turns. Every low spot was aboil with water and all of this poured into the draws and from the draws to the rivers. The Pecos rose in an 86-foot water wall and battered down the handsome new highway bridge that spanned its canyon fifty feet above the normal water level. The Devils River mounted its sheer canyon walls like an elevator. When the rain started its depth was measurable in inches. Monday it smashed a flood gauge at more than 100 feet, carried away the wreckage and continued to rise.

Johnson's Draw runs right through Ozona, a pretty little ranching town of 3,000, known for its dry and pleasant climate and the rather startlingly big and handsome mansions of its oil-rich cattlemen. The draw had that flat, scoured look. A sheet of water carrying stones and gravel from miles above boomed down it, spread out its banks and swept through the town. Buildings folded and hurtled away. House trailers floated and tumbled for miles. A refrigerator was found thirty-four miles downstream in a ranch meadow. A man remembers swimming frantically to avoid a great tractor-trailer truck that was tumbling grotesquely along behind him, slowly gaining. At the last moment he swept over an underwater obstruction that momentarily caught and held the truck and allowed him to escape.

Fifteen people died in Ozona alone, but I remember best the eyes of a young woman who survived. The sudden thrust of water caught her and swept her away, down the middle of the stream, and she thought she would drown when she saw bearing down on her the big inflated tire and wheel of a truck. She caught it, pulled herself up gratefully and saw a rattlesnake coiled on the other side and poised to strike. The snake was terrified. Like the thousands of others that gave the flood such a macabre tone, it had been washed out of its hole, and had swum for its life, found the tire and managed to slide aboard. In an instant it struck straight at her face. She screamed and fell back in the water, but she did not let go because she knew she would drown. The snake recovered, its rattles buzzing, its head weaving. It struck at her face again. It struck for her hands. She dodged and turned and snapped back her head and dropped one hand and then the other but never both and it became sort of a sick ballet that went on and on until the tire carried her momentarily into shallow water and saved her.

The produce of the draws and streams and rivers flowed into the Rio Grande itself, and that wide, winding, august and usually nearly empty river came to sudden malevolent life. At many points it lifted from its banks and burst the levees, but perhaps the most savage treatment it dealt was to Piedras Negras, a town of 35,000 in Mexico, across from Eagle Pass. It was obvious that disaster was coming, but most of the people ignored the exhortations of Mexican soldiers who cruised the streets in trucks and pleaded through loudspeakers for the people to leave. Mexicans are cheerful, emotional, somewhat fatalistic people little given to worry, and of course, in the small cities along the border, they are ignorant and provincial. The river had risen before and had not damaged the city; why wouldn't the levees hold this time? The rain had been upriver;

they had not seen it fall. And then there was the really quite valid view which one man put this way: "I've worked fifty years for my house and I won't leave it now."

José Galvan operated a small corner grocery store, but he had never earned enough to buy the building. At the reports of danger he walked down to look at the river. The muddy, turbid water was a mile wide, filled with the debris of Jiminez, a village of 1,000 people some forty miles upriver which had surrendered every building. He saw a thirty-foot section of picket fence slowly spinning, a roof lined with chickens, the side of a house. The river rose several feet while he watched. Then he saw a man swimming with powerful but futile strokes. The water pushed the man against the concrete pillar of the bridge. A whole wooden house, perhaps five rooms, came rocking and bobbing down upon him. The house broke into pieces against the pillar and Galvan did not see the man again.

Shaken, he went back to his store. Soon the water crept into the city, a slow brown tide moving gently but steadily through the streets. Inch by inch it rose and Galvan saw it would reach his store. He and his wife began stacking the merchandise on the sturdy wooden counters, shoe boxes and clothing and dry goods and sacks of flour and cornmeal, until everything was safely stored four feet off the floor.

But it turned out that this brown tide which had so gently invaded Piedras Negras was mere backup water, coming from below the city. As Galvan climbed onto the roof of his store to watch, the levees to the north crumpled and a current of river water leaped across the city. It filled the streets, tore at houses and knocked men down and dragged them. Galvan saw it carry a man head down and feet kicking in the air for nearly a block before he disappeared. He felt the foundations of his store shake when the water hit it and when the tide spread into the intersection it slapped against houses on the other side like surf. Now there was a distinct current and the water rose quickly. It flowed through Galvan's store. He was leaning over watching the doorway when he saw the first shoe box float out the door and knew he was ruined. The water was above the level of his counter and was taking his merchandise piece by piece. Soon everything Galvan owned was gone.

He spent the night on the roof, listening to the cries of his neighbors. The water coursed through the city a dozen feet deep. Adobe houses crumbled. Adobe is a desert material, clay mud and straw baked under the sun, and it will last hundreds of years, withstand bullets and fire and violent storms, but it will not withstand solid water. Some of the houses cracked open and collapsed with tired sighs and some went with noises like pistol shots, and over the noises of the houses were the cries of the people who died that night.

In desert country, flash floods fall nearly as quickly as they rise. Sometime before dawn the river crested and the swift current that had pounded Piedras Negras slacked. The sound changed as the water began to fall; now it was running out of the city by its own weight. By afternoon, Galvan could crawl down and examine the carnage. Already the stink of desolation, of dead bodies and overturned privies and mud, was in the air and it would grow much worse. Galvan walked around the town and spoke to the survivors and tried to tally the loss. At least 200 persons had died that night in Piedras Negras. Perhaps 5,000 had died in the entire flood. No one will ever know. Countless bodies were buried in the mass of shifting gravel banks the rivers built and countless more simply were carried out to sea.

It began on Saturday with the rain. It was pretty well over on Tuesday afternoon. Galvan went back, finally, and inspected his store. Everything was gone or ruined except 150 one-kilo packages of lard. He still owed the man from whom he had bought them.

CHAPTER

1

It was a Saturday night in Dallas a bare fifteen years ago and two young men were sitting in a honky-tonk café, talking and drinking beer and shaking out their differences. They were tough men, rutters and fighters and full of pride. They had known each other for years, fought side by side and against each other, but now real trouble had come between them and it may have been no more than the trouble that comes between bulls on a conflicting range. It is clear—witnesses afterwards were certain about this—that there was no specific point of rage that brought them to ignition.

Their talk ran down with nothing settled and one of them stood up to put a coin in the jukebox. The other half-turned on the stool, leaning against the cheap formica counter with its racks of potato chips and Fritos and peanuts, and almost casually issued his ultimatum. It was like cheap drama, except that it was real: beat it, he said in effect, stay out of my way, get out of town or I'll kill you. Or you can draw your damned pistol and fight and you can do it right now.

The other man nodded in full understanding. He walked across the uneven linoleum floor to the jukebox. It was big and bulky with colored lights that glowed and ebbed and changed inside like an endless kaleidoscope. A clock on the wall with turning lights advertised Lone Star Beer and a picture near it showed Judge Roy Bean's famous old saloon at Langtry, and the only really clear thing in the picture was a pile of cases marked Pearl Beer that stood on the saloon's porch.

The man put his nickel in the jukebox. He leaned against it and listened to the coin click through it. He studied the titles and made up his mind and punched the proper button. The mechanism jerked and whirred and an arm lifted the record and set it spinning and the needle found the groove and caught the first heavy thumps of the guitar. The man stood with his back to the room and tapped his foot to the music and listened, head nodding in appreciation, and when he turned around he had a cheap little chrome-plated .32 caliber break-action revolver in his hand and he fired one shot from the hip. The slug took his friend square in the middle of the forehead and knocked him off the stool and spilled him across the floor, his own pistol still in his belt.

I was on the night police run for the Dallas *Times-Herald* then. The press room was in the old Detectives Building and the ambulance was parked in the alley by the back door and sometimes the driver invited me to ride. He did this night and it was an extraordinary experience—the gunpowder smell still heavy in the café, the ride through the night to the hospital with the siren pulsing out ahead, the twenty minutes it took the man with the .32 caliber hole in his forehead to complete the act of dying. I had not seen a man die before and I found the whole night stunning and I always will. But it was my newness and nothing more that made it so and I did not even find this surprising. I knew that it was not an important story, that I would call in a couple of paragraphs at most for the Sunday paper and that this was so because the circumstances were not uncommon. In retrospect, this is the significant point —that two young men should find shooting a logical solution to their mounting antagonism and that the community in which they lived should not consider it unusual enough to be interesting.

There is a propensity for violence that runs like a bloody thread through Texas and her people. It is in their history and it touches their daily lives and does not shame them. There is an element of paradox here, of course. Most Texans are not violent people. The state is not a dangerous place. In the last available ratings, Texas ranked not first but tenth in murders per capita. Nevertheless, I am convinced that violence remains in the back of the Texan's mind as a sort of ultimate to which he might move naturally and logically if sufficiently driven. It creeps into his conversation and his thought processes. It affects his actions and his reactions.

I think that to understand Texans one must understand this, for the effect on the Texas mind is profound. And there is a powerful if indirect relationship between this heritage and the thrust and drive that marks the state, the sense of an active people, confident and proud of the individual's capacity to break new ground, to build dreams and castles and fortunes and even a new society.

The violence that takes place in Texas is not the mindless violence of the great cities, not sadistic or insane or an inarticulate attack on society itself. It is of the individual. I remember a little barber who brooded all day because a customer had called him a son of a bitch; that afternoon he went home for a pistol and killed the man. A minister's son met an old antagonist in the country and shot him to death when the man raised a shotgun. Police records are filled with affrays, street fights, barroom maulings, stabbings, slashings, pistol whippings. There is an old saying, "hot as a two-dollar pistol on Saturday night." One night in Starr County a combatant bit off his opponent's ear, swallowed it by accident and went queasily in search of medical advice. Two well-known cattlemen were tried and convicted of castrating a man who paid attention to a woman they knew. A prominent political figure is reported to have spent months recuperating when his wife shot him in the buttocks as he fled their house during a marital spat, and while the story may be apocryphal, the important point is that it sounds creditable. Two of the most recent fistfights in the U.S.

Congress involved Texans. Michaux Nash, President of the Empire State Bank in downtown Dallas, keeps a .45 caliber automatic pistol in his desk drawer and a .30 caliber carbine in a cabinet nearby; he has a clear sweep of the bank floor and he is deadly with either weapon. There is a story told with great relish in San Antonio of the time the Chicago gangster came to town to organize the gambling and a local gambler pistol-whipped him clear across the lobby of the Blue Bonnet Hotel and dumped him onto a northbound train. The journalist Tommy Thompson, himself a Texan, recalls a night in a luxurious Dallas club a few days after the assassination of President Kennedy. Thompson was delivering himself of opinions of his native state conditioned by years of having lived elsewhere. The conversation ended with his host clutching the table with veins standing on his forehead and shouting, "I'll kill you, goddammit, I'll kill you."

Killing is not hard to justify to a Texas jury and often is lightly penalized. Murder without malice carries a five-year maximum penalty. Until recently, at least, a man who could prove his position under the "unwritten law" could safely kill his wife's paramour and even today he is not likely to suffer serious penalty, nor, even more important, incur the disrespect of his fellows.

Texas juries used to be regarded as pushovers for any woman murder defendant who could manage tears and a demure look and who had not been arrested for prostitution. In the early 1950s, a Dallas woman of considerable wealth and breeding shot down her husband. He had been penniless when he married her and now he not only kept other women and refused her a divorce, he laughed at her. Everyone agreed that if she simply had told the jury that he had done her wrong and she had let him have it, she would have been sent home with garlands. But, perhaps in maintenance of her social position, she insisted it was all an accident. It is very hard to fire a revolver *twice* by accident (it is possible with an automatic pistol) and a jury reluctantly gave her five years. In general, the community regarded it as a pity.

It is unlawful to carry a pistol, but one may keep a weapon in one's car while traveling, which merely means demonstrating intent to cross a county line in the next twenty-four hours. Only a few years ago it was regarded as proper to kill a man who had threatened your life, provided he made some immediately threatening motion, such as reaching into his pocket for one reason or another, and I believe that a jury would listen to such a claim today with considerable sympathy if it were validly made.

There is a tendency, therefore, for trouble to accelerate. It may not be dangerous at the beginning, but there is an unwillingness on both sides to accept a beating or to run. Texas law, in fact, sets out that one is not required to run to avoid a beating. One may choose an alternative, which means something that changes the odds—a board, a knife, a pistol. The assurance that the other fellow is quite capable of such a move hurries one's own move to a weapon. So what begins with a harsh word can become deadly with sickening speed.

I believe that there is a linkage between this sense of easy violence and the natural courtesy of Texans. The soft word, the easy voice, the quick smile, set out one's intentions not to be antagonistic. Of course, other factors led also to courtesy. Texans were gregarious by nature and made the more so by their sparsely settled country. It was hard country and the people who broke it saw themselves as allies in a common cause. They were proud people and their insistence on courteous treatment led them naturally to extend the same. An unhurried way of life leaves time for courtesy, which in turn makes it mandatory, which in another turn reintroduces the idea of violence. The fact that even today discourtesy can lead so swiftly to such harsh results has its own powerful effect.

It is different in the East. People say things in New York which they simply could not say in Texas. Cab drivers shout obscenities at each other, apparently without thought of consequence. For a Texan in New York, it is startling to be in a cab when these violent shouting matches begin, especially if one has an appointment that surely will be delayed by a homicide investigation—and then the lights change, horns blow, the car lurches forward and it's all over. One snowy night on Fifth Avenue near St. Patrick's, I heard two vendors of roasted chestnuts assail each other in terms so violent that I stood rooted, sure that a killing was in process. It was not just the words but the other talismans, the stance, the thrust of the shoulders, the cocked fist, the little shuffling sallies. But death wasn't there. He was down in the subway, perhaps, or in the eyes of a moronic rapist in some apartment house elevator, but not there on the street. After a while the vendors walked off, pushing their carts from which came the warm aroma of chestnuts roasting over charcoal.

Years ago a friend of mine on a visit to New York illuminated a party with the Texas point of view. Suppose, he said, that you came home to your apartment and found your wife bruised and crying, her clothes torn, and she said that she had just that moment been raped and that she had recognized the man and that he had just gone to his own apartment on the next floor. What would you do? Why, said his listeners, call the police immediately. Said my friend, a bit boastfully, I expect, somewhat callow but still demonstrating accurately the Texas attitude, "Well, what I would do, I would get my shotgun and I would kick down his door and I would kill him."

Much later, after I had left Texas and my own attitudes had begun to change, I told that story to an Easterner, a sensitive man of demonstrated physical courage. He was outraged, partly by the story but even more by the approval that he sensed in my voice—and this brought me up short. For, indeed, there had been a time when I approved wholeheartedly of such individual action, which is the antithesis of a workable social structure, of rule by law instead of by force.

But there is such a strain in Texas. It is softening now, and changing. Juries are tougher. Thoughtful Texans know that a heritage of killing is no basis for a stable society. I doubt that my friend would repeat that story now. But just the same, if he came home one night and found the circumstances he had imagined, I would not want to guess what he would do.

2

In rather dry fashion, the encyclopedic Handbook of Texas relates the fact that in 1881 the town of Lookout, a railroad watering place on a high spot in Lamar County, changed its name to Petty. It seems that calling the station frightened the railroad passengers. One can imagine the conductor leaning into the car and bellowing "Lookout," and the Texans falling to the floor and clawing for their hardware.

The idea is more amusing than surprising. Texas was, in Tom Lea's phrase, "a big contentious place," and it did not change much as the twentieth century rolled in. Frontiers on rich land don't remain frontiers for long. The land draws people to cultivate it and gives them good incomes. They demand towns and services and transportation for their produce, and if for no other reason than to protect what they have achieved, they demand a stable society, its balance enforced by law. But a big rough country that requires a hundred acres to support a single gaunt range cow and her calf draws no such influx and does not rapidly achieve a stable society. Eventually the Indians were driven away or killed. The railroads laced across the great distances and the highways followed and deeds of specific ownership were struck. But there were still miles of trackless space, empty and silent but for the wind, the immediate mastery of which lay with a wolf or a rattlesnake or a man with a six-gun and a Winchester.

In East Texas the cotton economy of farms and plantations was active by the Civil War, but this cotton culture was an appendage of the Old South. Texas as a whole is essentially a Western and not a Southern state. Its people orient emotionally and philosophically to that great open section, three quarters of the state, which lies west of Dallas.

And in that dominant area, while the rest of America pushed on to the West, Texas remained a frontier. It kept the frontier life and attitude, the essence of which is self-reliance. It continued to draw men who liked to make their own way, control their environment and live unhampered and who accepted as a consequence the necessity of taking care of themselves. They were a rugged people, thrusting, courageous, resilient, aggressive, fair, good-humored, confident, and they were selectively so, because the frontier defeated those who were not.

This frontier life extends well into the twentieth century—indeed, it is not yet fully gone—and despite its continuing romance with the Alamo, Texas really is a new society. This has a profound effect on the state today, for the fact is that a mere half-century ago when the men who are running Texas now were in the most formative years of their lives, the frontier was real and immediate. It is impossible to examine what the state has done in the last fifty years or what it has become without considering this conditioning.

Of all the delineators of a frontier society, violence is probably the clearest. Well into this century, violence was endemic in the sparser parts of Texas and men habitually went armed. They were prepared to use their arms without hesitation and from time to time the necessity arose.

During the bandit troubles on the Mexican Border in 1915, James B. McAllen acted instantly and instinctively when heavily armed men rode up to his isolated San Juanito Ranch in Hidalgo County. He was alone except for a woman named Maria de Agras, who had been a feminine soldier, a *soldadera*, in the Mexican Revolution. In his book, *Trails and Trials of a Texas Ranger*, W. W. Sterling, former Ranger captain and then Adjutant General of Texas in command of the Rangers, describes the action:

> When the bandits arrived, Mr. McAllen was taking his siesta in the front room of the one story ranch house. It had four large windows which were covered by wooden shutters, painted green. The chief rode to the front door where he was met by Maria. He ordered her to tell the ranchman to come outside. She saw at a glance that they meant to kill him.
>
> The *soldadera* awakened her employer, handed him a glass of whisky and told him about the heavily armed men at the doorstep. Mr. McAllen picked up his ten gauge shotgun which was loaded with buckshot, and fired both barrels through the closed

blinds. The leader and his horse were killed instantly. This was the most deadly blast from a shoulder gun that I have ever seen . . .

. . . the surviving bandits . . . scattered to the shelter of the smaller buildings. These were grouped around the main house in the traditional plan of a Southwest Texas ranch. They were out of shotgun range and he started using his 30-30 Winchesters. Several of these handy rifles were always kept within easy reach in that part of the country. The bandits sniped at him from their hiding places, and he returned their fire. Maria reloaded his rifles . . . he killed another bandit outright and wounded three more. Two died a few days later. These casualties caused the marauders to give up the fight.

After help, including Sterling, arrived, McAllen said:

"Let's go look at the dead man." He had not been moved, and his gray horse was still lying half on top of him. The dead bandit had many freckles on his face. Mr. McAllen looked down at him and exclaimed, "You dirty dog, you tried to murder me on my own doorstep." He started to stomp the dead bandit with the heel of his boot, but I restrained him.

The key is the prompt righteousness and full acceptance of the realities with which Mr. McAllen cut loose with his shotgun. Most of the people of that day and place would have acted similarly, which probably is the reason that most of them lived to handsome ages. They had been trained by circumstances, which is to say both the necessity and the opportunity, to think in terms of backing their actions or even their wishes, in ultimate extremity, with gunfire. This was less true in the towns and still less true in the cities, and it is not fair to portray Texas as a land settled solely to the tune of exploding caps. But in the country the ranchhouses were far apart and the roads were lonely and even after the penetration of the telegraph and then the telephone, even after the automobile, a man was largely on his own. Smugglers worked along the border and renegades found this comfortable country. Cattle rustling was common and the big ranchers were glad to have men who could take care of themselves and they did not ask a great many questions. When the first drillers tapped oil in the desert, whole towns of shanties and wooden derricks sprang into being in a matter of weeks and the men they attracted were fully as wild as those who used to whoop in the cattle trail towns. Long before the boomtowns could get around to building a jail, harassed lawmen were chaining strings of offenders to trees. They dispensed a great deal of what they saw as justice with the pointed toe of their heavy boots or with their pistols. It was not a time for timid men.

Writing in 1935, the late historian, Dr. Walter Prescott Webb, recalled a trip into the brush country along the border: "Upon leaving Laredo, I buckled on the six-shooter, less conscious of it than I had expected to be for the reason that nearly every American on the border carries one when out of town."

The sentence is from Dr. Webb's book, *The Texas Rangers*, the only definitive history ever written of that extraordinary and storied band of lawmen. The Rangers exist today, as potent as ever, just sixty-two men to cover the whole state, and they are certainly the most elite force of lawmen in the country. They also are among the roughest.

Dr. Webb's history opens with their formation in 1835, the year before the Texas Revolution, and continues through bloody encounter after bloody encounter with Mexicans, Indians, and desperadoes well into the 1920s. It is a very thorough book, but in a curious way, it is almost totally uncritical. Dr. Webb had a deep grasp of the significance of the frontier. It is interesting, therefore, that his sympathy was totally and plainly with the violence practiced as a matter of course by the frontier Rangers. The point is not to diminish his authority or scholarship; it is to note that he was himself a frontiersman and that he was writing in 1935. The violent heritage was still fresh; Indian raiders and then bandits—Texans and Mexicans—had used torture and murder as standard practices; violence begot violence; the hand of society often was as brutal as the hand raised against it. And as late as 1935, the state's most prominent historian saw this violence casually practiced by society's protectors as natural and necessary.

This attitude is most clear in the final chapter of the book, which concerns Captain Frank Hamer, who could serve as the prototype for the modern Ranger. Stalwart, honest, brave, ferocious, Hamer is the man who in 1934 tracked down Clyde Barrow and Bonnie Parker and oversaw what turned out to be their execution near Plain Dealing, Louisiana. Webb describes the night in 1918 near Brownsville when Hamer was in a party of officers who were waiting to catch a smuggler named Incarnacion Delgado:

> On the way out, the officers in charge agreed that if anyone approached, the command to halt would be given and if not obeyed the men were to fire. Ranger Frank Hamer, though a private, vigorously objected, stating that Delgado was a dangerous man, who would not surrender, and that he would kill someone if possible.
>
> "I am in favor," he said, "of giving him the works first and the orders afterwards."
>
> "We might kill an innocent man," said one of the officers.
>
> "No, we won't kill an innocent man because no innocent man is going to be on this trail at this time of night," said Hamer. His judgment was overruled.

The officers concealed themselves beside the road where the smuggler was expected. They knew his probable route and his signal to his confederates, the bleat of a goat. The party included Hamer's superior and best friend, Ranger Sgt. Delbert Timberlake.

> The men had been in position about two hours when they heard the twigs breaking under catlike tread, the bleat of a goat and the brush scratching leather boots that were coming along the trail. Hamer and the sheriff rose quietly to their feet, leveled their guns and the sheriff gave the command, "Halt!" Delgado held his pistol in his right hand and fired instantly. The ball struck the ground eighteen feet from Timberlake who had not risen, ricocheted, and penetrated his body. Timberlake went over saying, "Cap, he got me through the guts." [Sheriff] Vann and Hamer fired at the flash of the pistol and as successive plumes of flame burst from the Ranger's Winchester, one man remarked,

"Good God, watch Frank use the pear-burner on him." The Mexican ran a few feet and fell dead with his forty-five pistol in one hand and a dozen pistol cartridges in the other.

Timberlake died at 7 A.M. the next day with Hamer beside him. Hamer pulled a sheet over his friend's face and went outside to report to the waiting officers.

"Well, he's cashed in," was the way he informed them.
"Hamer," said one of the officers, "if we had followed your advice, things would have been different. We made a mistake."
"Yes," he assented, nodding to the white sheet that could be seen through the window, "and there is your mistake."

Any policeman's life is hard; the pay is low, the thanks few, the risks high. This is the more true of the Texas Rangers. A tiny force with near impossible traditions of bravery and action, it is elite by its nature, quite without parallel in America, and its members must perform as such. The Ranger is thrust automatically into the most dangerous and violent situations, and because there are so few of him, he often goes alone, or at the least as the point-man and leader of lesser officers.

Capt. Bill McDonald, a colorful phrasemaker whom fellow Rangers early in this century saw as rather a publicity hound, summed up the Ranger dictum: "No man in the wrong can stand up against a fellow that's in the right and keeps on a-comin'." McDonald once met Bat Masterson in a café in Sanderson and remonstrated when Masterson started to hit a Chinese waiter. In the suddenly quiet room, Masterson said, "Maybe *you'd* like to take it up." McDonald had mild blue eyes that could get very cold. "I done took it up," he said, and ended the situation. McDonald was responsible for that old chestnut of a story, now emblazoned in bronze on a big statue of a Ranger in the lobby at Love Field in Dallas, of the Ranger and the riot. As he told the story later, he responded alone to a call for a company of Rangers to quell a mob. When he stepped off the train and met the dismay of the citizens who had summoned him, he said, "Well, you ain't got but one mob, have you?"

The tale is almost unforgivably hoary, but it does sum up the tradition which in turn delineates the man. The Ranger is courageous, physically oriented, capable of great violence, but more than that, he has presence. He has a capacity not just to command but to dominate other people and entire situations by some inner force. Certain men have that capacity and it really has nothing to do with size or toughness or strength, and these are the truly dangerous men. There is something palpable about this danger; other men recognize it with their nerve endings and they walk softly and with care; it is not a matter of fear of being hit or even of being killed, but rather it is deep, primeval, quite instinctive.

I remember approaching Capt. Alfred Allee one day in the lobby of the old Ringgold Hotel in Rio Grande City. It is a cool, thick-walled hotel, hardly changed since the days when cavalry patrols from Fort Ringgold jangled through the dusty streets and out to the Mexican Border beyond. The lobby, with its dark woods and old-fashioned desk, would make a natural setting for a Western movie. The captain, whose reputation for violence is as great as that of any man in Texas today, was registering. He had come to town to oversee a bit of trouble and three of his men who were already there now returned to the hotel. Suddenly—like a movie—the front door flew open and all three appeared at once. They stood for a moment in a little half-circle, each well clear of the others, with an air of coiled tension like pistols on full cock; they were good-looking men, clean shaven, wearing boots and twill trousers and shirts with pearl buttons, and there was a special neatness about them; they wore gun belts with pistols in holsters cocked out to the side where they could be easily reached, and their hands hung loose and easy; one of them was immense but the other two were smaller than I; and they stood there for a shimmering moment and they were *dangerous* and only a fool would fail to sense it; and then the moment passed and Allee said easily, "Hello, boys," and they said, "Hello, Cap." I talked to Allee for an hour and when I left the old hotel I looked back and saw the captain, now elderly and not very big and not a bit less dangerous for that, with the three Rangers backing him up, standing in that little half-circle behind him, poised, ready.

The man who is prepared to walk alone into great danger must be prepared to make instant decisions and act upon them, to demand instant obedience and get it. Years ago Capt. McDonald faced twenty soldiers at Fort Brown who had rifles trained on him and had been ordered to keep him out. He walked right in the gates. "I'm Captain McDonald," he roared, "and I've come to investigate you scoundrels. *Put up them guns!*" And they did.

It is just this quality that makes the Rangers hated men. Actually, they often are pleasant company. They usually are polite and sometimes affable until crossed. They have the dignity that comes with great confidence and they are usually temperate men who drink lightly if at all and are clean mouthed and incorruptible. But they have become an anachronism and this is never more apparent than when they are dealing with that mass of honest and significant people who are the militant poor of Texas—and whose hatred for the Rangers is bitter and unrelenting. Like any police force, the Rangers represent the status quo, which automatically is in conflict with social change brought about by protests, demonstrations and strikes. What's more, the status quo in Texas, as we will see later, is particularly archaic, made so generally by the same factors that produced the Rangers. So resistance to change is strong and when the Rangers are on the spearpoint, the resistance becomes implacable.

But the anachronism of the Rangers goes much further. Its real thrust lies in the fact that their traditions and their violence are characteristics not of a modern society but of the frontier. They provide one of the last direct and active links with the immediate past in Texas. In fact, their very existence is a significant demonstration of the proximity to its own frontier in which Texas still lives.

As witness, one should examine the killing of Gene Paul Norris in 1957. Norris was a Fort Worth bandit who was thought to have killed some thirty-five persons, including a Houston businessman and his wife who were covered with blankets, tied to chairs and beaten to death with ballbats. He was believed to be killing his accomplices too, and dead thieves were turning up all over Tarrant County. But the state had not yet convicted Norris for these crimes.

One day lawmen who were tapping his phone learned that he intended to make a trial run the next day over the getaway route for a bank robbery he was planning. The lawmen, mostly Rangers, were waiting the next day and when they jumped him, Norris fled. Near Springtown he turned down a clay road slick from rain and soon spun his car into a ditch.

Nearly a quarter-century earlier, when Bonnie Parker and Clyde Barrow did not surrender, Frank Hamer helped shoot them down. Now, on the flat plains a few miles from Fort Worth, Norris and the man who was with him were shot to death. The full circumstances were not made public, and though it was intimated at the time that Norris had opened the firing, this was considered doubtful. It is clear, however, that there no longer was any need to try to bring Norris to trial.

3

It was spring in East Texas and there had been a rain and grass was growing green and new along the highway in Rusk County. The trees were tall and strong and between them shafts of sunlight struck the crimson clover so that it flamed deep red. Verbena and daisies and little dots of white clover flowers marked the grass on the side of the road and the air was soft and clear. The Ranger was driving the car slowly, the windows down, enjoying the day and the job. He was going down to the Angelina River bottoms to look again at the scene, to nose about and talk and watch sharp-eyed and yet casual for anything that was new, anything that would suggest who had murdered old man Thompson.

H. J. Thompson had been sixty-eight, divorced, eccentric,

better known than he was liked. He lived in Laneville and ran seventy-five head of cattle on six hundred acres south of town, and one day just before Christmas of 1965 someone had waited in the pasture where he came every day and shot him and took the thousand-odd dollars he carried in his pocket. There was a particular brutality to the way it was done, a coldness and a cruelty that frightened people, and they got together in Laneville and asked the governor to send in the Rangers. Now the case was old, the murderer yet uncaught, and the Ranger, confident, patient, had spent many hours poking, ruminating, waiting for something to turn up.

Jim Ray is a tall, slender man in his early fifties. He has big hands and gives an immediate impression of calm strength. He wears bifocals with clip-on plastic shades and a khaki-colored Western suit with black boots and a businesslike policeman's pistol, a snub .38 revolver, blued and not at all flamboyant. He is a pleasant, quiet, good-humored man, capable of savagery and somewhat ambivalently disturbed by that fact, but on the whole satisfied with himself and the terms of his life. He spent years on the Highway Patrol, but finally the horrid matter of lifting shattered people from wrecked cars became overpowering—"You learn to dread the sound of the phone and to hate traffic offenders until you can hardly look at them." He joined the Rangers in 1957 and works long but not unpleasant hours. His wife, who has never fully reconciled herself to the lawman's life, teaches school in Tyler, where they live, and they get along.

"Old man Thompson was killed on a Wednesday. His boy came home from the Army on Friday and couldn't find his daddy. He finally went down to the pasture and found the old man half in, half out of his car. Shotgun had blown his head all apart. It had rained the day before. Washed out tracks and all and killed the scent for the hounds. And then the first people on the scene tramped all around. I reckon if there was any sign, they tramped it down.

"He'd been divorced and there was some money trouble with his wife. That may have been why he carried so much around, kept it in cash instead of the bank. We established beyond question he had a good thousand dollars on him the day he was killed. He used to flash it all around. Likely that's what got him killed. There's folks in Rusk County who would do plenty for fifty dollars, let alone a thousand."

He was still driving slowly, both hands on the wheel, ruminating over the ground he had covered so many times.

"This is rough down here. The people in this country are ignorant and backwoodsy. They believe in revenge. Most of the men run coons and drink busthead whisky and live by their own law and if they're in trouble they're not likely to go to the sheriff, they'll try to settle it themselves.

"Hell, there's lots of suspects. His wife's family, they're a tough bunch. I ran them on the polygraph and they came out clean. There's an old man keeps bobbing up as a suspect, but every time I trace the rumor down, it always goes back to his son and daughter-in-law. He's got a little piece of land and they'd like to see him put away, in the penitentiary or the asylum, and they could get the land. Then there's another old boy. I think he's had some brain damage. He's a bad one. He whips his mama and his poppa and his brothers, he whips his wife and he runs them all off. He bootlegs around here, stays drunk all the time, wants to whip everybody. He's just a typical character for this part of the country. I remember a trial one time down in the Big Thicket country to the south of here, when one of the Harrises, some relation to the boxer, Roy Harris, was on the stand. The opposing attorney wanted to discredit him. He says, 'Mr. Harris, what do you do for a living?' and Harris says, 'I run a few hogs and I steal a few.' Attorney says, 'Well, what else do you do?' Harris says, 'I drink a little whisky and I make a little,' and the attorney asks, 'Do you ever break the law?' Harris says, 'Yes, I do. I make a little whisky, I shoot deers when I feel like it,' and that was enough for the jury. They believed every word of his testimony. They knew he was solid."

We drove into Laneville, a tiny town on a secondary road, and stopped at Thompson's house. There are only a couple of filling stations, a couple of stores, a few houses. When a stranger stops, everybody watches. They recognized the Ranger's car, but no one approached. The house was closed now and forlorn, but it obviously had lacked the grace of a woman's touch for years. Thompson's dented 1958 Ford sedan was in the driveway, the blood on its front seat now a great rusty stain.

"Thompson was a talker. Few days before he was killed, he was in the general store. He was telling people, 'Well, I'm going to have to kill me a nigger who's been down there hunting on my land. I reckon I'll just kill the son of a bitch.' But no one thought much about it because the old man had been talking that way for years and hadn't killed anyone yet, least not that anyone knew. Used to be a young fellow, about five years ago, who operated a hog farm for an owner who lived in Houston. The farm was beyond Thompson's place and he had right-of-way over Thompson's land to reach his place. He and Thompson got to jawing and one day Thompson put up a fence across the road and said he wouldn't let this fellow through. When the fellow drove up and saw the fence across the road and Thompson sitting there in his car, he jumped out of his pickup with a .410 shotgun—man, he was ready, he didn't give a damn, he wasn't calling no sheriff—and Thompson started up his car and drove like the devil. He went home and called the law and when they wanted him to go back out and see this fellow, he wasn't about to.

"'Course, could have been a hunter who killed him, but I don't think so. I think he was killed for his money. Whoever it was knew him, I'm sure of that. A stranger never would have blundered into that isolated pasture and anyway, we know the man who killed him stood and waited for him to come and that means he knew the old man's habit was to come there every afternoon. I believe the man who killed him lives right around here, maybe right in Laneville, and he's watching us, jumpy as hell and trying to hide it, and I think we're going to shake him out one of these days."

We rolled on down the road, out of Laneville in a moment, covert glances flashing at us. The people were edgy. Ten years ago a couple burned to death in their farmhouse in suspicious circumstances. The people here believe it was murder. They think the killer knew his victims, that he lived here, that he's still here. And now Thompson, the same story; it's enough to make people think.

Several miles down the highway we turned in at the Risinger Store, where Thompson had stopped on the last day of his life to buy a piece of penny candy and talk to Jim Risinger. It was a weatherworn old store, gloomy inside, cobwebs hanging, floor so dirty it looked at first like hardpacked soil. It was a country place and its shelves were lined with corn meal, baking powder, snuff, chewing tobacco. The Justice of the Peace, Mrs. Austin Chapman, was inside. She is a small, round woman and when she saw the Ranger a spasm of worry went over her pocked face. She beckoned him to a corner and they exchanged information in whispers. She looked grim and upset. When we left, he said, "She didn't know anything. Just worried. But I always check. You never know when you'll get a lead."

He ruminated, driving along the road where the grass was such a new green. "That's what really breaks cases, you know, when you get some information. I remember one time an old Ranger near here got a call from an officer in Dallas who said he had some information that some thieves planned to knock a safe in a big store in a town near here. The Dallas officer came on out and they figured it must be the Safeway store the burglars planned to hit, so they staked it out, figured they'd wait and catch them in the act. The Ranger was out in the back where there was a field of Johnson grass high as your head and pretty soon he heard this burglar coming. The burglar was out on bail for a half-dozen jobs and probably was trying to raise money for his defense. He got up within about twenty feet of the Ranger and he was going to run right over him to get to the back of the store. The Ranger had his old shotgun and as he started to move away from the building to get out of the burglar's path the shotgun hit the side of the building. It was corrugated metal and there was a loud clatter and this old boy dropped in the Johnson grass and he and the Ranger both lay still, not knowing exactly what to do, and after a while the Ranger said, 'You stand up there or I'm going to mow down the grass with this shotgun just like a scythe and kill you.' And in a minute the burglar says, 'Don't do that, don't shoot.' And the Ranger said, 'Well, get the hell up where I can see you and don't make a move.' He stood up with his hands high and the Ranger said, 'You move over close to me and keep your hands up because if you put them down I'm going to kill you.' It wouldn't have been the worst thing if he had killed him, that's a surefire warning to burglars, but he couldn't just do it. So he didn't know what to do. He'd messed up, really, by making that noise. So he said, 'You son of a bitch, you came here to burglarize this store and I know you did and I'm telling you that you'd better go on and do just what you came here to do or I'm gonna kill you.' Well, the burglar found an air-conditioning duct and he went right up it with his bundle of burglar tools swinging from a loop on his arm and directly the Ranger heard the skylight breaking and then he went down inside. The Ranger just lay there hidden in the Johnson grass and directly a Safeway truck that makes early deliveries drove up to the back. The driver, without ever seeing the Ranger, got out of the truck and unlocked one of those lift-up doors. When he got it up he saw this burglar just inside knocking the knob on the safe. And he said, 'What are you doing?' And the burglar said, 'There's a Texas Ranger lying out there in those bushes who says he's gonna shoot me if I don't open this safe.' And the driver turned and went back to his truck and left, scared as hell. But out in front he saw a city policeman and the policeman called up reinforcements and in a minute here come the police force and they popped open that door and they discovered themselves a safe burglar and they arrested him. The next day he told the district attorney that he'd met a Texas Ranger out in the Johnson grass and the Ranger'd told him to go up on the roof and break in and commit that burglary. And the D.A. said, 'You are a damned liar and isn't that the most ridiculous thing you ever heard of and what chance do you think you have in front of a jury if you tell a stupid story like that?' This old boy got out on bond and went back to Dallas and told the story and from what the officers learned, all his friends laughed like hell and nobody ever did believe a word he said. 'Course, it wouldn't have held up in court and the Ranger'd never have let it get to court, but a little while after that, that burglar was convicted on a bunch of burglaries in Dallas and went to the penitentiary and that was the end of it."

But the killing of old man Thompson was different. No one was talking. There was no set-up, no place to dig and apply pressure. Several miles from the store, Ray slowed the car and turned off on a dirt road that led onto Thompson's land. We were retracing Thompson's last steps. We passed an old deserted house and wound into the pasture, and though it really was near the highway, it was perfectly screened to sight and sound by the trees. There were willows and elm, sweet gum, oak, birch, black walnut, hickory, cedar. Grapevine ran up their stout trunks and the car's passage knocked over thorny Russian thistles and crunched tiny wild strawberries underwheel.

Ray stopped his car where it had been Thompson's habit to stop his, just past a rude shack perhaps twelve feet by twelve with a dirt floor. The cows had walked into the shed and their hooves had marked the dirt, but in one corner the dirt was smoothed down. A man had stood there for some time on that bloody day, watching the road into the pasture through a wide crack at eye level, waiting for Thompson to come, knowing he would. When the old black Ford had lurched into sight and passed the shack and stopped, the man had stepped out with a 16-gauge shotgun in his hands. He had come to kill, because he intended robbery and the old man knew him, or perhaps just for grudge. But he had come to kill.

This is what Ray believes happened: Thompson was out of his car when the man appeared. He turned and made for the car and the man fired a charge of No. 4 shot that struck him from his beltline to his hat. Thompson staggered on and the man ran closer and fired again, tearing a five-inch hole in Thompson's back. Thompson managed to get in the car, close and lock the door, start the engine and get the car moving before he fell over on the seat. The car rolled down into the river bottom and jounced to a stop. The killer followed, put a bar of some sort in the door handle and twisted so violently that the whole handle assembly came off. He opened the door and fired again. The charge missed Thompson completely and went through the right window, leaving a two-inch hole. The man pulled Thompson out onto the ground, his feet still in the car, and put the shotgun to his forehead and fired again. He blew the old man's head apart. Bits of Thompson's false teeth were found in the car and under it. The killer flipped the body over, the feet still in the car, and grabbed for Thompson's wallet so furiously he tore out the whole rear pocket. Then, with the wallet, the shotgun, the shells it had ejected, the bar and even the door handle, he walked down into the river bottoms and vanished.

Ray looked around carefully, a tall, loose figure walking head down, scuffing the ground thoughtfully with his shiny boots as he always does when he comes here. He reconstructed the whole thing in his mind, moving as he thought the killer had moved, searching for an anomaly until then overlooked that would open new insights and give him new avenues to pursue. It was tantalizing there in the pasture where it had happened, and now it was more than merely a mysterious puzzle. Now it was real. The ground on which we stood had soaked up the old man's dying blood and it had cushioned the footsteps of the man who had killed him. The wind stirred in the trees as it might have that day and a bird cried. But the new insights did not come and finally, regretfully, Ray turned the car and we drove out of the pasture and back toward Laneville.

"There are lots of suspects, lots of 'em. All sorts of people knew he had money and knew he went out to that pasture. And he wasn't the most popular man around." He sighed. "But I think we'll catch our man. We're going to keep asking and talking and waiting and putting on pressure and something is going to turn up. I can wait a long time on a murder, I'll tell you that.

"Fact is, I'm doing a little psychological warfare right now in a case several years old. There was an old gal up here a ways married to a fellow a good bit older than she was. She milked him pretty hard and got his money and made him buy insurance, and all the time she was sleeping with a bunch of different men. One of them was her main lover, a fellow from Dallas, a mailman, and he would drive up to see her. Well, her husband played poker every week regular as could be and he always came home the same way. One night this mailman came up from Dallas and blocked a cattleguard near their home and when her husband stopped, the mailman stepped out of the shadows and shot him twice with a .38 and killed him. Now, I went to work on that. I found her alibi was so pat that I was pretty sure she was involved and I began running down the men she'd been sleeping with and there was a plenty of them, including a game warden, she'd slip out in the woods hunting and getting a little to boot. Well, I finally turned up this mailman and he had suddenly acquired a lot of money, bought his way into a gambling joint and was living high. So we brought her in and she denied everything. We put her on the polygraph, though, and she bumped the peg—drove the polygraph needle right off the board whenever we asked about the killing. We brought in the mailman and he like to blew up the polygraph. But both of them denied it and polygraph evidence is not admissible in court. We put on lots of pressure and eventually they got married, maybe because husbands and wives can't be forced to testify against each other. But we never could get any usable evidence and finally we had to back off. Well, that was some years ago and not so long ago she divorced the mailman and married someone else in another town. So I got out all the old pictures we'd made of her husband's corpse still in the car with blood all over and I had a big batch printed up and now I'm sending her one every once in a while, about every week or so I send her one in an envelope with nothing else in it. I put no return address and I just mail them to her at her home address under her new name from all over Texas, wherever I happen to be. And I'm going to keep on doing this and I'm going to see if it will shake her up a little bit. I'm going to see what's going to happen."

It was nearly sundown when we got back into Laneville. We stopped for a soft drink, the Ranger unfolding himself from his car and stretching easily and all the time looking around in little cat glances. He opened the bottle and stood by the corner of the building in the soft fading light and in a moment a little man hurried around the corner and almost ran into him. He was a tense, uneasy-looking man, ulcerous perhaps, not yet fifty but graying and getting old, and he leaped back, startled by the big Ranger, and then recovered and thrust out his hand.

And of course he asked, "Anything new on the case yet? Anything turn up?" The Ranger eyed him gravely. He was one of a half-dozen men who headed the suspect list and naturally he knew that.

"Oh, there's some new things, but they haven't panned out yet, not quite."

"I guess there's lots of suspects, ain't there?"

"Sure, lots of them at first, you know—but the list is sure as hell narrowing down in a hurry now, down to just a few people, right quick now."

The man gulped. His head bobbed in a nervous, nodding gesture. He was wearing low working boots and he shifted from foot to foot.

"I hope it does," he said. "I'll be honest with you. I hope it does."

"Well, we're going to poke around here and we're going to keep on poking until we turn up the man who did it."

"I hope you do," the little man said. "You know, Thompson was a good old buddy of mine."

The Ranger did not answer. He stood staring at the little man, a tall, stern, dangerous-looking figure. The silence drew out and the little man turned suddenly and went up the street, hurrying, and the Ranger stood motionless, his face unchanged, watching him go.

4

When President John F. Kennedy was assassinated in Dallas, the whole world noted instantly that it happened in Texas. It hit so hard. It was such a dirty thing, so cruel and aberrant as to make every man feel vulnerable. I think Lee Harvey Oswald fired on our hope that day and that is why the pain was so intense; hope that lay in a brightening vision of man's capacities, that insisted that the future would be better if just we cared enough. Some of us had made of Kennedy a prince in our lives, elegant and graceful, riding about with a glass slipper that might someday fit us. And then there was the electronic speed with which the inexorable facts piled up, ruthlessly destroying all the little cushioning doubts that man puts up. Who doesn't remember that afternoon when the electronic media focused the pain and left us defenseless? (I was in another country, in a library, and the librarian came panting up the stairs to whisper in a Scottish brogue and I went down into the street where the transistor radios were destroying the lingering hope that it was all a mistake, and caught a plane for Dallas.) The man in pain wants a scapegoat and there stood Texas, big, loud, crass, with its hard-rock Western ethic that in the terms of today's society leads automatically to conservatism and commercialism. There stood Texas with, as we have seen, its undoubted propensity for violence. Who else to blame?

This automatic assumption was vastly ironic, however, because it happened not to be true. Or so I believe. After considerable examination and thought, I have come to the firm conclusion that neither the atmosphere in Texas nor that in Dallas itself had any bearing on the assassination. That it took place in Texas was happenstance, and in Dallas still the more so. The irony of the situation lies in the fact that people in both the state and the city have conducted themselves over the years in such a manner as to lead the rest of the world to blame them quite logically for that in which they were blameless.

The thing that separates Oswald from Texas, to which he moved when he was six, was not that he was so often gone, in New York, New Orleans, the Marine Corps, Russia, but that his violence seems inner-directed instead of outer-conditioned. (The same point appears true, incidentally, in that other great orgy of individual violence, which also happened in Texas, when a mad student firing a rifle from the University of Texas tower killed sixteen people and wounded thirty.) Oswald just did not seem to be affected much by his surroundings or by the people he met, except that his rejection of them and their consequent rejection of him heightened his powerful drives toward self-destruction.

At thirteen he was having trouble relating to other children and a psychiatrist who saw him diagnosed incipient schizophrenia with paranoiac overtones. The psychiatrist found Oswald isolated, suspicious, defiant, hypersensitive with a deteriorating grasp on reality, a boy who believed himself singled out for rejection and frustration and who had given up any hope of being understood. In his teens he was more and more the loner with a flattened personality. A boy who had known him as a child and saw him again in his middle teens was surprised. "He just hadn't turned into somebody. He hadn't turned into anybody."

His personality was fixed by the time he joined the Marines. He was flat, withdrawn, and, when he did have contacts with others, aggressive. It has been speculated that by this time he had turned a psychological corner: he no longer felt that people rejected him but that he rejected them. The move to Russia seems more psychological than ideological: he found life intolerable, which is to say he found himself intolerable, and he hoped a drastic change would improve things. It did not, naturally, and so he came home, puttered about minor jobs and causes, postured as an intellectual and a political activist, and leaned more and more toward an expression of himself in violence. His wife reports that it was he who fired the shot at the rightist general, Edwin Walker, several months before the assassination, and there seems to be no reason to doubt her. It is plain that in the last months of his life, Oswald was increasingly erratic, increasingly the failure, rejected by society and by his own family, and more and more the haunted man for whom nothing goes right.

By chance he got a job at the Texas School Book Depository, before President Kennedy decided to come to Texas and, of course, long before the President's motorcade route was announced and Oswald's opportunity thus was presented. Psychiatrists say that the typical assassin of an important man is a person with paranoiac ideas of grandiosity who can achieve psychic comfort in his own view of himself only by shocking the whole world and forcing it to recognize him. In the twisted smirk on the captured Oswald's face there is the look of triumph: now the world knew him.

But if Oswald was not a product of the Texas society, that other character who placed the seal of irredeemable horror on that terrible weekend, Jack Ruby, most certainly was. Whatever his motivation, however sick his reasons, Ruby acted within the heritage of the state he had adopted. He killed on impulse.

It must be so. He was at the Western Union office at 11:17 that morning. It is a three-minute walk from the Western Union office to the city police station. He killed Oswald there at 11:21 and no one had known just when Oswald would be brought down from the police station detention cell to be moved to the county jail.

Policemen fascinated Ruby. He liked to be around them. He had come from Chicago years before, picked Dallas because he liked it and now he was a frustrated little man who operated strip joints and lived with a pack of dogs. He had an obvious business relationship with the police, but his affection for policemen went far beyond that and he often was at the station. A detective I know recalled seeing Ruby in the station's crowded halls the day after the President was killed and not being surprised. "I opened a door and there was Jack, squeezed in with all the reporters. I grabbed his coat and jerked him into the room. 'You son of a bitch,' I said, 'what are you doing here?' He grinned and giggled. He had a way of wiggling himself like a little dog. 'I'm here with the press,' he said. I said, 'Press, hell, you're not with the press.' He said, 'I'm a translator for the Yiddish Herald.' And I said, 'Get out of here,' and I opened the door and threw him back into the hall with the reporters." Ruby was an old hand at the police station.

He came down the ramp that morning with the pistol he had a permit to carry and they were bringing Oswald out and the television cameras were on him and uncounted millions of people were studying the man who had killed the President and Jack Ruby, that red-blooded Texas boy from Chicago, made his move. He stepped up, pistol in hand, and in the approved phrasing of the world of police and hoodlums in Texas, shouted, "You rat son of a bitch, you killed the President." He fired once and fell down in an instant, which police later said saved his life, since they certainly would have shot him down if he had remained on his feet. And he was yelling, "I'm Jack Ruby, you guys know me."

He had thought he would kill Oswald if he got a chance, he said later, when he saw the sarcastitc sneer on Oswald's face. Ruby had a streak of violence in him despite his small size, and had seriously assaulted several men. He admired tough guys. And he saw Oswald: *Oswald, that jerk, had killed the President and messed up Dallas and now he was sneering and not cooperating with the police. Somebody oughta shoot the rat son of a bitch.* A policeman testified at Ruby's trial that when Ruby was asked after his arrest why he had done it, he said, "Someone had to do it, and you guys couldn't do it." It was grotesque and perhaps insane, but it was in the Texas pattern.

And now the counterpoint irony developed. While the world denounced Texas, and particularly Dallas, for Oswald's act, a feeling grew that this in no way explained Ruby's act. He, the suspicion went, had killed Oswald as part of a larger plot against the President. The notion was immensely frustrating to Ruby. He died of cancer in Parkland Hospital imploring people to believe that he had shot Oswald on impulse, only because he happened to have the chance.

CHAPTER
VI

It was a Sunday in late spring and the First Baptist Church of Dallas was full. The old minister's mellow voice filled the great room, capturing the listening people and moving them steadily and willingly toward the fire of his message. They were handsome and well-dressed, these members of the biggest and probably most sophisticated Baptist church in the world. There was a sense of radiant well-being: air conditioning drew off in silence the body heat of nearly 4,000 people and there was not a dust mote or a sun ray or an errant noise to interfere. The people sat in burnished wooden pews and walked on red carpets and the walls were a soft, cool green with molding that was excellent but not ornate.

It was all smooth and precise, timed to the television camera that was beaming this, the 10:50 A.M. service, to believers for miles around. The hundred-member choir in white robes and red sashes had lifted its soaring voice in the kind of hymns that catch a man's heart and turn him toward the faith. There had been announcements and prayers by various assistants, the words clear and neatly turned, and then the minister had come on.

He was one of the great fundamentalist preachers, straight,

spare, with a strong, squarish face that radiated sincerity. His name was Dr. E. S. James and he was appearing this day as a guest pastor in the regular pastor's absence. He was from rural Oklahoma and Texas, and though the country accents were there, the voice was magnificent. It hurled every word to the farthest reaches of the room and after a while it took on life of its own, rolling across the pews and recoiling, sometimes gentle as a caress, sometimes violent as a storm. It was conversational, understanding, comforting, and then as the fervency mounted and the excitement grew it thundered in exaltation and cast lightning bolts against the ungodly; and it seduced the mind and caught it and swept it toward the promise that lay ahead.

He had taken for his text and had read from the second letter of Peter, which was written to assuage the doubts in the days that followed Christ. Christ had promised to come again to earth and the people who had stood in the sun and listened to him had assumed it would be soon as men count time; the fathers of the church had expected not to die but to be swept up to the kingdom of heaven in their own lifetime. Now these fathers were dead—"fallen asleep," the writer said—and nothing had changed. Hence, of course, doubts; but these doubts, the writer cried triumphantly, are themselves part of prophecy, for in the last days before Christ reappears, scoffers shall arise; indeed, the presence of scoffers shall mark the end times. With relish and affection, the minister read the beautiful, bell-like words from the King James Bible, ". . . there shall come in the last days scoffers, walking after their own lusts, And saying, Where is the promise of his coming? for since the fathers fell asleep, all things continue as they were from the beginning of creation." But, the writer goes on, the scoffers ignore the facts: that "by the word of God, the heavens were of old," and that the flood came and destroyed the world that was known and now there is a new world, "reserved unto fire against the day of judgment." And the words went on, ". . . one day is with the Lord as a thousand years, and a thousand years as one day. The Lord is not slack concerning his promise, as some men count slackness; but is long-suffering to us-ward, not willing that any should perish, but that all should come to repentance. But the day of the Lord will come as a thief in the night; in the which the heavens shall pass away with a great noise, and the elements shall melt with fervent heat, the earth also and the works that are therein shall be burned up." Therefore, ". . . what manner of persons ought ye to be . . . look for new heavens and a new earth . . . be diligent that ye may be found of him in peace, without spot, and blameless."

Thus he set the pattern of his sermon and launched into it with relish. In a curiously direct way, the sermon described his faith and, in turn, the faith of his church. Repent, for the Lord is coming; cleave to the old values, honor the fathers, live that you may not be found wanting on the day of judgment. This is fundamentalism. There are 1,700,000 Baptists in Texas and vastly more fundamentalists of various other faiths and sects, and they have a powerful effect on the state and its outlook. This is much more than a few simple and somewhat puritanical attitudes—particularly opposition to drink—backed in some cases by law. Rather, it goes to the very root of the people and it is an indispensable part of what they are and what they believe and what, as a result, they have accomplished.

The First Church of Dallas has some 13,500 members and six buildings on three blocks in the heart of the downtown city. Its members shy a little at the term fundamentalism. They associate it with the old extremes, the foot washers, the shouters, the holy rollers who roll on the floor when the spirit is upon them, and they are not *that* kind of fundamentalists. But the difference is one of manner. At bedrock, the faith is the same. Issues are simple and plain. Virtue is to be rewarded and vice punished. Righteousness is a shield against the enemy. Naturally, it also is simplistic and therefore easy to manipulate, which is significant not for the excuses that men of evil may take from it but for the self-justification that men of goodwill may find in it. All together, it makes for a strong people, confident, direct, accomplishing.

These were the people who were listening to the minister

that morning as he warmed to his task, his big voice spilling happily into the words of the Book of God. He was focused, as always, on that time which is the climax moment for all Christians but most particularly so for the Baptists, the end days when God will come again to earth and punish the wicked and summon home the faithful. Later the fire would come, but now he was conversational and easy, taking them gently to task, showing them their foibles:

> Now Peter had several reasons for writing this letter. He deals with the theme of human suffering, the suffering we should be willing to bear in the hope of the glory that lies beyond. But we don't like to think about suffering very much and besides, if we seem to ignore the world in which we're living, others will call us other-world-minded, they ridicule us and we don't like that. Now we ought to be concerned about the world in which we live, ought to do everything we can to change it and make it right, but like the people of God of old who were unmindful of the country from which they came because they were traveling to an invisible city whose maker is God, our objective is beyond and we ought to be willing to suffer, but we don't like to think about it.
>
> And he warns us about those who make false profession, and says, it had been better for them not to have known the way of life than having known it to have turned their backs upon it, and he said it has happened to them like the dog that went back to its vomit or the sow that returned to the wallow after being washed. He's warning against people who profess to have had a change when the only change was on the surface, and we don't like to think about that, either.

Earlier, before the 10:50 A.M. service began, I had walked around the church with the assistant pastor, Melvin Carter. It is a thriving place with a happy air, well appointed and obviously moneyed, that has grown like a mushroom, shouldering its way among the city's buildings with serene confidence. It reached across the street to absorb an entire eleven-story building for Sunday School space and still the classes spill into other buildings. There were 4,500 people in Sunday School that morning, in 87 different classes that ranged from three-year-olds to their grandparents and included a class for the deaf, one for the retarded and two in separate dialects of Chinese. The teachers were lay people, teaching on careful schedule all from the same Bible passages, sharing their searchings in voices that carried the flat twang of the plains into the corridors as we passed. A nursery tends the babies and each week the newest draws the honor place. Presently we passed a big window set in the wall. Behind it was a crib in which Dale Lee Stechman, two weeks old, lay wrinkled and asleep over a large sign: Baby of the Week.

This is a formidable church, so elaborate and well organized that it seems like a big business. It has its own five-story parking garage, a gymnasium, skating rink and bowling alleys, a full kitchen, 121 employees and an annual budget of more than $1.6 million. There are twenty-one choirs and an orchestra which have a total membership of 1,304 people, led by a music director who sings duets with his wife at some services. Van Cliburn plays here occasionally when his concert schedule permits and Dr. Billy Graham counts this his home church, though he lives in North Carolina and preaches all over the world.

Down in the big kitchen, volunteers were filling thimble-sized cups for the communion service that was to follow the old minister's sermon. The red, winy fluid ran down a plastic tube from a plastic bottle and with a start I recognized it as a blood bottle lately of some hospital. It was almost grotesque: a blood bottle for the blood of Christ. But I put the thought aside. Of course, I said, the holy wine, my mind suddenly full of priests and golden goblets—and a burly man who was filling the cups looked up and said, pleasantly but with rising challenge, "Tell him it ain't wine, Brother Carter."

And he said [cried the old minister, warming now to his message], I want to stir up your memories. I'm going to die pretty soon, and before I leave I want to stir up your memory so you can have these things always and remember them, and the thing I want you to remember is that what I told you wasn't a fable. It wasn't a fairy tale, it wasn't fiction, it wasn't a fantasy. I was on the mount of transfiguration and saw Jesus in his transfigured form. I saw him together with the other two disciples. It wasn't any fairy tale that we've been telling you, we saw the Lord glorified, we saw him in his power, we saw him overshadow Moses and Elijah, and we heard the voice saying, "This is my beloved son, hear ye him." I want you to remember that, said Peter.

As you stroll about the church with Brother Carter, there is on every side that quality which the Baptists call fellowship and the rest of us call sanctimony. They smile endlessly. They call each other brother and sister with the regularity of military titles. They shake hands on every encounter, hug each other and give each other little pats as if to guarantee a goodwill that really seems not so much their true selves as it does the shape of their best impulses and this makes it artificial and even syrupy. But Sunday ends and Monday comes and it is my impression that on Monday morning most of Sunday's smiling brothers leap up with sharp eye and hard face and set about assaulting their fellow man in search of profit.

Of course, I have stated opposing stereotypes. For obviously, the Monday morning Baptist is no more ferocious than anyone else on Monday morning (though on balance, neither is he any less) and the Sunday morning Baptist is only expressing the yearning for goodness and love which we all share, except that he acts his yearning out in a sort of exuberant pantomime that is, after all, quite in keeping with the open outlook of the West. Nevertheless, this contrast between his manner on Sunday and on Monday leads some people to suspect him of hypocrisy.

It is always a mistake to confuse manner and substance and you see this very plainly in the senior Sunday School classes. The senior women's class was made up of women with iron-gray hair, well dressed in a subdued, matronly way, who gave an impression of dignity and strength. They were listening with grave attention to a woman who had mastered the real sense of the Bible in a way that a preacher or a professor might have admired. I recall her saying firmly, "Now I think we can see that Jezzybelle obviously just wasn't really helping her husband at all." And again, "Ahab was plain old wallowing in self-pity."

The senior men confirmed the impression. They were lawyers, doctors, bankers, heads of businesses. A few were old, their hair gone white. The others were graying, with thickening bodies encased in good wool suits. They were close-shaven and time had broken their squarish faces into many separate planes which were enhanced by the small, bright panes of their glasses. The room was finely paneled in old wood and lighted from high windows. The men sat a little apart from each other, in the way of men of power and achievement, as if their presence extended physically beyond them in an aura which demanded respect and distance. They were the sort of men— and were among the actual men—who shake Texas, power it and make it go. Now they sat quietly in a Sunday School class, something that many of us reserve for children, and listened to a member and a friend make still more meaningful the book by which, most of the time and as best they could, they tried to live.

This is the root strength of Baptists in Texas; this is what counts. The sentimental acting out of their best but not quite real impulses is manner. These men and the decency for which they stand (decency always by their own lights, but not always or even often socially enlightened) are the substance. And later, during the 10:50 A.M. service, I realized a startling thing, which must have been a reflection not of face but of spirit. As Dr. James moved into his sermon from the pulpit, his big voice sweeping his listeners along, I realized that he looked like all the men in the senior Sunday School class. Or perhaps they looked like him.

Now, if you want to know where you are living in time [the great voice gentling, expository, ruminating about this question that absorbs all Christians and most of all the fundamentalists, when will Christ come again?] then forget about the fantasies of figures in the Bible. Any adept student can take the figures in the Bible and make them fit almost anything he wants. Forget about the troublous times that the Bible predicts. There was troublous times when Israel was carried into Babylon, there was troublous times when the Romans destroyed Jerusalem, it was troublous times when Kaiser Wilhelm set the world on fire, it was troublous days when Hitler tried to exterminate a race, and we have no hope of anything but troublous times for time yet to come. You can forget about the fantasies of numbers or figures, forget about troublous times, forget about wars and woes and listen to what men preach. Listen to the theology of the day and you'll get some idea of what place in time you are living. In the latter days scoffers shall come, scoffing at the promise of the coming of Christ. You're not going to find out where you are in history through the study of geology or archeology or anthropology or paleontology or ontology or any other kind of an 'ology. Listen to the theology of men and you'll know that when they deny the coming of the Lord, bringing to themselves damnation, it is a sign that you are living toward the end of time.

Fundamentalism is plain, simple, decent, going back to the faith of the fathers and ignoring the forms of the men who followed. There is no ritual. The minister appears in a plain suit and speaks from a lectern. The emphasis is on lay participation and the idea of a priesthood is abhorrent. So extreme is the lack of dogma that although the minister is regarded as a Bible authority, no one is required or even expected to accept what he says. The minister and the simplest member interpret the Bible with equal weight. Indeed, Dr. W. A. Criswell, the church's regular pastor who was conducting a revival elsewhere on the Sunday of which I write and who is himself a famed fundamentalist preacher, has written, "It would be unusual for two men anywhere who sought the truth of God in the Holy Bible to see it exactly alike. The mountain of God's truth is too large for one finite mind to encompass. We are Baptists in the faith and that means we have the high and holy privilege of studying the Bible for ourselves and of allowing the Holy Spirit to teach us its meaning." Thus the essence of fundamentalism is independence of view, simplicity of form and confidence of spirit; for every man knows where he stands and if by his own lights he stands foursquare with God, he knows that he is all right.

In the last days these false teachers shall come and you can recognize them because they will be scoffing, they will be ridiculing, laughing, pointing a finger of scorn at the illiterate believer who in an age of enlightenment still believes that Jesus is coming again. They will scoff at the thought of the promise of his coming, they will say, "Where is the promise of his coming, for since the fathers fell asleep all things continuously were from the beginning of creation." Do you note the words? Those are Bible words. They indicate these are churchmen, they are teachers and they are ridiculing—everybody is saying if it isn't logical it isn't theological; if it can't be tested in the laboratory it's not trustworthy; if it isn't scientific then it surely must not belong in the scriptures; if it isn't provable then it isn't probable; if it isn't immediate then it's not important.

There is no such thing as the Baptist Church. There are only Baptist churches scattered across the country and particularly the South and even more particularly Texas, where there are about 4,000 of them. The Southern Baptist Convention is merely an association, with no central structure or authority, no bishops, hierarchy or control. Each church has its own property, raises its own funds and hires, and sometimes fires, its own pastor.

This lack of central authority explains a certain undisciplined quality found in Baptist churches. There is no established dogma, no standard pattern of church operation and no overseeing of the minister by an outside and relatively uninvolved authority. The result is an occasional explosion of unchecked aberrance which can shatter a church and destroy a minister. But the result also is the sense of independence, confidence and self-assertion that so clearly mark these people and their church.

It also makes the Baptist preacher a bird of very bright plumage. One might think that his total dependence on the local church and the absence of either the vested authority or the protection inherent in a hierarchical system might tend to make him subservient and fearful. It has had the opposite effect, however, probably because the circumstances of his tenure are such as to weed out the fearful at the outset.

Almost without exception, Baptist preachers are powerful fellows of dominant nature. This is most obvious in rich urban churches, but I think it equally true in the smallest churches. Even those unpaid preachers who must work at a regular job through the week and only assume their real roles on Sundays are just as respected and as powerful in the framework of their own church as their sleek brethren in the big cities. The point is that if either failed to dominate his congregation, he would be turned out for a preacher who could.

Churches, like any other organization of humans, are political substructures and successful preachers are also good politicians. Instead of being spread along a hierarchical structure, however, Baptist politics are contained in each church, which makes them considerably hotter. The result is to attract ministers who are temperamentally geared to taking risk and who enjoy living on fine balance. There is an element of all or nothing here, for manipulating church laymen who are awed by one's learning and piety and the majesty of one's sermons is considerably easier than manipulating one's bishop in another faith; on the other hand, one's failures are much more easily rationalized to a bishop who is a fellow professional than to an angry church board. So long as the preacher maintains his control he is secure beyond any recourse, but when he loses it he is out on his ear. Therefore, with a show of great confidence, he must walk a very narrow line among his people. He must be one of them and yet above them, he must inspire and lead them but not offend them, he must know more than they do but not let them feel ignorant. They want to look up to him but they don't want him looking down on them. He can function securely only by establishing such power of leadership that while he is never above his people, he is always ahead of them. He flatters them and I suspect that he encourages them to flatter him, for to maintain his position at all, he must seem a most desirable prize.

The preacher, then, is a mesmeric fellow, not necessarily intelligent (his temporal advice often is fatuous) but schooled in the Bible, a masterful speaker and an accomplished showman. Showmanship is the sensual side of religion. Other faiths grant its importance and offer it in pageantry and pomp. In the fundamentalist churches it is focused entirely in the sermon, which of course centers still more attention on the preacher himself, for alone he provides almost the entire thrill and emotional release of going to church. He must be very good to last in such a demanding situation, but if he is good his power is unlimited, for he *is* the church.

Oddly enough, however, this did not quite apply to the man whose sermon thundered down upon the silent congregation of the First Baptist Church of Dallas. For Dr. James was not a regular pastor in any church, though he had been in the past and he understood the pressures. But as editor of the authoritative *Baptist Standard* for years, he enjoyed an across-the-faith relationship that generally only the great traveling evangelists achieve. He had preached here many times, and as it honored the church to have him, so it honored him to appear in this church that for its size, wealth and excellence is a pinnacle in the Baptist faith. Years of practice, study and thoughtfulness had gone into his sermon, and now, as the words soared in the great church hall, coming faster and with rising passion but no less clarity of inflection, he was splendid.

> Peter said they [the scoffers] are willingly ignorant of the fact that the heavens were of old. How old do you think the sun is, the stars, the heavens above us? Well, maybe six million years? Maybe six billions? More probably the heavens in our galaxy are at least six hundred billions; matter is probably as eternal as God himself. And they forget that there was an old world overflown with water that perished. What world was that? Noah's world? Maybe. I don't think so. I think it was this world, long long before God created it in its present form, a world in which substance was partially liquid, partially gas, partially solid, and the liquid overcame and overflowed the solid, destroying all that world, and finally God made it over into the world that it now is.

And God placed upon the world that now is the things we now find and the climax of God's creation was the creation of man, made in the image of God himself. So it doesn't matter when, it doesn't matter how old the universe, it doesn't matter how many worlds there have been, the only important thing is that they are by the word of God. By the word of God they were created, sustained and brought to their ends. And by the same word, he says, the earth now is reserved in fire unto the day of judgment and perdition of ungodly men. They are unwilling to admit that; they are willingly ignorant of the fact that he who created matter created the manner of matter's destruction. In the search of the whole universe for truth, modern man ignored the central, first and final truth of all truths, that in the beginning, God. The most significant statement ever penned. The first four words of the Bible. IN THE BEGINNING, GOD!

The fundamental faith was natural on the American frontier. Frontier people were direct, simple, open. Their lives dealt in plain things—in breaking a piece of land to use, in raising and feeding a family, in simply surviving. The faith fitted these needs and it fitted the kind of courageous and above all confident people who were drawn to the frontier. It preached hell and damnation and the redemption of man with no sophisticated qualifications. It justified the harsh things that men had to do to survive. It offered a comfort of certainty that helped make their lives bearable, a sort of guaranteed future in a risky present. They knew from the faith that things really were simple: if you sinned, you went to hell, but there was something you could do about it. You could get right with God. You had the Book's guidance and the right to fit its words to the terms of your own life. You probably didn't hear a sermon every week or even every month, but with the Book you didn't need a sermon to be saved. You had left an ordered society to come out here where you made most of your own rules and you didn't much care for dogma in your faith. You read the Word and acted accordingly. And you could face the future brightly, for you were four-square with God and that was that.

Fundamentalism still flourishes in Texas. The people still

take pleasure in its teachings for much the same reasons their fathers did. Despite its modernity, Texas and its institutions and its attitudes are not very far removed from the frontier. You still see it in the people, if you look.

God promised and God is not slack. He hasn't forgotten that he made a promise. The day of the Lord will come. Christ IS coming. The promise hasn't failed simply because he hasn't come yet. Yes, the disciples expected him to come when they were still here upon earth and men have been expecting Christ to come ever since. And I've been expecting him ever since I can remember and I shall always look for him, he may be here today, he may be here before the close of this hour. The promise of God hasn't failed, it's simply the faith of men that has failed, and it all was done by the word of God and the same word of God says he's coming, why should we doubt it? Don't let their scorn dampen your ardor, don't let it nullify your faith, don't let anything call you to doubt that Christ is coming.

Peter said, therefore brethren, what manner of persons ought we to be, if all these things are to be fulfilled? God is holding the world reserved in fire against the day of judgment and the perdition of ungodly men, what kind of persons ought we to be so that when he comes we may be found of him? We'll be here. He's coming, as a thief in the night, not stealthily but unexpectedly. We will be found of him, and when this heaven and this earth shall have been destroyed, we'll look for a new heaven and a new earth wherein dwelleth righteousness. Are you ready for it?

There was the challenge, as old as Christianity itself—are you ready? Christ is coming and you will have to answer. Are you ready? The people sat transfixed in the burnished wooden pews, caught by the great idea as the fine voice warmed and softened over the words and cast them gently against the lofty ceiling and the pale green walls and the bright red carpet until they washed over every person there. And the words fired the people and swept them along toward the point of it all.

He won't come until the last person ordained to eternal life has been saved and when he gets that person in, Gabriel's trumpets will sound and our Lord will come. Are you one of those? He's waiting on you to repent. Will you repent today?

This is the emotional apogee, the chance to declare yourself in public, to purge yourself of sin, to position yourself so that when Gabriel blows his horn you will be, in the old Baptist phrase, right with God.

> While we have an invitational hymn, will you come right along, will you come? For Christ? For the Church?

Thus, the invitation. If you are so moved you may walk down the aisle and present yourself to your God (and your fellows) at the front of the church. You may come in tears if you like, riding the emotional thrust of the sermon with the Lord's word bursting in your head. Or you may come to repledge yourself, to repent for special sins which need not be enumerated, to dedicate yourself to service to your church, to transfer your membership from another church or simply because you feel like doing so. Whatever your reason, it is a powerful experience. In the more extreme sects, this is the time of release—the shouters, the people who babble incoherently which is called speaking in tongues, the ecstatic foamers. But today we are in a dignified church in downtown Dallas and the people are well dressed and educated.

> Surely if you are not ready to meet God, you would want to get ready this morning, wouldn't you?

After the talk, explanations and exhortations, this is the point of it all, for this brings them up and offers them to God. This is why Baptist sermons tend to be Biblical instead of temporal and why Baptist attitudes tend to be conservative and traditional instead of progressive. Everyone was standing at the pews, singing the full-bodied hymn, "I Am Coming to the Cross," and with great expertise the minister's voice, gentle toned but strong, overrode the music.

> All you can do is trust Christ to the salvation of your soul. It's up to you to repent, to turn your back upon sin. Will you do it now? Will you come?

And no one came. The people were standing, watching, caught in the emotion but not moving. A pleading note came in the minister's voice and I thought there was a touch of anguish on his face as he waited before his people. And suddenly I saw the man's courage. He had preached a mighty sermon, he had given his best, and now he waited to see if it had seized their hearts.

And it struck me that the Baptist preacher, who has such influence on his people, is one of the real high rollers. Every week, whether he's sick or depressed or frightened or any of the other things we fall prey to, he must commit himself before his people. Every sermon must inspire, for it ends in the invitation and the invitation is its proof. Every minister hopes on every Sunday to bring at least a few forward, for thus a soul is saved and that is the point of it all, the difference between success and failure. A minister whose sermons failed to draw souls forward would, in the words of Brother Carter, "probably re-evaluate his ministry and his mission and wonder if he wouldn't be better in another field."

Will you come to Christ? It's up to you. He begged you to come. Will you come now? Right now? Come right along, from wherever you are.

So every Sunday morning the preacher lays it on the line. He puts up a big piece of his capital—his prestige, his effect, his control of an always volatile situation—and he throws out his sermon like a roll of the dice and he waits to see what will happen. Watching that morning as the spare, dignified minister waited a last lonely moment at the lectern, I thought that it is not lost on Texans that the man whom they admire, honor and seek to emulate reveals himself every Sunday morning as a classic high roller.

CHAPTER

VII

From the air the country was harsh and dry-looking, with none
of the rough beauty of miniature trees poised on rocky hillocks
that you see on the ground. We were in a big military helicopter and after a while the colonel who was piloting turned
around with a smile and gestured down. The sharp whacking
noise of the rotors changed in intensity and the machine settled
toward the ranch below, which is, when the President of the
United States is there, the alternate White House. There were
sheds, garages, and a big barn with a corral beside it. Strong,
blocky Hereford cattle of obviously superior bloodlines gleamed
red and white in the sun. The President's house was handsome,
though unpretentious, a white frame building with some of its
walls in fieldstone, flanked by a swimming pool and surrounded
by a white fence made of crossed planks. It was partially
hidden in a grove of fine old liveoak trees that extended gracefully down to the river. Out behind there was a communica-
tions tower and a landing strip that would handle small jets.
The chopper touched the ground and settled. In the distance
I saw a cream-colored Lincoln convertible jounce slowly along
a ranch road. Several Secret Service men came out of the shade
of the trees and one came across the runway and met us as we
ducked low and ran from under the whirling blades.

I was visiting President Johnson to talk about Texas. I think he granted my request so quickly and pleasantly because he was relaxing at home and he *likes* to talk about Texas. I wanted him to discuss the capacity of Texans for taking and holding national political power, a trend of which he himself was the latest and most obvious proof. The fact is that since 1928 there has not been a time when a Texan did not have a dominant voice in Washington. John Nance Garner became minority leader in the House of Representatives that year, Speaker in 1930, and Vice President in 1932. Lyndon Baines Johnson went to Washington as congressional secretary in 1931 and was elected to the Congress in 1937. Sam Rayburn became Democratic whip in the House the year Garner took the vice presidency. Tom Clark was Attorney General in the New Deal days and later a Supreme Court Justice (he resigned when his son, Ramsey, became Attorney General). Jesse Jones was Secretary of Commerce under Roosevelt. Rayburn became Speaker of the House in 1940 and remained until his death, the longest tenure in history. Tom Connally was chairman of the Senate Foreign Relations Committee. Johnson went to the Senate in 1948, was Democratic whip in 1950, minority leader in 1952, majority leader in 1954. For the last six years of the Eisenhower administration, he and Rayburn ran the Congress. In 1960, Johnson had 409 votes for the presidential nomination itself at the Democratic Convention, and it seems unlikely that John F. Kennedy could have won without him. John Connally, who had been associated with Johnson for years, was Secretary of the Navy in the Kennedy Administration before he became Governor of Texas.

In a democratic society one tries to be casual even about the majestic quality of the presidency, but it is not easy. The President is the most powerful single man in the world and quite possibly the best known as well, and as you approach him you are aware that you are on a rare adventure. There were several of us that day and we went to Randolph AFB to meet the White House helicopter. We were escorted onto the apron, past the white and blue Air Force One, the President's personal plane with the gold seal of his office and in black capital letters the words, THE UNITED STATES OF AMERICA.

When the helicopter landed at the ranch, the Secret Service agent took us to a big picnic table on the front lawn and presently Mrs. Johnson came out to welcome us. She is a great lady. Her gracious charm often takes the edge off her husband's blunt manner and the affection she displays to him warms everyone. She went back into the ranchhouse and soon a small man staggered out under a big tray on which stood icy cans of Texas beer. Then the President's cream-colored convertible drove up and he emerged from behind the wheel, a tall, paunchy figure in ranch clothes, twill trousers and a matching twill jacket with the round presidential seal over the left breast pocket. He had been showing friends his cattle and now he shook hands in a way that was at once faintly ominous and somewhat diffident, so that one felt encouraged to speak softly and as little as possible. He said vaguely that there would be lunch soon and that we would be called and then he disappeared into the house.

It was nearly noon and the sun was hot. We sat on the grass and drank the beer and talked quietly to Dale Malechek, who runs the ranch, and it was very pleasant. The grassy bank slopes down to the Pedernales River, which the President calls the Perd'nales, and all along it the big old liveoaks, many more than a century old, cast their pools of shade. The river is a small lake, impounded by a little dam downstream over which you can drive, with the water spilling across its top at your elbow and splashing away beneath your wheels. All together, with the irrigated grass so strong and green, the stretch of placid water, the neat white fence, the high-bred cattle all looking proud as Lucifer, it is easy to forget that every bit of this was created at the President's pleasure. It is easy to forget how hard and tough is this country that produced him.

This is the Hill Country of Texas. Its main characteristics are its hardness and its beauty. It is a rolling country shot with rock and cut with little streams that are almost always dry. Its low hills are covered with cedar and liveoak. Sumac flames red in the autumn and giant wild pecans shake down an endless supply of sweet little nuts to the animals that prowl the grassy stream banks. There are squirrels and raccoons and possums, well armored armadillos, and foxes that neatly trap the pheasants. The morning sun splashes gold all across this land and in the winter new little shoots of oats come up as green as spring. At dusk the deer slip out of the protective woods to graze the oat fields, as many as fifty at a time, and at a sudden noise they clear the fence like arrows loosed from fifty bows and vanish quick as mist. Stalwart wild turkey prowl the woods, gobbling complacently. Once on a friend's ranch the foreman's young son, goaded perhaps by a turkey's pomposity, leaped from a truck to give chase. The bird ran strongly into the woods, springing from side to side, gobbling furiously, and the young boy, still all arms and legs, pumping in his heavy boots and knocking aside the brush, ran after it until they both disappeared.

I have seen this country overhung with rain and cool mist, grass leaping up eagerly from the ground, wildflowers thrusting themselves from the crevices of rocks, the smell of settled dust clean as new-mown hay, with the sun flashing through occasionally and lancing its bow to the ground. But all the same, the dominant factor in this country is its dryness. In the heat of the summer sun the caliche powders white and rises under wheel and boot in a cloud until the liveoak trees by the road turn gray with dust and still the rain does not come to wash them clean and green. The grass gets brown and brittle, dust blows out of the fields and the livestock mill testily against the fences. The oil leaches out of women's skin and their eyes squint against the white glare and the wind blows on and on.

This is drought-prone country, but even when wet it is not very fertile. It is rocky as any New England hillside and its hard slopes produce the barest cover of grass. Only its little bottoms are worth tilling and then only for pasture grasses. The last Indian battle was within a century past. The people who chopped a living out of this land worked from dawn to dusk to do so, raising more sheep and goats than cattle and operating little spreads of a hundred or two or three hundred acres on which the whole family worked. Survival depended on the virtues—hard work, frugality, diligence, a capacity for suffering with good cheer.

It is changing now. The little spreads are no longer viable. The young people are moving away and the land is going to city men with excess cash who buy it because it is beautiful and is a tax shelter, or to consolidators, of whom the President himself is one. The point is to put together spreads that run in the thousands of acres and are big enough to be handled efficiently and economically, often converting, as the President has, to cattle. His total holdings exceed 4,000 acres, though his famed LBJ Ranch is only slightly more than 400. Still, a few of the old people remain. On a tiny ranch on a back road of Blanco County not long after Johnson became President, I saw an ancient iron kettle suspended over a fire. Mrs. Henry Danz, a dignified lady with white hair who said she then was seventy-eight, interrupted her lambing to tell me that she used that kettle for everything—for boiling the wash, for rendering lard, for making lye soap.

But the view of Mrs. Danz' kettle irritates President Johnson. Once when he was shown a collection of pictures emphasizing the beauty, hardness and age-old virtues of his home country, he reacted with real anger. Fine, yes, very pretty—but where are the farm-to-market roads all paved and properly shouldered, where are the miles and miles of REA lines that run like silver laces through this country, how about the flood-control dams that have made a whole chain of lakes to the north? Do you know how many houses in Blanco County have hot-water heaters? the President asked, and reeled off proudly some figure of totality, ninety-nine-point-ninety-something; one had the impression of just a couple of old holdouts who didn't want hot water ruining the whole picture. The President is proud of the rural electrification, the dams that ended the annual flooding, the roads that freed people to the towns for their pleasure and their produce. As a young Congressman in the days of the

New Deal he was responsible for many of these programs. He is proud also, I think, because this is his idea of what government should do for its people: it should work to make their lives better. There is a good deal of the American populist in President Johnson; he is a liberal, but an exceedingly pragmatic one, which is a characteristic liberals often do not share and rarely admire.

In many ways, I think of President Johnson as a personification of the Texas character—or, and therefore, an extension of the national character. He is a big man. He has capacities for real violence. He is strong, tough, stubborn, and he expects to win. But he also is sentimental and emotional. He can be kindly and occasionally generous and he has a hunger for approval; indeed, he wants to be loved on a large scale and when he is not he is both hurt and somewhat surprised. His manners are often crude, not because he doesn't know better, I suspect, but because he doesn't care. He is in fact highly sophisticated and when necessary his manners reflect this fact; but he doesn't consider manners very important and usually doesn't bother. He is an insatiable talker with a genuine literary talent. His renditions of homespun stories and aphorisms have a sort of dialect genius. When the mood is upon him, when the crowd is warm and right and the sun is setting and the day has been good, he spins out marvelous tales that are paced and pointed even as they seem rambling and artless. He is immensely intelligent but not particularly literary, and his knowledge of history and literature, which are keys to man's actions and thoughts, is probably relatively slight considering the magnitude of his thoughts, capacities, and responsibilities. He has a good deal more respect for engineers than for philosophers and he has an inherent distrust of the holders of all doctorates save those of medicine. Above everything else, he is a pragmatist. Don't talk about it, his father used to tell him, do it; he didn't give a damn for all they said, he once cried of Kennedy, Eisenhower, even Truman, because he was getting done what they talked about doing. The wise man works within the limits of the problem, to lose is simply foolish while to compromise is natural and necessary, and the proof of any pudding is its success. All of which is to say that the President has a great deal of that quality which Americans prize so highly, the knack for getting things done.

This strikes a familiar air in Texas. The President has a huge instinct for power, which no doubt has been sharpened by nearly four decades of experience in the power center of the world but which grows basically, I believe, from the man. One of the most striking things about Texas is the sense of personal power found in individuals, the same basic quality that the President has in much greater degree. I have seen this sense and feel for the exercise of power in many places in Texas—out on ranches, among big businessmen, among police and particularly rural police officers, in rodeo riders, in lawyers and perhaps most of all, though obviously to a lesser degree of individual concentration, in the anonymous people simply encountered on the street. I suppose it includes a huge self-confidence and grows from a sort of inner force, and I suspect also that it is based on a quality that is somehow physical. It involves a feeling for maneuver, and even more, for action; again, it is pragmatic, dealing with deed instead of hope. It is probably this physical aspect to the power quality that makes the President so overwhelming in person. Most people find him so and it is a characteristic that goes far beyond the power of his office. It may sound naive, but I have found that on nearly every occasion I have dealt with him, his very presence has been awesome. I believe this, rather than his logic or his guile, is the root of his famous persuasiveness; he is not a man who, in the flesh, you have much desire to challenge.

So we sat on the grass that day at the LBJ Ranch looking out over the lovely countryside and presently there came a summons to the luncheon table. Afterwards the President led me into a small combination study and sitting room. It is a comfortable place near the front of the house with a view of the yard and the liveoaks and the river. The President sat in one of those patented lounge chairs that throws up its bottom part for a foot rest when you lean back in it; it had the presidential seal in the center of the headrest. The President casually gestured me into a solid chair beside it in which the beagle, Him, lay sound asleep, his Washington dog tag No. 1 rising and falling with his breathing. Tell him to move, the President said. I used my friendliest tone—this, after all, was not just any mutt—and the dog did not so much as grunt. Suddenly the President let out a roar and raised a mighty hand, whereupon the dog lifted his head and without the slightest sign of fear, but with a certain recognition of the inevitable, grumpily climbed down.

I sat down and asked my single question: Would the President discuss the qualities in Texans that had, in his opinion, made it possible for so many Texans, and most of all him, to achieve such position in Washington? He ruminated over this for a full two minutes, which is a long time when one is sitting in silence beside the President, and then he began to talk. One quotes a president directly only at his pleasure. A half-hour later he turned to me easily and said that I was not to quote his words but that I was free to report the sense of his ideas.

To begin with, these elections that so many Texans had won—Garner as Speaker of the House, Rayburn as Speaker, himself as majority leader—were surely the most elite elections in the country, for they were conducted by men themselves elected and thus they were something like the highest distillation of the will of the people. They were conducted in calm, with none of the rhetoric of public elections, and those chosen were the men whom the members of the House and the Senate thought best suited to lead them. Now, why was a preponderance of Texans chosen?

It was not because of any inherent weight in Texas. It was not for the state's wealth or its political power or its geographical position. For years it had been regarded as part of the South, which in those days was a liability. Its political weight was relatively small, and even with its oil money and its cotton, it has never had the real money of the East.

This led him to reflect on the East, and not in happy terms. It is hard to describe the bitterness with which Texans regarded the East. Easterners ridiculed Texans. They laughed at Texans' accent. Their big-time journalists, especially the big Eastern magazines, were always picking at the state. They hunted up the oddballs, a handful of new-rich oil men who never did have any power in Texas and made them stand for all Texans, and they ignored the state's men of grace and literature. People have no idea of the basic resentment in which the East is held in Texas. Texas had to go to the Easterners for money with its hat in its hand, it had to explain that it wasn't what they made it out to be—and then if what it had was any good, they wanted a big piece of it.

So Texans weren't rich or influential. They were frontier people. He fell to reminiscing about Earl Rudder, who became chancellor at Texas A. & M., and who had led his troops up the cliffs of Normandy in 1944 before the invasion to knock out the machine-guns at the top. General Bradley had wanted Rudder to stay below and direct his troops by radio; Rudder had refused; if he didn't lead, he couldn't be sure the operation would go. What caused him to function so well?

A frontier people learn not to be afraid, or they learn to live with fear and to control it. This was a country where women lived ready to stuff a diaper in a baby's mouth to keep hostile visitors, Indian or otherwise, from hearing it. He recalled that his own grandmother, not far from this very ranch, had done just that—his grandfather had been away when the Indians came and she had taken the baby into the basement and closed the trap door and stuck a diaper in its mouth and late that night, when her husband came home and called her, she brought the baby upstairs, still with the diaper in place. This was a country where there were coyotes and wolves that howled within hearing of your home. He recalled that only the day before on the way to church he had killed a couple of rattlesnakes, rattlesnakes that were six or seven feet long—just going to church.

These people grew up around animals on the range, learning to handle them and work them. This has a calming effect on a man. It gives him a sense of his own competence, teaches him how to direct and manage things and the penalties for making mistakes. It puts him in the habit of deciding what's to be done and directing whatever is around him to do it. There is a lot of time to think when one is out alone with animals in the open country. One develops a patience and a powerful sense of reality. These people were not crowded in with streetcars and telephones, bells ringing all the time, the city pressing them. They are a thoughtful people, a thinking people, an independent people, a valorous people. All of this is related to a knowledge of the elements, of the power and violence of storms, of the strength and the demands of the open land in a hard country.

All of these things combined to give them good judgment. Education is fine and important, but it is on a man's judgment that he and others live or die. Of course, information is essential, but given that, judgment is a personal thing which is made on instinct and experience and a sense for reality. Talk is fine, but results are what count. Results are reality. Mr. Rayburn used to say that the most valuable thing a man had was his judgment.

The President got up, the patented chair creaking and clicking. He stood at the screen door looking out on the hot afternoon, through the liveoak trees to the Pedernales shining on beyond. The beagle had gone to sleep on the floor and in the drousing quiet I thought I heard the cicada's distant chatter. He stood by the door a long time, looking into his memories and his heritage, and then, moving restlessly about the room, he began to talk again. He remembered that when he went into public life, nine of the fifteen major committee chairmen were Texans. He thought of all the others, himself, Garner, Rayburn, Col. House, Jesse Jones, Tom Clark, Texans chosen to lead. He didn't think it was mere coincidence that so many Texans were named.

He remembered the splendid old story of Sam Rayburn's visit to the Bond Club of New York, invited in the '30s when Rayburn was working out the legislation that set up the Securities and Exchange Commission. The Bond Club members hadn't expected Rayburn to come and they were startled; the chairman gave him an introduction that was brief to the point of rudeness, adding that he didn't know why this man from Texas had come, but he had and here he was.

And Rayburn had taken the podium and said that he had worked all his life, had never married, had saved and scrimped, but that he had never been able to assemble a million dollars and so he had thought he would come up here and rub elbows with men who had and maybe some of their expertise would rub off on him.

And then he added, almost casually, that the second reason he had come up was to show them he wasn't scared of them.

The President ruminated over this. Rayburn hadn't been scared and when the President was gone he believed his worst enemies would agree that he hadn't been scared and that he hadn't been in anybody's pocket either. He was sympathetic to business but not in its control. He leaned toward labor, but labor didn't own him. He was for doctors, but the doctors were under no illusion about their power with him. He was for lawyers, but just the other day had found occasion to tell the American Bar Association to go to hell on some idea or other.

When his fellow Senators voted him their leader, the President recalled, they didn't do so because he was rich or his daddy was famous. They did it because they trusted him and his decisions.

Texans, he thought, are forthright, fearless, confident—too confident, sometimes, so that they are mistaken for braggarts—and their over-all image is one of men with a prudent view, conditioned by experience and judgment and not likely to be changed by pressure. The frontier bred courage and independence and tenacity. And then there was a good bit in the breeding. Texans believe breeding in cattle is important. A lot of Texas bloodlines came down from Tennessee and Kentucky, good bloodlines infused with a love of freedom and a willingness to fight tyranny. A leader needs every quality—diligence, passion, imagination, quickness, courage, good humor, love for his fellows, optimism, a sense of obligation, intelligence, integrity—but none of them are any good without judgment.

He thought about this. Judgment was the thing. And he thought that you'll find judgment in Texans and that it comes as a natural outgrowth of the way they live and the heritage from which they came. Nobody knows for sure what is right on the big issues. One can only guess and judge. He remembered that he was always glad when Mr. Rayburn came down on his side of a question because he respected Mr. Rayburn's judgment and his leadership. He'd found by testing him over many a year that his judgment put him on the right side most of the time and that is all that any man can ask.

CHAPTER

1

Now comes that hell of a fellow, the frontier trader, heir to all the problems, violence and dangers of the frontier and having to worry about turning a profit as well. Naturally he was vigorous, rough, often dangerous, uncouth, deceptive, an agate-eyed horse trader who accepted great risk and therefore demanded great profit. He dealt in cotton, cattle, land; he was rancher, planter, trail driver, banker, and very often he failed, but if he did succeed, if he got his foothold and had the wit and courage to maintain it, then in the constantly expanding frontier there were hardly any limits on how fast he could move or how big he could grow. It was wide open and immense traders began to develop. It is a pattern that continues today.

The first of the really big action was in cotton. There is an old saying that Texas began on hide and horns—the produce of the range country—but it didn't. It began on cotton. Long before the Civil War, East Texas was plantation country, the great cotton tracts inching westward until they reached the blacklands south of Dallas. As the terrain expanded, Texas cotton production went up until by itself it formed an important part of the world market. It was the only money crop and it led to very high stakes trading. There were so many things that could happen to a crop—drought or flash floods that washed out newly planted seeds or rainstorms that soaked and muddied the maturing bolls or the ubiquitous boll weevil itself. Some of the biggest trading of all was in cotton futures and bankers learned to bet regularly on a crop that often was all or nothing. It made the adrenalin run to trade in cotton.

After the Civil War cotton was still important, but the traders were expanding westward into a new opportunity—the modern cattle business. The range country was opening up as the Indians were driven out and the desperadoes brought under control. There were millions of rangy longhorn cattle roaming the brush, thousands of war-weary men coming home and looking for occupation, and a booming meat market in the post-war North. The idea was to round up those cattle and walk them to market. It seems simple and natural, but in fact it was revolutionary, for it involved a whole new concept. It belonged to no single man and there had been big if haphazard drives as early as 1846. But the systematizing of it can be said to have started one day in 1853 when a twenty-eight-year-old steamboat captain named Richard King paid three hundred dollars for his first parcel of land in the Wild Horse Desert and thus started his King Ranch.

Until then grassland cattle raising had been a Latin affair. Spanish brought the first cattle to the New World in 1521 and long before the first English coastal colony, there were big herds in Mexico. In *The King Ranch*, Tom Lea writes of a single owner in the Mexican province of Jalisco branding 30,000 calves a year. And, he notes, it was Mexico that developed "an unprecedented type of New World herdsman: the vaquero," who "invented a technique for the horseback handling of half-wild cattle on an open range." The vaquero developed the rawhide rope with a sliding noose, a saddle with a pommel to which he snubbed his rope, a specially trained pony that could outthink and outwork the cattle. Thus he developed a practical method of harvesting those vast plains areas "where natural rainfall would never bring crops but always brought grass."

King was born in Manhattan of Irish immigrant parents. He ran off to sea as a child, became a seaman, then a river pilot, then a steamboat skipper on the Rio Grande, sailing out of Brownsville during the Mexican War. He was a burly man with dark blue eyes and black curly hair and Lea's paintings show his heavy square jaw and look of iron determination. Years later a trail driver described him: "I never knew a rougher man, nor a better man."

When he started his ranch, King turned naturally to Mexico for cattle and for expertise. The American settler so recently come to Texas was essentially a farmer or a woodsman and it would take him some time to grasp the idea of great herds on the open prairie. What's more, there was no big beef industry as such in those days. Cattle on the prairie far from the populous East were slaughtered for their hides and tallow, and most of their meat was wasted. This was even more true in Mexico. King, however, had different ideas. He drew on the Mexican vaquero for his expertise in handling cattle, Lea writes, but "he added an Anglo-Saxon dynamic, a new thought. Ranching was not a subsistence, it was a business. It was a financial enterprise, susceptible to an organized efficiency [and] a systematic yield of profit."

King had been in the steamboat business and "it was not difficult for him to understand the reward awaiting a man who could raise herds of cattle where the great grass was and ship meat in volume to cities where the great market was."

In the wild years after the Civil War, thousands of Texans, including Richard King, were cashing in on those rewards. There were millions of head of cattle, manpower to drive them, an eager market awaiting them and real money to be made. Thus began the era of the great drives up a variety of trails, the best known of which probably was the Chisholm. Generally speaking, it began in Brownsville at the tip of Texas, passed near Waco and Fort Worth, crossed the Red River out of Texas, crossed the Washita, the North Canadian, the Cimarron, passed into Kansas and the town of Wichita, and ended at the railhead in Abilene, a distance of more than a thousand miles—

and the longhorn was such a hardy creature he could walk a thousand miles and gain weight on the way. In the years of the trail drives, which began soon after the war and ended when the railroads reached Texas in 1884, three million head of cattle went up the Chisholm alone and a total of ten million went to market from Texas. It established firmly the ranching concept that survives today—and of course, it was to that nervy fellow, the frontier trader, as honey to the fly.

For endless risk was cast against marvelous profit and it was no place for the faint-hearted. The value of a cow trailed to the railhead could multiply by five or more—but oh, the risks. There were wolves, disease, stampedes, violent rivers to cross, drought failures of grass and waterholes, rustlers, fights with landowners along the trail. Disaster could come from any quarter, and often did. Lewis Nordyke tells of a cowpuncher who realized that dream of the cowboy, a herd of his own. He trailed 4,500 Texas steers clear to South Dakota to finish out on the grass there, ran into a blizzard and emerged with 123 head still alive.

Ranching itself was just as risky. The profits of gathering wild cattle on unbroken land could be great, but it was lonely out there and when trouble came, whether rustlers or pneumonia, a man very often could not expect much help. Western films of today always show the ranch conveniently near a thriving little town with a kindly doc and a stalwart sheriff, but the reality was somewhat more grim. The rancher was in charge of all he could see and it operated on his order and, indeed, his whim, and that, as President Johnson noted, bred independence and confidence in a man, but it also meant that he was on his own. He faced predators, illness in cattle and men, fire, drought, grass failures, water shortages, flash floods, rustlers, balky hard-case cowboys, to say nothing of his product itself, wild cattle that could run like express trains under a spread of horns that sometimes reached six feet. In the face of all this he never could guess accurately what his calf crop would be. And even when his calf crop was good, the market might well fail. The great profits available when the trail drives began fell off, and eventually the market set up the pattern of fluctuations and occasional collapses that continues today. It was enough to try the nerves of the hardiest trader, wilder and riskier even than the cotton market a few hundred miles to the east, and the banker who bet on either was a brave man.

Of course, there were many factors at work as the great cotton fortunes grew and the ranching empires stretched across the empty grasslands from which the horse Indians and the buffalo had so recently been driven. There was, for instance, the influence of Texas law, which is an amalgam of English Common Law and Spanish Civil Law with some special characteristics of its own. One of these was its tendency to favor debtors. Most of the settlers remembered with no pleasure the harsh treatment of debtors in the states from which they had come (a harking back to old England) and more than a few were fleeing that treatment. When they wrote the Texas rules, they did not allow garnishment of a man's wages for debt. They did not allow the seizure for debt of his home or the tools of his trade or certain of his lands and livestock. It was somewhat harder to borrow because collection was harder, but all told it was a beneficial law because it did not break people, which tends to create a static society. It left them always with the means of working themselves out of trouble and thus contributed to a forward-moving, optimistic society.

There was a special spirit generated on the frontier by the constant vista of free land beyond the horizon. One might have thought that the power inherent in the fortunes that began to grow, especially on the great ranches that a man could spend days crossing, would have created as a corollary to the barons a serf class, men bowed by the power of their masters. In fact, it appears to have had the opposite effect. There tended to be something like a class democracy, in personal relations, at least, if not in political or governmental fact, and the lowliest cowboy took no dirt from the boss. Any time a cowboy felt mistreated, or even just for the hell of it, he could draw his time and ride on down the line. Free land over the horizon plus the constant expansion generated by free land made this possible. A man who was dissatisfied or who simply wanted to get ahead a little faster always had the alternative of going farther out, where the dangers and the hardships were greater but the land was free.

And of course, as is well known, free land powered the whole economic growth. It was like a gift, something that in the terms of this society had not existed before, and it had the effect of infusion of new capital.

And then, in every aspect of this, there was the impact of magnitudes and extremes. The areas were staggering. The cotton tracts ran for miles and miles, the weather was apt, the soil rich (before the cotton exhausted it) and the bales covered the wharves at Galveston. In fact, the trade was so extensive it made Galveston a rich city before its time. In 1880 it was the largest city in Texas with some 22,000 population and a considerable culture, and it survives today with its fine old buildings and inherited customs as a sort of baroque monument to the past in a country that otherwise manages to look raw and new. To the west the cattle ranges seemed endless. Trail herds of bawling, ambling, grass-cropping longhorns stretched from horizon to horizon and sent dust pillars into the sky. Richard King's ranch reached nearly three-quarters of a million acres and the XIT Ranch had three million acres in the Panhandle along the New Mexico border. The size turned every factor into an extreme, and this was particularly true of the weather. Thus a good rain over huge holdings could make a man, and conversely, a drought magnified into disaster. The old patterns of the frontier held good: the circumstances probably busted you, but if you survived, the magnitude of those same circumstances tended to make you boom.

It was true of the landowner and the cattle buyer and the cotton factor and the banker who bankrolled them all. The Texas trader was a big operator dealing in big money and he had learned how to take great risks and enjoy it and prosper—and oil was yet to come.

2

Oil didn't change things radically in Texas; it just expanded them. It made the action bigger, faster and even tougher. If free land was like a shot of capital, oil was the supershot. For oil really *was* capital, worth hard cash on the barrelhead the minute it came up from the depths. The acquisition of free land was slow by comparison, governed by changing circumstances, by the westward migration and the Indian wars, and therefore it offered at least a partial view of what lay ahead and what might become of the economy. But oil blossomed like an overnight flower. You sank a well on a piece of scrub land where there'd never been a thing but marshgrass and a week or two later brand-new capital, the existence of which people never even suspected, would come roaring up the pipe and into the economy. It came all at once with a splendid bang and its suddenness and its magnitude gave the state a tone and a pattern that it maintains yet.

Oil is a mixture in various balances of the elements hydrogen and carbon. It began as decomposing organic matter and was transformed into oil in a mysterious synthesis spread over the geologic ages. It occurs in layers of porous sedimentary rock, often sandstone, over which are heavy layers of non-porous stone. Water seeps through this porous rock, lifting and carrying the lighter oil along. The great changes in the shaping of the earth's skin have caused all these many layers of rock to lift, buckle, and break, and occasionally in the movement of the porous rock a high spot occurs into which the oil is pressed by the water beneath it until it can go no further. This is a trap and is the basis of the oil business. Sometimes it holds billions of barrels of oil and sometimes it is quite small. The trick is to decide where it might be and to drill from two to twenty thousand feet to see if you are right. So fine is this gauging that it has been determined that wells which brought in big fields would have been dry if they had been drilled a mere hundred feet beyond the site chosen. It is a chancy business.

There were a number of oil fields in the United States, from Pennsylvania to California, before the first serious find in Texas. But when Texas did start it was with impact—a field called Spindletop which was discovered in 1901 near Beaumont and proved to be the largest field then known in the world. I think there is little doubt that this dramatic beginning, following an already established pattern of magnitudes in cotton and cattle, had its effect on the outlook of the people and on their future. It was a marvelous sight. The first Spindletop well blew in as a gusher, spouting a column of oil at the sky and settling down to a steady production rate of nearly 100,000 barrels a day. Down on the docks in Galveston, in the cotton brokerage houses in Houston, around the stockyards in Fort Worth, men who were high rollers by inclination as well as by necessity sat up to watch this spectacle of money surging out of the ground.

The business had no controls then. Within weeks the original Spindletop rig was surrounded by drilling rigs packed so densely, it has been written, that you could cross the field from platform to platform and never muddy your boots. Wildcat drillers with little rigs made of wooden timbers that bolted together, easy to put up and easy to take down, went across the state looking for new fields. Their wells were shallow. With any luck they could sink a well in a week, tell when they were in paydirt from the whine of the bit and hit oil or walk away to try again. Each new field brought swarms of drillers and gradually the great fields that made Texas the pre-eminent petroleum producer of America began to hit. Even today, the names of those old boomtowns send down over half a century the heavy smell of crude and of money—Humble in 1904, Electra in 1911, Burkburnett in 1912, Ranger in 1917, Desdemona in 1918, Mexia in 1920, Laredo in 1921, and then through the twenties and beyond the finding of the many fields that pock the great Permian Basin, that huge West Texas semi-desert area that centers on Odessa and Midland.

But the great one, the one that changed the course of Texas history, was the East Texas Field, discovered on September 30, 1930. An old wildcatter known as Dad Joiner, drilling blind without benefit of geology, sank his famous Daisy Bradford No. 3 on that day. Four months later another well ten miles north of the Daisy Bradford went into what obviously was the same field—and a month after that, another well, this time twenty-five miles north of the discovery well, established that this was a monumental field. It was then and it remains today by every criterion the biggest oil field in the United States. It was some fifty miles long and up to twelve miles wide, reaching through five East Texas counties, with an estimated seven billion barrels of oil in place. It was bonanza. The wildcatters, the roughnecks and roustabouts and drillers, the technicians, the gambling men, the whores, the bootleggers all rushed in. The rather staid town of Longview nearly tripled its population and soon there were hundreds of wells along the red dirt roads slashed through pine forests. By July of 1931 there were 1,300 wells in production and they were pouring out an incredible 1.4 million barrels of oil a day. (There were 3,612 producing wells by the end of 1931 and the figure went to 25,976 by 1939.)

The result was chaos. The nation was in depression and already there were the beginnings of a glut. With the new oil supply, prices collapsed. There came the day when oil sold for a dime a barrel (a barrel holds forty-two gallons; there were instances of penny barrels) and for many there simply were no buyers. But there were no regulations then. If you didn't take your share, your neighbor pumped your share out from under your land. If he pumped, you did; if anyone did, everyone did. Storage space was exhausted and people dug big tanks with earthen walls to hold the oil. They put earthen dams in canyons and stored the oil behind them. Sometimes the dams or the tanks would break and send a cascade of crude oil bubbling down the river, killing fish and birds and ruining for decades large sections of that lovely piney woods country. A man who was there, still caught by the excitement of it, said, "I remember a pit a good five hundred acres, maybe fifteen or twenty feet deep, washed out one day and flooded the river with millions of barrels of oil. It floated on the surface and we built escarpments trying to trap it and hold it until we could get pumps into it. It was very volatile. It could have fired whole towns. God, what days those were."

Those days produced men to match. The oil boomer was the legatee of the frontier traders in cotton and cattle, but he was different, too. His business was based on science and it oriented to industry instead of the land. It also was much faster than the old trade and contained even more, if that is possible, of a gambling element. He made his best estimate for a drilling site, drilled knowing the chances were against success, and when his hole came in dry he dismantled his rig and licked his wounds and moved on. But if he did hit, oh, he could hit big. He could bring in a whole field. He could bring in a single well that would produce twenty or thirty thousand barrels of crude oil a day and keep on doing it. Or he could bring in a well that didn't contain enough oil to pay the cost of reaching it, or one that soon began producing water instead of oil. In cotton and cattle a man bet on a crop and while disaster was common, at least he could watch over and try to protect his crop. But oil was wide open and wild. If someone brought in a field on the other side of the state you could race over there and get a piece of it, and then when you bought in, you might find that your well still was dry even though the field around you was flowing. You could bet on yourself if you wanted. You could wander around where no one believed there was oil and poke at the geology and look at the land and let yourself down into every farmer's well for miles to see the subsurface shape of the rocks, and if you thought there was something there you could bore your hole. Or you could copper your bets by drilling all over the state or you could follow your hunches or follow rumors overheard in taverns or follow the crowd. Whatever you did, it was fast and rough. And finally, perhaps most important of all, there was the tonic of constant hope. Whenever you had a drillbit in the ground you went to bed with the certain knowledge that you *could* be—literally—rich in the morning. So the adrenalin shot of victory and success backed by instant wealth was just around the corner. It made for an ebullient atmosphere.

It made for men like D. H. Byrd. His parents named him David Harold, but for many years in the oil business the initials stood for Dry Hole Byrd for his famous streak of fifty-six dry holes in a row, drilled up and down the Balcones Fault. Byrd is an oil boomer. Now he is a heavy old man, very wealthy, with wispy white hair combed straight away and china blue eyes cold and hard as stones behind his rimless glasses, just as they were when he was a dashing dealer on the oil frontier. We sat at lunch in the Dallas Club on the fiftieth floor of the Republic National Bank, where you could see Fort Worth in the distance if you wanted to, and his brassy voice filled the room with oil talk and no one looked up because they are used to Harold Byrd.

He took a degree in geology in 1923, received membership No. 237 in the American Association of Petroleum Geologists, an organization that now boasts more than 70,000 members, and jumped into Texas oil. He went to work for a company, and he found immediately that he had an intuitive flare for geology and a hungry, independent streak that would not allow him to be another's man for long. Three years later he was on his own, drilling his first well in Mexia. He had spent $750 and when the well appeared to be a strike, he sold out for $86,000. He remembered it well.

"The people who'd bought me out made a couple million out of that and it didn't take me three months to lose my whole $86,000, drilling dry holes with it. I had a lot of dry holes. Three times I went broke and had to go back to work for the company, but each time I'd learn a little more and get up some more financing and pretty soon I'd be back at it. Well, I got to drilling along the Balcones Fault, runs the breadth of Texas almost, good five hundred miles, and you know a fault, which shears the formations below, is a good place to find oil traps. I had a Pierce-Arrow automobile, which was an uncommon car, and I had my own driver. I'd sleep while he drove and he'd sleep while I dealt and we were moving all the time. I tried to keep at least five wells going at a time and I was always looking for new formations and new possibilities. I'd go prowling down those dusty roads in that big car and jump out and climb among the rocks and check the formations and then I'd turn into an oil camp to try to make a deal and I got so I was known as 'that fellow in the Pierce-Arrow.' You kept so many wells going at once, you had to spend a lot of your time worrying about financing and visiting with bankers and backers and all the people who wanted to throw a little cash into a well and see if it would grow. Then I ran into this streak of dry holes. One well after another came up dry, not a sign of oil, and I'll tell you it was frustrating. My geology wasn't so bad—since then a lot of those wells that came in dry have been redrilled and the oil was there at greater depths, greater than the rigs in those days could go. Best we could do then was about 3,500 feet. I didn't lose faith and people didn't lose faith in me, I could always get some backing for my next well, but just the same, when you get fifteen, twenty, thirty, forty dry holes with never a lick in between, never a dollop of oil to patch up your finances, it gets discouraging. When you've put your last dollar in a well and all the indications look good and it's riding high and then it comes in dry, it's hard. But I kept going, right through fifty-six failures, and on the fifty-seventh I brought in a field up in Coleman County. That wasn't a bonanza, but after that it seemed like I couldn't keep from hitting. I got into the East Texas field, made a strike over near Longview that put me into solid financial condition for the first time. And I drilled just east of Dallas, where other geologists said there'd never be a thing. The signs were very subtle, only about a ten-foot outcrop on the surface, but I plunged and hit . . . but that first go-round, down in Mexia, oh, that was exciting. I bought in for $750 and I sold out for $86,000 and that was a lot of money for me."

After a while the wells got deeper and the deals got bigger until the oilmen became such operators that the whole nation began to take notice. And because they were naive and credulous and most very excited by what was happening to them, the oilmen began to exhibit a considerable flamboyance, to which Byrd, who eventually ran his fortune into the tens of millions of dollars, happily contributed. He enjoys the title colonel, from his days as Texas commander of the Civil Air Patrol, and his office is filled with pictures of himself, often in uniform with aviation dignitaries and Air Force generals. He was a cousin of the late Admiral Richard Byrd and financed some of the Admiral's activities; an obscure peak about three hundred miles from the South Pole appears on maps as Harold Byrd Mountain, and the Admiral's fur suit now hangs in Byrd's office. He is an honorary captain of the Texas Rangers and an honorary member of the University of Texas band, to which he gave, as he once put it, the biggest damned drum in the world. It is ten feet or so in diameter and made of a single skin from some massive African animal. It has its own wheels and a man to pull it down the street while the drummer runs along behind whacking it and the Colonel takes great pleasure in hearing its boom on the streets of Dallas in the parade held every year before the big rivalry game between the Universities of Texas and Oklahoma in the Cotton Bowl. After this game, which is full of nostalgic and often drunken sentiment for Texans, Byrd used to throw an extraordinary party. He was always a handy man for a party. Once he took a whole train to Mexico City, a performance to which an important national magazine gave considerable play, to the Colonel's mingled irritation and pleasure. But such parties have gone out of style in Texas and Byrd stopped his old Cotton Bowl celebrations several years ago and now discusses the old gaiety and the fact that it is past with a curious mixture of regret and relief.

Colonel Byrd is a dignified man today, comparatively modest in his activities, and most of his fellow boomers are gone, having yielded to the somewhat more graceful new aristocracy of Texas. Yet at his best—or perhaps one should say his loudest —he was the very personification of that familiar caricature the loud, antic Texas boomer. There were never many such men, but they had a tendency to show up at the Waldorf with cow manure on their boots and conceit in their voices, and Easterners took endless pleasure in detesting them and cari caturing them so that today they live on in myth though in fact they have almost all disappeared.

But despite the oil boomer's image, there is reason to think that the really significant Texas traders, the men who in the first half of the twentieth century made Texas synonymous with big deals, were not lineal descendants of the oil boomer at all but came directly down from the old frontier trader. The distinction is fine but worth making. The Texas trader was a fellow of frontier-developed capacities who when powered with the extraordinary impact of oil capital, both on his own outlook and on his economy, achieved a magnitude far beyond what the oil boomer could manage with his essentially technical orientation. This is important only in order to note that the Texas power attitude goes far deeper than its oil. In practice, of course, the trader jumped right into oil himself, though it seems to me that oil never limited his horizons or his interests; it just gave him more power to follow his natural inclination.

That is the pattern out of which came the group sometimes called the Athenians. They were hardly in the classic mold of Athens, for they were country traders, high rollers, money makers. But they all grew up in the little cotton town of Athens in East Texas and a good twenty of them went on to make fortunes. There was Sid Richardson, who often was considered the richest man in America; Arch Underwood, who built a fortune in cotton and cotton compresses; Toddie Lee Wynne, who dealt in everything but concentrated in real estate; and most of all there was a small, relaxed man with a nondescript face whose name was Clint Murchison and who helped shape the national image of the Texas trader as a hell-for-leather fellow.

They grew up together hanging around old Doc Sturman's drugstore on the town square in Athens, listening to the traders talk and the drummers and the politicians. They weren't poor. Underwood quit school after the fifth grade to work in the family cotton firm. Murchison started college, but left hurriedly after a crap shooting episode and went to work in the family bank. Richardson liked to say in later years that he'd been so poor in his youth that he'd slept on pool tables, but his friends would counter that that was only when he was too lazy to go home. When they were still boys they began dealing in horses, cattle, land, and anything else in which they found profit, sharpening with experience their already acquisitive instincts.

And then came oil. Of course, oil is what powered them, made them grow and made their later exploits possible. But their approach was not that of a prospector but of a trader, and they used their oil money like any other money, to go into any number of things including more oil deals. Murchison polished the technique, particularly viable in a rising economy, of borrowing money and putting it to work at a return sufficient to retire the principal as well as meet the interest. Of course, to succeed at this pleasant enterprise, one must not only nose out the deals that can make such a return but have both a record and a personal capacity that will convince the bankers who put up the money. Murchison had both, and undoubtedly his attitude toward trading helped him. Like most of the other great Texas traders, he liked what he was doing. He was relaxed and easy, rarely worried and not easily shaken. He and his fellows were hard drivers, but they were not driven men and there is reason to think they didn't even work so hard.

Arch Underwood once told a friend, "Hell, all this about us *working* so hard—not a damn bit of truth to it. We spent more hours around Doc's drugstore than we did working. We played a lot and we traded. Trading was one of the main sports in small towns and we were sports, all right. Clint and Sid started out trading horses and cattle, and then they got in oil and gas and everything. Clint was a real trader and he was the leader. He set such a mean pattern. Clint moved fast. In fact, he went so fast some of them dropped out. When it got going so big, all over the United States and Canada, old Toddie Lee says, 'Hell, give me my money. I want out. You're traveling too fast.'"

Murchison was in big-city real estate, ranches, gas, oil, banks, insurance companies, motels, steamship lines, office equipment, taxicabs, movies, theaters, race horses, restaurants, fishing tackle, pipelines, book publishing, newspapers, magazines and even such unlikely things as the Royal Gorge in Colorado and the Martha Washington Candy Company. Murchison used to tell his sons, "Money is like manure. If you spread it around it does a lot of good. But if you pile it up in one place it stinks like hell." He spread his around. He was in a hurry, he was always looking for a deal and he was not particular about where he found it. When he was in New York buying control of the old publishing house of Henry Holt he told an Eastern financier, "The trouble with you guys up here, you're too slow. You spend months shuffling those papers and going to board meetings. We trade, make the deal and let the paper work catch up later."

The Athenians were powerful operators, but they retained their rather easy-going, smalltown curbstone trader outlook. When Murchison and Richardson helped Robert Young get control of the New York Central in the early 1950s, Richardson threw some twenty million dollars into the pot largely at Murchison's request. Later, the story is told, after a conference with his tax man, Richardson called Murchison back to ask, "What's the name of that damned railroad we bought?" Apocryphal or not, the story suggests a man not notably awed by big dealing. When he was seventy-three, Arch Underwood sat in the headquarters of his cotton compress empire and said, "I always figured that after I go, I'd like to lie in state in Doc's drugstore there in Athens and let the band go march around the square. And let all the old boys march in and say, 'Now, don't he look natural!'"

3

The East Texas Field was running wide open when, on August 17, 1931, the Texas National Guard was called out to shut it down. It had been wild. Production had hit 1.4 million barrels a day and was still climbing, though the market had broken and some oilmen could find no buyer at any price. When oil was stored in earthen tanks its most valuable parts tended to evaporate and dirt and debris contaminated what was left. People watched offset wells running continuously despite the glut and draining oil from beneath their land. Tempers rose, fights broke out and there was a dangerous air over the big field.

Armed cavalrymen went on patrol in the deep pine forests. Troops in trucks wound along the red dirt roads up to the hidden wellsites. It was hot and steamy and the soldiers sweated and cursed as they moved across the field and well by well pinched off the endless flow of oil. As a restless, uneasy quiet hung over the field, the state established and prepared to enforce a system of proration. While complicated, proration is in effect an arbitrary limitation on the quantity of oil that can be taken from the ground in a given period. It applied to the whole state, has been in effect ever since and for most of that time has been under attack. Without examining its current merits, it did have the effect then, when the East Texas Field opened the following month, of stabilizing the price structure and conserving the total supply of oil. It is more efficient to take oil slowly because a higher percentage of what is in the ground usually can be recovered. No well will deliver all the oil in the trap, but those drained carelessly have been known to stop producing with as much as 90 per cent of their oil still in the ground and permanently lost.

Proration, however, had a larger significance that went beyond conservation or price. The moment the state limited the rate at which a man could produce his oil, it created the concept of reserves of oil still in the ground. The reserves were there, good almost as gold, but not immediately obtainable and the technique by which those reserves could be proved began to develop. Test wells around the field determined its size and the depth of its producing sand. The porosity of the sand determined the percentage of oil it contained and there were other factors that suggested what portion of that oil could be brought to the surface. So the time came when a man could, with due margin for error, get a fair and, more important, provable estimate of his underground wealth.

Until this point, oil had pumped capital into the Texas

economy as it came out of the ground and sold at the going price. Often enough in those early days of the motorcar industry and of the boomtown period in oil, the supply outran the demand and the price was weak. So until now, that capital input that meant so much to the Texas economy and, only slightly less directly, to the Texas personality, had come in haphazard surges.

But the science of proving reserves combined with the protection of proration solidified the reserves into something like capital itself. In effect, the capital flow became strong and steady and of continuing importance, compared to the heady but occasional surges of the past. Naturally, this contributed still more to the sense of thrust and excitement inherent in new capital. There remained but one more step fully to systematize its use.

Meanwhile, this had an immediate impact on the oil business itself. Oilmen had chronic financial problems, which, considering the instant gold that oil had been for them, amounts to a curious anomaly. The fact is that they could and did strike bonanza overnight and some became rich beyond their dreams. But the business was such that often these same men were broke the following year, for they kept right on drilling and it did not take many dry wells to exhaust the proceeds of their last strike. Since they were often broke, they tended to pump as quickly as possible when they did hit, in order to convert the oil immediately into cash. They expected a well to be exhausted quickly. It might produce for years, but there was no way to determine that in advance and so no way to capitalize on it. It had always been difficult to find really big financing. Banks made only short-term loans. A producing well was good for a loan on what oil might emerge in the next thirty or at most ninety days. Sometimes the banks took a man's equipment as security, though that covered only a fraction of his needs, but usually they bet on his reputation for integrity and success. (As Col. Byrd once said, "Anything will do for brains if you've got luck.") In the early days financing had not mattered so much; drilling didn't cost much and there were always workers ready to throw in for a share. If a man had a run of bad luck, he might take a job for a spell until he could afford to try again. But the character of the oil business began to change after the East Texas Field, and financing began to be critical. The shallower finds had been made and new exploration was going deeper with newer, heavier, and more expensive equipment. There was less prospecting on wildcat intuition and more on scientific geology backed by expensive testing, and increasingly the operators were fewer but bigger.

This was the situation when the Dallas banks stepped into oil, a move that in terms of the meaning of oil to Texas probably was second in significance only to the actual finding of the oil. The leader of that move was a slender, gentle man named Fred F. Florence, who may have been a financial genius. He was born in 1891 in New York City and moved the following year to Rusk, in East Texas, where his father operated a general store. The boy grew up with a soft East Texas accent and a powerful capacity for work. He had relatively little formal education. When he was fifteen and was selling newspapers on the street, he was offered a job at the First National Bank of Rusk, sweeping out and learning the business. He accepted instantly and, as he recalled years later, "I ran all the way home to tell my mother I was going to work in the bank." Once he had thought he wanted to be a lawyer and he had walked the country railroad tracks practicing courtroom oratory. Now he worked just as hard at learning the hazards and responsibilities of country banking. They are not so very different, he observed later, from big-city banking. It is just a matter of magnitudes. When he was twenty-four he was president of a small bank near Rusk and when he was twenty-eight he joined as first vice president the newly formed Guaranty Bank and Trust Co. of Dallas, which became the Republic National Bank. He was thirty-seven in early 1929 when he became president of the Republic, which was to become under his guidance and remains after his death the biggest bank in the Southwest.

Florence was not in the traditional banking mold. He was a

warm, friendly man and he believed that banks prospered by helping people prosper. He was aggressive and always on the move. Bankers should wear out shoe leather and not the seats of their trousers, he liked to say. Once he told Holland Mc-Combs, "No is the last word we say. Traditionally the banker is the man who starts with No and you try to convince him. We start by saying, Let's work it out, and the most regretful thing we say is No, if that finally becomes necessary."

Largely because of Florence, and Nathan Adams at the First National and R. L. Thornton at what became the Mercantile National, Dallas began to be the banking center of Texas and the Southwest, taking the projects that were too big or too demanding for the smaller banks. So these were the men with the financial foresight, the resources and, most of all, the downright courage to take the next step in oil: they began lending against the reserves.

They were lending on an asset that no one had ever seen. It was a radical departure from the old oil financing and it was made possible by the proration laws. The reserves were measurable so that an expert could make a fair estimate of what was there, how much it was worth and how much could be recovered. The proration rules were a guaranty on which a banker could rely that those reserves would not be drained with such speed as to depress the market, thus making the oil less valuable, or to damage the well, thus reducing the amount of recoverable oil.

It was this new stability in financing that systematized the use of oil reserves as capital. Proration turned the reserves into a sort of latent capital. Now the bankers found the way to spring that capital out of its sandstone vault and into the mainstream of the economy. It seems almost simple and obvious in the telling, but of course it was not. It was new, daring, dangerous; it was all the things that horrify traditional bankers.

Nathan Adams probably made the first such loan, but it was Florence who developed the system fully. He made the head of his credit department an oil loan officer. He hired petroleum engineers as advisors and the bank began making its own study of a man's reserves before it wrote his loan. It took an assignment on his production runs so that it received a share of whatever the well pumped under proration. Florence was cautious at first, but never harshly restrictive, and as the engineering techniques improved and the bank's information became more accurate, he eased the terms.

This had a cumulative impact on the oil business, for it led success to breed more success. Once a man developed reserves he could raise money to develop more. There were oilmen who started with $100,000 borrowed against a small field and worked up to many millions, all secured by new reserves found in strikes financed by previous loans. Since they could use their oil while it was still in the ground they were under no compulsion to pump it out at once, which meant in turn that it was worth more. It was the cumulative quality of this financing that began to produce the really big oil fortunes that startled the rest of the nation. As a man got bigger and bigger, realizing his return as soon as he found it, he could afford better geology, more efficient testing, the gamble of drilling to depths of up to five miles at perhaps a million dollars a well (by the middle 1960s, as equipment became available), all of which contributed to still bigger reserves and thus still more available money. Further, the depletion allowance freeing the first 27½ per cent of his income from federal taxation (set so high, theoretically, to offset the high risks of exploration) gave him a big cash advantage which, with the aggressive policy of the banks, increased still more his power of movement and exploration. The result of all this—the immense deposits of oil, the demanding, gambling outlook necessary to find it, the cumulative backing of the banks and the tax advantage—was to give oilmen a momentum which touched the whole society.

Col. Byrd gave up the old Pierce-Arrow automobile and learned to fly airplanes. "One day in the late thirties I was flying across New Mexico and Arizona when I noticed surface structures there in the Four Corners area that sure suggested oil to me. I went back out and checked my geology on the ground and I bought the drilling rights to a million acres and went to work. I drilled eight wells and brought in six big fields and started a boom up there in the San Juan basin. Now I'm in a combine in Australia, with Delhi-Taylor, you know, the Murchison outfit, and others, and we've got drilling rights on 186 million acres. We've brought in some wells already but we need a 500-mile pipeline. That may cost two hundred million dollars, and we're going to have to drill some more wells to support it." Could they bust out? "Oh, sure, but we probably won't. What's more likely is that we'll have to bring in still more capital and split the pot further to make it work."

Byrd casually reflects the facts of Texas economic life today—facts that have strong bearing on what the state has become. Opportunity is much more important than having money. Money is available. No one expects to operate on his own money. He expects to borrow and, given a background that establishes his solidity, he can borrow nearly anything he needs if his proposition is right. The money is available and many people use it and in the psychological sense, this is the real meaning of the capital pools provided by oil.

"If a man wanted to borrow a million dollars in San Antonio," said Michaux Nash, president of the Empire State Bank in Dallas, "there would be a ceremony like trying to see a potentate." In Dallas they regarded money as a tool and the bankers bet on the man who used the tool. This was the atmosphere that made Clint Murchison possible. The banks bet on Murchison because he usually won, and in a smaller way and in every sort of field, they bet on others and helped them grow.

It was this money atmosphere, this sense of no limits action imposed on natural frontier exuberance, that gave rise in its beginning stages to that Texas boor, big-hatted and big-mouthed, who, as I have said, was so storied in the East. Most of the classic boors are gone now, and today's men of power tend to be educated, usually moderate, grown up. Their maturity is reflected in the economy. The real power has shifted to Houston, in both population and industry. The oil business headquarters there for the entire free world and men trained in Texas fields are operating fields everywhere. Texas builders and real-estate developers are active all over the country. The building boom in Denver in the late 1950s and in Atlanta in the mid 1960s were Texas plays, made by Texas builders. It is interesting to note that the money that Texas used came from the East. Texas money power has always come not from quantity but from use of money and attitude toward it. It is a favorite American myth, perpetuated by the suddenness of oil money and the exuberance of oil operators, that Texas rolls in money. Obviously in a state ranked thirty-fourth in per capita income, the average man isn't rich, but in the sense of riches as they're understood in the East, only a handful of the biggest Texans can compete (and the Republic Bank, first in Texas, ranked twenty-seventh in the nation in 1966). Texans understand this. They draw great power from the Republic Bank's attitude, but when Pennzoil wanted to take over United Gas, the Liedtke brothers went to New York for their money. Murchison went to New York for his money, too, though he liked to say that New York money was musclebound, tied to restrictions and rules and boards of directors, so that his independence made his lesser money actually more effective. Trammell Crow of Dallas, one of America's biggest builders, though his modest nature and his method of organizing his business into separate units keep him out of the public eye, once said, "There are many more men in New York than in Texas who could write a check for ten million dollars—but there are probably fewer who would." For that matter, this disparity in favor of Eastern capital is merely the modern reflection of historical fact: Texas has always been short of money. The frontier's free land constituted capital, but because it was always reaching ahead of itself, it was constantly under-capitalized and hungry for immediate transfusions. The cotton culture in East Texas, partly as the aftermath of the Civil War, remained for years in bondage to the Eastern financial centers and paid destructive interest and discriminatory rail rates. That is the source of President Johnson's bitter recollection, culled from his young manhood, of economic bondage in which Eastern money held Texas. It was quite real.

In a surface sense, Texas has changed a great deal. It puts much more emphasis on industry now, for instance, particularly refineries and petro-chemical plants that are publicly owned and developed by outside capital. Industry changes the society that forms around it. Industry offers a steady paycheck, a premium for education and training, an increasing standard of living. It wants a stable labor supply living in a stable society. All of this is antithesis to the old frontier. Even the oil boomer is almost gone, with the new emphasis shifted to major companies dealing in size and science.

The effect of the change, however, can be overestimated. The old trader is still around. The banks are still behind him. He now is interwoven into every aspect of life and commerce and moving faster than ever. There no longer are such clear patterns of cause and effect: now the trader, the oilman, the industrialist and always the banker merge into one with joint projects, profits and, inevitably, attitudes.

I think that the Texas attitude of today grows in powerful degree from these combinations. Even those people employed by industry and living with all the urban problems are touched (perhaps in a way that is emotional, misleading, even false and damaging to their real interests) by the sense of optimism, independence, and excitement that is inherent in the trader. They are not traders themselves and most of them never will be, but the sense of the banks and the oil boom and the availability of money rubs off on them and their society. It opens doors, even today, even in a modern, industrialized society, to those who want to go through them. If most are content to stay outside, that is not to say that they are not influenced by an atmosphere in which it is possible to go through the door.

CHAPTER

1

David Witts, master of the Terlingua Ranch, sat in the big corner room of his law office on the tenth floor of the Vaughn Building in Dallas. It was late in a summer afternoon and the white glare outside was softening to gold. The office was cool and shaded and there was that sense of dry ease that accompanies silent air-conditioning. Witts sat with his shoes propped on his big desk. He was wearing an expensive silk suit and his dark face was burned even darker from lying the week before in a lawn chair on the white dirt in front of the Terlingua Inn with the desert sun full in his face. This is a very handsome room, not at all like the raw Terlingua Ranch or like his life as a boy. There are rugs and drapes, deep chairs around the polished desk, old books and silver fittings and framed documents. The working day was finished, the office empty, the phone silent, and Witts sat cocked back in his chair, smiling and easy, remembering how it all began, before there were silk suits or a Jaguar automobile or a 220,000-acre ranch in the Big Bend country. Witts is something of a rarity, a successful man who has not lost sight of himself. He knows that he made it not by some special grace or innate superiority but by scrambling, by working hard, being smart, taking risks, coming along at the right time and in the right place. On his desk is a heavy piece of jagged metal six inches long, sharp and lethal, the fragment of a Japanese shell that sliced above his head one bloody night on the island of Morotai and imbedded itself in a palm tree. He dug it out and keeps it now where he sees it every day and he says, "Whenever I get to taking myself too seriously, I look at that shell fragment and I say to myself, 'Hell, man, who are you kidding?' "

Witts was born in 1920 and, in the old frontier phrase, he lit running and he's been running ever since. He burns with a sort of hyperactive energy and he is enthusiastic, optimistic, generous, and good humored, all until he is crossed and then he shows a hard and implacable streak, which is to say that he is a latter-day child of the frontier. He loves the land. He finds it natural to settle deals on a bonding handshake, as he did that day in the El Paso airport when, over a friendly drink, he sold half the Terlingua to Carroll Shelby, who was himself merely between planes on his ceaseless passage between the world's racing meets and the production barns for the manufacture of his sports cars. When Harold Wynne contracted political ambition and decided to run for office from the Terlingua, Witts foresaw all the problems, including the retaliation against the big and vulnerable ranch which a losing race would bring. But it takes a considerable arrogance to interfere in such things: "How the hell am I going to tell any man he can't run for public office and particularly a tough old boot like Harold? So we backed him up, put five hundred dollars in his campaign account and the opposition went around saying it was five thousand dollars and that we thought we could buy Brewster County, and of course he lost and we've been hearing about it ever since. But what the hell."

Witts grew up in Denton, a farming community north of Dallas. He doesn't talk much about his boyhood. He had a magazine route when he was six, selling *The Delineator* from a canvas sack, he said one day, brightly, as if it was a fact that had popped up suddenly from the gloom of recollections in which he takes no pleasure. He was poor and ambitious and, as were so many poor boys of that generation in Texas, hungry for a piece of land. He went to college, served as an FBI agent, joined the Air Corps and flew his fifty combat missions in bombers in the Pacific. He held a pilot's rating but he flew as navigator and even now when he visits the Terlingua Ranch he likes to stand in the crystal night and call the well-remembered constellations that used to guide him home. He came back, finished law school with honors and went to work. "I could pack everything I owned in my B-4 bag," he said. "A couple of attorneys already in business in Dallas let me use the couch in their reception room for my office for whatever business I could get plus anything that slopped over from their practice that they couldn't handle, and believe me, there wasn't much of that. I made fifty dollars the first month."

He was quick and energetic and soon the attorneys hired him. He began to build a reputation in trial work, having in happy combination agility of mind as well as tongue. His real interest, however, lay in business maneuver, the matter of how to move without mistake rather than how to repair mistakes already made. After three years he was receiving a great many compliments and three hundred dollars a month and he decided that at this rate he would wait a long time for that piece of land.

So he quit, opened his own law office and survived, which is a feat in itself. He was building steadily a reputation for legal ability, for business sense and, perhaps most important, for integrity and dependability. As he rushed about town, from the courthouse to his clients' offices to the endless luncheon clubs patronized by young attorneys hungry for business, he speculated with himself as to how he might get ahead.

"I had neither cash nor credit and no immediate way to get either," he said, smiling, remembering, shifting in his comfortable chair at the thought, "so I thought I might as well start at the top. I picked out the biggest company I could find, which happened to be Humble Oil, and decided to do business with them. The only place I could see where their operation might touch my level was in their filling stations, and I began studying the filling station business.

"And one day I walked into Humble and told them that I could build a filling station for them quicker and cheaper and better than they could build it themselves. I told them that if they would give me a lease that would amortize the full mortgage, plus interest, I would give them a price that their own people couldn't equal.

"It really was pretty simple. I had found a likely piece of property and I had an option to buy it for $20,000. I had a builder ready to contract to put up a station to Humble's specifications for $30,000, a turnkey job, meaning complete to the key in the door. That was $50,000, and I knew that Humble was paying up to $60,000 for a station. And they had to lay out all their money at once. That was before real estate became such an obviously attractive investment, and most of Humble's money went to hunt for more oil. In those days the company regarded its main operations as finding, producing and refining oil and tended to treat its retail marketing as a sort of stepchild. So I thought that in addition to the saving, having to pay for the station only as they used it also would be attractive. And of course, there was the tax factor too—they could write off lease money the year they spent it, while if they built themselves they would spend years depreciating the building and never could depreciate the land.

"For me, you see, the whole key was that lease. It had to cover everything. It had to be for a full fifteen years in the exact amount per month required to pay off the $50,000 plus the interest. The whole point was that I had the idea but I didn't have any dough of my own to invest.

"The people at Humble looked at me like I was nuts. They wanted to know why I thought I could build it cheaper. Well, I told them, I sure as hell could buy the land cheaper, me an individual and poor at that, than they could as representatives of a big corporation. And then, as an individual working for my own benefit, naturally I'd work like a dog to cut every corner I could. As an attorney, I understood and knew how to handle the problems that would arise, title problems, for instance, and contract, zoning, city regulation problems, all the things I was handling all the time for other people anyway. And I told them, sit down and figure it all out and see if you don't come out ahead. They thought it all over and a few days later they called me back and said, 'Okay, you deliver us a finished station to our specifications and we'll give you a fifteen-year lease that will amortize the mortgage.'

"So I was in—or at least, part way. The thing was, I had to build the station and give Humble the key before the lease payments could start. I still didn't have a penny, so the money to build the station was going to have to come from the bank. And that was the hardest part of all."

He paused, smiling at the remembered anxiety; now his mortgage accounts are routinely heavy, but that was the beginning. He picked up a silver letter-opener and balanced it in his hand so that it caught the dying light outside and fetched it into the office.

"I walked around town wondering where in hell I could get the money. It was one of those deals where everyone wins, which, of course, is what makes a good deal. Humble would get a station at a price it couldn't match and in a way that was financially convenient. The bank would hold a mortgage guaranteed by Humble's lease with the lease payments made directly to the bank. It couldn't lose. And after fifteen years, I would own the station.

"You might think this would strike the banks the same way, but you'd be wrong. Banks expect to have solid collateral when they let their money go and especially when they let it go to newcomers. Banks are not in business to help out penniless young men. I had small accounts in two small banks and neither would deal with me. Just a few months before I had tried to buy a little farm out near Grapevine. There was a farmhouse on it and the old man who owned it was going to throw in a houseful of magnificent furniture of mahogany and leather and marble tabletops. He'd been down to the drugstore in town and he'd fallen in love with that chrome and plastic drugstore furniture and he'd decided to buy some and move to town. The farm was thirty-two acres and he wanted $30,000, which was a fair price, but he wanted 10 per cent down. He didn't need the money, but he believed in 10 per cent, which wasn't unreasonable, and he wasn't going to deal without it. Well, I had a fellow lined up to lease the farm for a third more than my payments would have been on the three thousand dollars I needed to borrow, it was a solid deal, I had a solid reputation, but I couldn't do a thing. I got thrown out of every bank in town.

"I kept walking around thinking to myself, this filling station is the best deal I've ever had, it's ironclad, I know it's ironclad—and finally I walked into the Republic National Bank. I got in to see a senior vice president and I laid out the whole thing. I told him about the land, the contractor who was ready to build, the Humble lease, the exact figure payments to be made directly to the bank, and I told him there was no way any of us could lose. So, I said, I want you to give me $50,000 to handle this deal.

"There was a long pause and then he asked quietly, 'Now, Mr. Witts, what sort of collateral do you have?' I looked him square in the eye—I'd been waiting for that—and I said, 'I'm not in the habit of putting up collateral on small loans.' He knew I was bluffing and I knew that he knew and we sat there and the silence got longer and longer and finally he said, 'All right, Mr. Witts, I think we'll let you have that money.'"

Now, in his big corner office, remembering, he sat bolt upright and slapped the polished desk hard with his hand so that it made an excited crack. "God," he cried, "I'll never forget that day as long as I live. The surge of triumph that went over me—" The next day Fred Florence had called him in. "I want to see this young man we're giving $50,000 without any collateral," the old banker had said, but Witts, in his ignorance, had supposed that all the bank's customers received such treatment. Years later the senior vice president recalled the loan he had made to Witts and said that "from the standpoint of financial responsibility, he [Witts] was not entitled to the loan." But he had felt confidence in Witts and it was obvious that the arrangement with Humble was workable and would make Witts a good deal of money, so "I abandoned one of the basic rules of credit to extend him the funds he needed."

So, the bank behind him, Witts built that filling station. He bought the land, made the contract, arranged every detail, hovered over the carpenters and the masons, and when it was finished he gave Humble the key and the lease went into effect. It all worked just fine—so he found a new piece of land, went back to Humble and back to the Republic Bank and soon he had about thirty filling stations and as he put it, "I had a marvelous financial position. I was more than a million dollars in debt. I figured I was a millionaire in reverse." But month by month as those mortgages were slowly retired, his equity in his filling stations increased.

The filling stations were the start, the solid base on which he grew. They were tied up, of course, but they gave him position and reputation. His law practice expanded, his income increased and he began acquiring interests in various businesses and other properties. Eventually—ambition realized—he started buying ranches, which led him up to the Terlingua. And oddly enough, the filling stations played a direct and significant part in making the Terlingua work. He bought the ranch on an absolute shoestring, $25,000 down against a purchase of $1.3 million for 140,000 acres (when Shelby came in they added another 80,000 acres), and ran into immediate problems. The land had not been ranched for years and he had to start almost from the beginning. The herd of cattle he put in the pastures was not so difficult because he was able to mortgage it to the bank for most of its purchase price. There were many real property improvements necessary, however, that could not be financed. Equipment, buildings, wells and the pumps to draw their water, miles of roads, cattle guards, and miles of barbed fence demanded an immediate outlay of several hundred thousand dollars in cash. At this point, Humble, having become interested in the investment aspects of owning its service stations, exercised its option to buy out Witts' equity in a number of his stations for a figure that amounted to several hundred thousand dollars and most conveniently met the Terlingua's needs.

The light outside was failing. It was in that quiet moment between day and night when electric lights are not yet bright, and it was nearly dark inside the corner office. Witts' voice was low. "I don't know a place in the world where this financial climate exists. This was new frontier money, wealth generated by a preceding generation which fought the Indians and raised the cotton and the cattle and found the oil—and I slid in on its back. And it was a particular time in the world's history, too, a demand everywhere for new things and new facilities after a long war, and maybe if I'd stumbled along at any other time it wouldn't have worked." He got up, stretching, and began stowing papers into his briefcase. And then he looked up, grinning. "But just the same," he said, "if I'd walked into the banks in Chicago with some of the deals I've put together here, they'd have hit the burglar alarm."

2

It began as a little company in Dallas that bounced sound waves off the rock formations deep in the earth in search of oil and it only came to manufacturing by the back door. During World War II it started making military search gear that grew out of the equipment it used to look for oil, but the total of its contracts during the whole war barely exceeded a million dollars and afterwards some of its management was all for dropping manufacturing and getting back fulltime to oil. But a Brooklyn-born engineer named Erik Jonsson who had become vice president fought for and won a decision to maintain a small manufacturing division. All this was years before the transistor was even invented and long before the little company changed its name to Texas Instruments and became one of the great industrial success stories.

In Washington, Jonsson had met a thirty-one-year-old electrical engineer named Patrick Haggerty, a quiet, pleasant man of incisive intelligence who came from a little town in North Dakota and was finishing his wartime service as a naval procurement officer. They liked each other and often lunched together and talked of the technology of the future, which they believed lay in the then somewhat embryonic field of electronics. When Haggerty's naval service ended, Jonsson offered him the new manufacturing division. It was a fortuitous choice, for Haggerty had real talent for organization and for planning. When the new division was running smoothly, Haggerty began thinking far ahead. He wanted a fundamental position in electronics making something basic that would be useful in many applications and could be sold in volume, probably for use in equipment manufactured by others. The fundamental tool of all electronics is the valve that controls a flow of electrons, which at that time meant the many varieties of the vacuum tube, familiar from the big old radios of the day. Haggerty was considering going into specialized tubes when, in 1948, two men in the Bell Telephone Laboratories invented the transistor.

Without going into technicalities, the transistor also is an electronic valve. It is a solid piece of a metalloid element such as germanium or silicon formed in a single perfect crystal through which an electron flow can be controlled, amplified or otherwise handled. Though its significance was not immediately recognized, it would eventually change the whole course of electronics, which in turn has changed the course of modern life. Neither the exploration of space, for instance, nor the science of computers nor countless other things that work to the benefit or the detriment of man would have been possible without these minute solid-state electronic valves, of which the transistor was the first developed. Their importance lies less in their tiny size or slight power requirements than in their reliability. Vacuum tubes were inherently unreliable, so as the number of tubes increased in complicated equipment, so did their chance of failure. It is said that a modern computer made with tubes would break down at least every five minutes.

But the transistor's future was not at all apparent then and most of the industry saw it as a specialized and expensive device of limited use that would never replace the vacuum tube. Haggerty, however, saw something quite fundamental. As he put it much later, "I realized that the first quarter century of the electronics industry had been dominated strictly by circuitry. The advances were made in the way you put components together to solve problems. I was beginning to realize that another element was being added and that it grew from the knowledge we were getting of the materials themselves. For the first time—think of the atom bomb—we were going clear to basic levels. I'm not talking about metallurgical uses, alloys and such, but about going right down to the structure of matter itself. We were beginning to comprehend the structure of matter so well that we could manipulate its very components."

In the next eighteen months, Haggerty became convinced that the transistor would be basic to the future in electronics. If that was true, then Texas Instruments should be making transistors. It was an idea of marvelous effrontery. The firm had no theoretical electronics engineers, not a single holder of a doctorate in engineering, not an hour's background in solid-state electronics or in the predecessor vacuum tube and not even very much money to back it up. Whatever it did would have to be in direct competition with the huge mass manufacturing companies, RCA and General Electric and others, with their capital, their laboratories, their research staff and their years of experience and accumulated knowledge.

And yet, Haggerty thought he was right. If he was wrong, if transistors were merely an interesting blind alley, the results would be disastrous for the little company and for him. But one day he walked into Jonsson's office and made it official: after eighteen months of study and discussion with Jonsson and all the staff, he wanted to go ahead; he wanted to bind Texas Instruments to transistors, to go after Bell for the right to manufacture them, to make money commitments now that would assume a momentum of their own and be increasingly difficult to stop—and he knew that all this had to be done before there could be definite proof that he was right.

Patrick Haggerty remembers that decision very well. It was the most important he ever made or that his company ever made. He sits in the spartan offices of the chairman of the board (he succeeded Jonsson, who went on to spend nearly full time as mayor of Dallas) and he smiles faintly as he thinks of that day. His hair is gray and his face is getting pouchy. He remains a quiet, unpretentious, rather charming man with an almost sweet quality that does not belie the hardness of command, though one suspects that more than most executives, he rules from the force of his mind rather than of his personality. He constantly wonders about the meaning of things, probing with lean, quick efficiency into their depths, and altogether, he displays an elegance of intellect that makes him as unusual among engineers as it does among Texans.

"Ideas are such gentle things," he said. "When they are young and untried, they are so vulnerable. Now I made this decision and I remember quite well the agony of it. As you look back, if the decision was right, it seems logical and natural and the experience that piles up in favor of it ultimately makes it seem impossible not to have been made. But I remember that when we looked at the pros and cons, it was not so completely clear, there was plenty on both sides."

Erik Jonsson remembers that he thought it over most of that night and on the next morning agreed to commit the company. There were immediate things to do. They needed an elaborate materials laboratory, for materials is what the new field was all about, and they needed more trained personnel. It was all expensive. So Haggerty and Jonsson went to the Republic National Bank and laid the whole problem on Fred Florence's desk. Florence listened gravely while Haggerty spelled out the technological need which he believed the transistor would answer and described what he planned to do. Their net worth was low at this point and so was their cash position, but they had contracts on which they were working, a good record and, most of all, potential. To develop their plans for transistors, they wanted the bank to give them a credit line of $2.5 million on which they could draw as they needed it. Florence, who had watched their progress for several years and had reason to respect them as individuals, smiled and agreed: the bank would give them the credit.

"Now you must realize what this meant," Haggerty said as he recalled that crucial meeting. "There was a climate in Texas, an attitude that made things possible. Remember that I had only been in Texas a few years then. I was not a native and I could see the difference clearly. Take Erik Jonsson—he understood in general what we were doing, of course, but he was not an electronic engineer and he could not pass on the finer points. He was willing to go ahead and commit the company anyway because he was used to sticking his neck out. He had been living and working in that kind of society.

"This is even more true of Fred Florence. The fact that he would accept our plans when he couldn't possibly understand the technicalities of what we were doing and that he would lend us what then was for us a truly huge sum of money at a time when our cash position was low and our book value relatively poor meant that he was betting on people and on performance instead of sticking to banking standards. I don't think there were many places where that could have happened.

"And as for our decision, there were good reasons not to go ahead, too. There were cons as well as pros and they could have stopped us. A fear of risk, a fear of things big and important, trouble with the bank, difficulty in financing or terms too arduous and debilitating, any of these might have blocked the decision. We could have grown a good 10 per cent a year without any risk at all and in a really conservative situation, the question would be, what's wrong with that? Why not stick to a safe 10 per cent a year, which after all is a handsome growth rate?

"And then we wouldn't have gone into transistors and we wouldn't be what we are today. What's more, because our work in silicon transistors later put us three years ahead of the industry, I think that if Erik Jonsson had hesitated and Fred

Florence had been conservative, we can at least speculate that the whole thrust of electronic technology might have been delayed in this country and that would have had consequences beyond imagining."

In 1952 Western Electric, which held the patents, released the transistor for development to some fifty companies which had applied for licensing and paid a $25,000 advance against royalties. Of these, Texas Instruments was the smallest. Bob Olson, then its chief engineer, has been quoted as saying of his first visit to Western Electric: "They were not impolite. They were mighty nice people. But I got the impression they were both amazed and amused that our little company would have the effrontery to think that we could make transistors."

The new materials laboratory at Texas Instruments improved the original transistor and developed a machine to make them in commercial quantities. They remained expensive, however, running up to $16 apiece, and were used mainly in hearing aids. Haggerty reasoned that if the price could be brought down to about $2.50 each, there could be a big market in portable radios. In a major step, the laboratory developed a mass production system that met Haggerty's price level. Then he took the $2.50 transistor to a small company that made the Regency radio line and helped it bring out the first transistor radio.

That was in 1954 and the public impact was tremendous. People were astonished and then delighted with the brash little radio that spoke so clearly right from their hand. *Transistor* became a household word and even today it is commonly used to denote a small radio. It had almost equal impact for Texas Instruments. It demonstrated that the transistor was reliable, practical, susceptible to mass production at guaranteed volume and at a price that made it reasonable for many uses. The company was on its way to seizing dominance in the field, dominance it maintains worldwide today, and Haggerty's decision was beginning to pay off.

The original transistors were made of germanium and would not stand excessive heat, which didn't matter much in radios but limited their use in things like missiles and high-speed aircraft. A transistor made of silicon withstood heat readily, but there were numerous problems, and the industry agreed that serious production was still several years away. In 1954, however, which was the year of the transistor radio, Haggerty's laboratory also developed an ingenious machine that could produce silicon transistors in commercial quantities. It was a real breakthrough. There was an electronics conference scheduled at Dayton at which Gordon Teal, who had helped develop the new transistor, was to give a paper. He arrived at the meeting with the transistor in his pocket, listened to a colleague predict it would be years before silicon would be practical and stood up to give his own paper. Toward the end he announced casually that Texas Instruments was producing the silicon transistor and had it ready to market. When the startled audience erupted in questions, Teal gave a little demonstration. He wired an old germanium transistor into a small record player and spun a record. He thrust the transistor into a pot of boiling oil and the music stopped. Then he wired in the silicon model, put it into the pot and the music played merrily on. *Fortune* Magazine later wrote, "The silicon transistor was a turning point in T.I.'s history, for with this advance it gained a big headstart over the competition in a critical electronic product; there was no effective competition in silicon transistors until 1958. T.I.'s sales rose almost vertically; the company was suddenly in the big leagues."

It has been growing ever since. In 1958 it made another great stride and another followed: Haggerty believes that innovation is the success key, that profits for work without innovation are likely to be no more than a modest fee for use of assets, like bank interest. Texas Instruments sales have risen from two million dollars in 1946 to more than half a billion dollars in the mid-1960s. Its growth has increased at a compound rate of about 30 per cent a year and its profits at a compound rate of 31 per cent. It is the world's largest producer of semi-conductors, of which the transistor is the best-known form. It has more than 40,000 employees, a beautiful plant of strikingly intelligent design outside Dallas and other operations all over the world, and yet about 35 per cent of its effort is in non-electronic areas, including its original function, the search for oil. It has made rich men of its officers and major stockholders. Its stock has climbed and split and grown and done all manner of crazy wonderful things that, if you were lucky enough or foresighted enough to own a little, coated your affairs with gold. Nor is the story over. With the same attention to the future that put him into transistors, Haggerty has plans today that he believes will put the company into the three-billion-dollar range in the next decade, which by today's standards, would put it in the magic ring of the nation's dozen biggest companies. "This is not just ambition. This is hard planning, including contingency planning in case something goes wrong, as something always does. Of course, the three-billion-dollar figure is a goal and not a forecast and the decade is a target and is not precise. But I think we are going to get there."

This growth rested on many things, on the basic decision, on Jonsson's backing it and Florence financing it, on good planning and strong scientists and a constantly expanding market in electronics. But Haggerty believes that the atmosphere he found when he moved to Texas is responsible too, and he has thought a great deal about this.

"I expect the matter of feeling comfortable with change is as vital to growth as any other thing, and here the acceptance of change that is worthwhile comes very easily. There is quite a striking difference here and it is not limited to people at the top. When I came I was taken instantly with this quality in our people out in the shops. In other places, people fought new ideas. There was an inchoate resistance. There was the feeling that you must wait and examine and be certain before trying anything. Here, if the new idea is good, they're ready. In fact, there is almost a reverse factor—a hurry to change, an impatience with failure to change.

"And then there was the masculine nature of the big businesses that went before, the cotton and cattle and oil; they're all high-risk businesses, huge in scope, international in operation and very complex. Oil, which was the last, was more sophisticated and technical and it led automatically to the petro-chemical industry, which brought such great sums of money into the state. It was this industrial sophistication that paved the way for other industries, such as electronics.

"Oil helped create a rational atmosphere of measuring the risk against the potential, and there was a correspondingly bold and masculine quality to the financing. Bankers had learned to base their risk on technical indications of what lay in the ground and on their estimate of the men who were applying to them. So when we came along, it was easy to transfer from the idea of intangible assets in the ground to intangible assets in a man's head. It was this attitude that made the money possible. There were fewer restrictions and no feeling of a dead hand on the controls. Of course, there is more capital in the East, but it is tighter and more conventional. Electronics is a high-mobility business. Quick decisions are necessary and they are made possible by swift financing. And what's more, the bankers here lend you the money and then let you run your own business. In more conservative situations there were controls placed on money, either on its use or on the company that borrowed it, and this restrained things. People from other states simply couldn't believe the kind of financing they got here. So when industry came to Texas, it found an atmosphere receptive to fast growth, to speculation, to the vigorous imaginative use of money to accomplish new things."

He paused, sitting in his simple office that opens onto a small garden shared with other executives, and smiled. He had found more of this spirit in Texas than elsewhere—but why, he wondered somewhat puckishly, did it survive, considering the droves of new people flooding into the state? A selection process, he supposed: the spirit attracts a certain kind of people who feel comfortable in its environment and their presence in turn attracts more people like themselves. It is equally likely, however, that there also is a conditioning process: the spirit and the environment work on the newcomer, encourage him and open doors for him and finally, if he is at all inclined—and after all, most of us are—fit him into the mold of progress.

This free and open atmosphere is not at all primitive; rather, it is quite sophisticated, which Haggerty believes also is a result of oil. "Oil telescoped in time the transition from the frontier to the modern world. The change was so quick because of the suddenness and the size of oil, that it really carried over much of that early atmosphere into today's industrial world, directly from the old attitudes into what we are doing here today. This peculiar juxtaposition of the old and the intensely new, modern and industrial, explains some of the excitement and pace of Texas.

"As an economy and an area evolves it seems to move toward a more feminine attitude, more complex, with more pretense, more formality, more interest in and acceptance of the status quo and less push for the new and less willingness to take risks. In Texas, the evolution was so quick that things were up and running before this hamstringing effect could take hold. So there wasn't that stratification of society, the convoluted social patterns, the tendency to hold a man's parentage his most important qualification for trust and acceptance. Here acceptance was on face value and if a man did what he said he would do, he had no problems.

"So the atmosphere here had a lot to do with our success. It helped make possible a decision that had high risks but, as transistors proved, high potential as well. The important point is that we did not have to debate this beyond the rational. They were used to risks, size and judging men. All you had to do was convince them not of yourself, not of the reasons for taking the risk, not of the importance of the project if it succeeds, but only that it has a rational chance and that the approach to it is rational.

"So things here came down to the particular dream. Did it make sense? If you could show that the dream made sense, no one was afraid to dream."

CHAPTER

X

But there is another side of Texas, a considerably uglier side, that grows just as logically from the past as do the fabled traits of strength and independence. If you look at Texas as a humanist, if you measure it in things that relate to people instead of buildings and therefore make a great instead of merely big society, it falls sadly short. It has the resources and the energy to do anything it chooses, but in matters of the human spirit it chooses to do very little; and the saddest thing is that it does not even seem to recognize this most obvious fact.

Viewed thus, the Texas society that we have been seeing in such bright colors takes on a shabby tone, not from evil or ill intent but from the way that it has grown. Its predominant, guiding and even controlling quality is its intense materialism. Despite its proud talk of heritage and independence, its real interest is in making money, and it gets very grim with anything that interferes with this. Its politics are usually reactionary and sometimes cruel, because they are geared to materialism instead of to people. It is essentially noncultural, though it pays lip service to culture. It is anti-intellectual. It discriminates against its minorities and is cruel to its poor, who make up a surprisingly big percentage of its population, considering the emphasis it puts on money and success. This cruelty seems less the product of selfishness or greed, though there is that, too, than it does of a lack of tenderness, of simply not caring enough. The Texas society frequently creates physical ugliness and then defends it as the consequence of man's God-given right to pursue the greatest profit possible and regards those who protest as naive and somehow weak and unmanly. It exhibits the most intense satisfaction with itself, self-pride become flatulent. It is all these things because the establishment, which controls both the economy and the politics, feels natural and comfortable this way; and that segment of the population growing increasingly uncomfortable is not in control nor likely to take control and therefore is considered negligible.

It follows that the individual Texan produced by such a society, at least when seen with this critical an eye, is not the most pleasant fellow around. And admittedly, this is too harsh a view to be fully valid by itself, but my point is that it is just as much a part of Texas as is the picture of the gay, courageous, freedom-loving boomer of the frontier or the oil patch, and it is impossible to consider one without the other, for both grow from the same source and are equally part of the state.

Even more than America as a whole, Texas is a product of the Western ethic, the land ethic, predicated as we have seen on free land. Never before in the history of man had there been such a wealth of land not occupied by an organized people and therefore relatively free for the taking and breaking. Of course, this Western frontier produced its own man in a process of selectivity, first in who was attracted and then who could survive. He was first of all confident, and as a result, proud. He was self-reliant, since he could expect no help, and thus was independent. He lived with pain and death and he became hardened to suffering. He had no use for weakness or sympathy for failure; he was threatened with failure constantly and survived only by the hardest work. He met his responsibilities and cared for himself and his family. He was contemptuous of those who would not or could not work so hard or were less courageous or could not cope with the life. This, coupled with his own natural feelings of superiority and cultivated pride, encouraged his tendency toward arrogance. All told, it was not a combination that would rest easy in modern society.

Eventually the free land was all taken and many places in America settled down to develop and exploit it under fairly orderly circumstances. This was somewhat less true in Texas, however, because of the stretches of land so poor that it would not support intensive settlement, 'land like the Terlingua Ranch that even today is not far removed from the frontier. Still, the ethic born of free land undoubtedly would have passed on more quickly in Texas if free oil had not come along. Oil was not quite so free as the land had been, since there were immediate strictures of ownership, but it still amounted to a gift of the earth. This point is fundamental to the Texas of today and it is one that most Texans don't recognize. Oil was not manufactured or grown or developed. It was there, waiting for someone to stick in a pipe and draw it off. And it too demanded a man with a streak of the pioneer attitude, with the courage and the drive to find it and bring it up. The pioneer and the oilman were not the same, but one followed the other naturally and oil continued the atmosphere that began with free land.

But that has a counterpoint irony too, for oil also hastened into being the sophisticated society of today in which the old ethic doesn't work very well. This is a money society, urbanized, increasingly industrialized and dominated by big companies and big cities. Its problems are not much different from those of any industrialized, urbanized complex—urban blight, decay of the inner city, flight to the suburbs, eroding tax base, an indigent portion of the population increasingly unable to support itself, an electronic life style that discounts the individual. Like nearly all of America now, it is oriented to the collective whole and is marked by man's inability to care for himself individually. But the old ethic carried along by oil was just the opposite: it was oriented above all to the individual. It is this thrust of the old verities into the new realities without the interim time of adjustment given most of the country that accounts for much of the Texas personality and character today.

Obviously, under such conditions, the old ethic could not survive intact and unchanged. To replace it, I believe, Texas evolved a new ethic which might be called the action ethic. In the action culture that grows from such an ethic, the key is movement, accomplishment, building; action, not reflection; the builder, not the thinker. As Colonel Byrd put it, "I like private enterprise. I like to produce something. I don't care if it's oil or cotton or a building. I don't give a damn. That's what people here do. They plunge in, do things, and like as not, they lose their ass along the way, but in the end, they usually make it, they do accomplish." It is not for nothing that Texas has never excelled in education, art, literature, music, medicine, science, architecture, but rather in building businesses, refineries, cities, ranching empires, winning football teams, highways, financial houses, manufacturing plants. These are the flowers of the action culture and pragmatism is its creed. This is why when Texas is moved to do something right like, say, integrate some of its schools, it does so invariably in the name not of right but of business expediency. This is why President Johnson has such contempt for holders of doctorates. It is why people whose orientation is to the mind find Texas so barren, "the despair," said Sam Zisman of San Antonio, "of intelligent people." This is why such people band together as exiles and outcasts, rarely accepted by the real society, where they are regarded with suspicion or perhaps good-humored condescension and taken as impractical, visionary, unreal, unreasonable, and offerers of advice of little value. It is why such concepts as the importance of beauty to the human spirit get short shrift, why college professors are so rarely elected to school boards, why the world of ideas and intellect is so rarely entered, why Texans are so appallingly lacking in self-knowledge and self-understanding.

In an action culture, the builder is supreme and his tool is money. I believe that is the key to the Texan's materialism, far more than anything so simple as greed. He is reverent about money because it is a fundament of his culture. Texans are often generous individually, but rarely collectively. Individual generosity is the individual's business, based on his estimate of his abilities, directed as his sympathies choose, stoppable at any point. But generosity systematized through government helps those whom the builder disdains anyway, people who can't or, as he suspects, won't produce. And it is enforced in a continuing sense despite changing circumstances, and this threatens the care and conservation of money, which to be most efficient must operate in a free market for its own benefit. The Texan reacts violently to any systematic demand for money for a purpose not immediately related to making more money, for something like, say, an adequate welfare program, because of his instinctive feeling that it constitutes an attack on, and a possible weakening of, the action culture itself. Of all the Texans I have known who have made themselves wealthy, few seemed greedy for the luxuries and position that come with money. Instead, money was attractive for what they could build with it, and while the result of their continual building was still more money, I do not think that was their purpose. Their purpose was instinctive, for it was dictated by the culture itself.

I think this explains the commercialism that permeates Texas life, the anti-intellectualism, the coarse emphasis on money. I think it explains the Texas establishment and its reactionary outlook. The establishment, though probably somewhat less strong in the industrialized Houston-Beaumont area, runs not only the apparatus but even the thinking of the whole state. The establishment view works its way firmly down to the smallest aspects of society, to the conduct of the schools, the operation of the churches, the positions taken by the newspapers, the affairs of the towns and counties in even the most rural areas, the activities of builders, real-estate developers, merchants, editors, chambers of commerce.

This is not thought control, but guidance from above willingly accepted. The guidance is patterned to the need of the establishment and often opposes the true needs of the citizen who so willingly accepts it. Texans, however, are such a homogeneous people that they tend to identify with each other, with the state as a whole and with the establishment. Except for the two ethnic minorities and despite the surprising number of nationalities melted into the pot, the Texan of today is generally of Anglo-Saxon or Teutonic stock and in both outlook and background is very similar. Texans are proud of this homogeneous quality, and the men who operate the establishment praise it. It means that the people tend to think alike, to move together and to agree with whatever the establishment decides is for everyone's benefit (meaning, in an action culture, what will make things grow the fastest). There are few divisive elements. Labor is weak, the poor are silent, the minorities are largely disorganized, and since everyone else is inclined to identify with the establishment, there is little of that instinctive skepticism which questions whether the individual's needs are being served. The newspapers, which might be expected to ask such questions, are not only the captives of the establishment but in many cases *are* the establishment—or, at least, are so interlocked in its highest councils as to be indistinguishable. It is this lack of independence that makes the newspapers of Texas uniformly poor, serving as advertisement sheets on the one hand and unquestioning perpetuators of the establishment view on the other. For practical purposes, there is only one political party, which denies Texas that other great challenger of the status quo, the out-party. The result is that the establishment arranges the laws and the rules of operation largely to suit itself, such political issues as are debated are often spurious while the real issues remain unvoiced and hidden, and Texans in general, except for a band of liberals whose stridency suggests how sadly small is their number, accept this happily.

This is not to say, however, that today's Texan has lost his sense of independence or individualism. My point is that he too, no matter his size, no matter whether his true economic interests are being served (as usually they aren't), considers himself part of the action culture and shares with the establishment the full vigor of self-satisfied certainty that the way of the builder is righteous and beautiful. I think that a majority of Texans accept that as primary to their existence.

The irony of this is that it leads Texans to accept in popular culture so much less than what the state's capital, energy, and ability could produce if it were expended. It is wonderful indeed to have Texas' opportunity for greatness and then to achieve no more than the low average of the country's mass in what William Arrowsmith, one of the state's stronger social critics, calls "culture where it counts and affects the lives of everyone: the food people eat, the furniture they buy, the houses they live in, the books they can buy, the style of their city and its public and private buildings."

Considering the potential, the thrust and the drive of the action culture, what has Texas achieved in these areas which circumscribe the daily lives of its people? Well, always with a few, but usually a very few, exceptions, it has managed mediocre restaurants, dull entertainment, unexciting stores, inadequate libraries, limited colleges, uninspired homes, ugly cities and newspapers that are consistently poor in that they neither mirror their own society nor report adequately on the rest of the world. As for buildings, O'Neil Ford of San Antonio, one of the country's better architects, says, "They're trash. The vulgarities that are perpetrated in Texas shouldn't be allowed. We're becoming like Southern California or Phoenix."

There is a startling look of uniformity in the suburbs, where most Texans live, endless identical streets with nearly identical houses set back an identical distance from the curb. The pattern extends into the wealthy suburbs as well, where a surprising number of expensive houses are turned out from a builder's master formula. The avenues leading to the business districts are usually drab with forests of flickering, whirling, dipping, flashing signs interlaced with black cables draped from utility poles. Much of the downtown sections are drab too, though new buildings and a kind of urgent sense of energy make the newer parts seem lively and attractive. Nevertheless, there are few of the parks and squares that give a moment's flash of green respite from the concrete and all over the state there is a dearth of public statuary with its pleasing forms. San Antonio, which is older and was well formed before the action culture took full hold, does somewhat better, though the Conservation Society has fought for years against a plan to build a garage under one of the prettiest squares, at grave risk to its fine old oaks. The great exception to urban ugliness in Texas is the San Antonio River, which winds through the heart of the city. Its banks lie well below the street level and they have been made particularly beautiful, so that to walk there is to leave the city behind and to lighten one's spirit. The Conservation Society was formed years ago to combat the first plan for the downtown river, which was to pave over a section of it, creating in effect a giant storm sewer through the town and giving the businesses which backed onto the river a back alley for their convenience.

If one should want to take a country walk even in so lovely a part of Texas as the Hill Country, he must stick to the graveled roads, leaping out of the way and quite possibly onto a cactus as cars roar by and shower him with flying gravel and caliche dust while their occupants stare in surprise at the spectacle of a man taking a walk. This is to say that Texas, out of that incredible sweep of free land, preserved almost none for public use, a mere few acres scattered here and there across its broad reaches. Most of the beautiful spots in Texas are on private land, used by their owners as if no other course ever occurred to them. I know a spring and waterfall of particular beauty on a ranch in the Hill Country. You turn in on an unmarked road, wind through a pasture that is impassable after a rain, stop at a cattle guard and give a surly old man a dollar and drive to the water. It is worth the trouble. Cool crystal water bubbles over a limestone fault and splashes into a deep green pool below. It is a place for lovers and children and old men in need of peace and of course it should be and could be a public park. But it is not.

Only the highways, themselves the work of builders and well

done, are exceptions. Every few miles there is a little roadside park, tasteful and imaginative, with pretty little shelter buildings. A few are perched on impressive overlooks, like the one at Devil's Canyon, but most of them are simply along the road, a place to pause on the long drive. The Highway Department casts wildflower seeds along the shoulders to bloom in the spring, and plants occasional groves of liveoak trees and even the lovely oleander with its graceful bloom. The action culture, incidentally, views such activities as a great inducement to tourism, which is a considerable industry in Texas.

When Texans broke the free land to their own quite private use, they immediately abused it. They overgrazed it, destroying the native plants and opening it to dust storms and the tide of brushy mesquite that took over from the natural grasses until it covered much of the southwest part of the state, the part now called the Brush Country. That is why the old railroad rights-of-way, laid out at the beginning of the westward movement, turn out to be priceless arboretums, almost the only places left where all the state's native plantlife still flourishes undisturbed. The native wild animals, despite the vast openness of the state, were less fortunate, for they had no refuge even on railroad rights-of-way. Any animal which man conceived of as pest or predator was subject to systematic slaughter. That is what happened to the wolves, panthers, wild sheep, most of the coyotes and now is happening to the majestic golden eagle which, despite the naturalists' claim that its danger to livestock is negligible, is being shotgunned down regularly by professional hunters in West Texas who use small airplanes. The only sizable animal that survives in any numbers is the deer, which is coveted as game. Ranchers lease their land to hunters during the season, often providing a blind and guaranteeing a deer for a hundred dollars or so, and they have come to regard the deer that use their land as a crop and even feed them during seasons of drought.

If the popular culture that determines in what style people will live leaves something to be desired in Texas, the same certainly is true of its formal cultural activities. So formidable are the ladies who ramrod high culture in Texas that I make such a statement with trepidation and hasten to say that I am aware of the good and handsome things that have been done. There is the forty-million-dollar complex in Houston devoted to the performing arts. There is the Alley Theater in Houston and the Dallas Theater Center under Paul Baker, which also operates in a handsome new theater building at Trinity University in San Antonio. There is the museum in Houston under James Johnson Sweeney which is doing interesting things in modern art, and there are fine museums in traditional, modern, and regional art in Dallas, Fort Worth, San Antonio, El Paso and other Texas cities. There is good community theater in Midland. There are three full symphony orchestras in Texas, and there are opera seasons and ballet festivals and even a bit of summer theater. So I certainly do not deny the existence of islands of culture in Texas—but neither have I ever been able to see that very many people were touched by it.

The significance of cultural activity can only be in the effect it has on the society that produces it, and while there is evidence that theater is broadening its audience, the other activities remain narrow and limited. I think this is a result not of any inability to appreciate on the part of the average Texan, but rather because the imperatives of the action culture tend to shape cultural activity in just this manner. Parts of a paper given in 1965 in Corpus Christi by Dr. William Arrowsmith and reprinted in the *Texas Observer* go decidedly to this point. Arrowsmith, chairman of the classics department at the University of Texas, was educated in the East and abroad and discusses Texas with the interest of an insider and the perspective of an outsider. He is inclined to doubt, he writes, the "absolute, disinterested sincerity" of the Texas commitment to the arts, despite its generously endowed galleries, museums and auditoriums, and suggests that much of this emphasis

has been done in the name of civic zeal, a commitment to a place, a reputation, an image. What Dallas and Houston require, they will have; and large cities, with an unabashed hunger for cultural prestige, nowadays require rather sumptuous cultural apparatus. But much of it is precisely apparatus, and should not be confused with culture at all. . . .

The arts and humanities in Texas flourish, I feel, not because the humanities have any real roots in Texas life, but because it is a part of public and civic policy to make them flourish in order to prove something about Texas, or a particular Texas city. In short, the old Texan determination not to be outdone . . . and beneath much of the talk about education and humanities in Texas, I invariably detect the harsh ground-bass of self-interest and commerce and money-making . . . what they really want is industry for Texas. In order to attract industry, there must be good universities and a tone of civic culture. Thus interest in the humanities . . . is so often a matter of chic, snobbery and lip-service. It is chic to have operas, museums, to be *au courant;* but I personally see very little evidence that the immense cultural machinery of Texas has any real base in Texas life.

Arrowsmith finds the low level of the tone of daily life in Texas rooted in materialism. He notes what he calls the First Commandment of Texas—"Thou shalt not interfere with thy neighbor's God-given right to turn a fast buck at the general expense, lest the same right be someday denied even to thee"— and adds:

And all this greed is then metamorphosed into uplift: paeans to progress and civic growth, hymns to Free Enterprise whose fervor emphasizes the vulgarity and greed it is designed to disguise; a loud, hearty air of self-congratulation and the empty parade of altruism.

Culture, he thinks, is imposed on Texans from above,

a vast pretense organized on the spot, it seems, by millionaire magicians in the belief, apparently shared by the audience, that museums, libraries, operas, etc., *are* culture . . . one has the feeling that Texas confounds culture with cultural institutions, just as it patently confuses education with impressive school buildings. Here Texas materialism reveals itself fully in its confidence in the reality of stone and steel and physical plant, and in its appalling distrust of the individual, the teacher, the intellectual, and the artist . . . the Texas hunger for the life of the spirit, or for the reputation of it, constantly reasserts in its very presuppositions the primacy of money and material power. That is why high culture in Texas seems always to have something of manipulated pretense about it. At its worst, it seems a hollow sham created by professional image-makers; at its best, it seems thin and unreal . . . what we have, in fact, is businessman's culture, superficial because it is so rarely disinterested. It all too often contains, along with a real hunger for a higher life, a corrupting core of self-interest.

A man who sees Texas culture from inside one of its best-known cultural institutions and who cannot be identified here, since he must continue to work with the people he describes, has this more sardonic view: "You know, I don't think Texas has ever grown out of the royalty idea—the way a patron of the past would support an artist and get a consequent ego growth of his own. Of course, what this really means is supporting the artist if the artist fits the royalty concept and dumping him otherwise. Take Dallas: that's a medieval place. Each big building represents an inflated ego and each one of those towering egos would like to buy into the arts. I don't think they have the slightest feeling of what a theater or an opera really means. Any place in Texas if 3,000 people attend a cultural event, it satisfies those people. They say, 'Everyone was there.' In fact, only 3,000 people were there and they are the same 3,000 that support all the events and the rest of the populace remains untouched.

"This tight little group—this royalty group—dominates the theater, opera, music all over the state. You can't do anything or get anyone to do anything that would step on the toes of the royalty that controls culture. And this is because everyone knows that in the end, the royalty will pay the bills. In Dallas, for instance, culture becomes the possession of a tight little group—that same 3,000 people pay for the symphony, the ballet, the opera. The average person won't come and he certainly won't support, but the thing is, no attempt is made to reach him. Culture is in the hands of the royalty-ego few and they like it that way and generally intend to keep it that way. They're the people who go to the concert to see who's there.

"And there is a terrible problem with the effete, effeminate and plain homosexual types who manage to take control of so much cultural activity. They are very cliquish people. They don't have to have money, though many do and are brilliant and clever as well. They have no wives, no children. They spend incredible amounts of time maneuvering for what they want. They have a natural devotion to the arts and they get in control and then they run off through simple nausea people who might otherwise become excellent patrons. But they're interested in culture mainly as an adjunct to their social life. This is dilettantism at its worst, which goes right back to the royalty concept, which in turn usually eliminates the craftsmen and the professional men who provide the real strength of the citizenry in any city."

But we have been examining the sometimes dismal tone of the action culture in terms of those whose basic needs of food and shelter and an assured place in the society are fully met. In fact, however, the place at which the action culture's hard conservatism and lack of sympathy and care for the human condition are most evident and most destructive is in politics, which controls government and thus determines what sort of lives will be led by those people who do not function well in such circumstances.

It is in government that the establishment becomes quite implacable. In fact, government *is* the establishment, and vice versa. Only rarely does a maverick politician succeed without the establishment's blessing and it is even more rare when a politician who has succeeded strays more than momentarily from the establishment view. That view, incidentally, is benign enough, for it is simply the voice of the action culture. It holds that man's purpose is to make progress, that progress means physical growth and that business is the vehicle even as money is the tool. What helps business, therefore, is good; the expenditure of money to make more money is sound and for any other purpose is weakening. Not only is the way open to the special interests, therefore, but the way *is* of the special interests, for they are no more than the businesses which are engaged in thrusting the action culture forward.

They are helped greatly by the one-party political system that still flourishes in Texas. Since the days following the Civil War the Republicans have had no serious voice in Texas internal affairs, and despite the swing to Eisenhower in the 1950s and even the election of a Republican to the U.S. Senate, that is still basically true in the mid-1960s. That means that everyone runs for office under the Democratic Party, with not the general but the primary the significant election. But when there is only one party, there is in effect no party. Every candidate must run on his own, for there is no party structure on which he can rely. There is no continuity that runs from election to election with fixed purpose no matter who is the individual candidate. So each man must build his own following, a sort of personal machine, and he must maintain it or renew it every time he runs, which for most state offices in Texas is every two years. That explains the extreme emphasis on loyalty as the sticking plaster of politics. It is the only thing in a non-structured every-man-for-himself system that holds things together and that a man can rely on. When that goes, everything goes. That is the reason for President Johnson's extraordinary emphasis on political and personal loyalty which certainly colors the way he functions in the White House: it is a harking back to the Texas one-party political wars. It also explains the intense bitterness that pervades Texas politics, for the drain on the candidate and his followers, the strain of mastering every detail, meeting every problem and taking all the blame for failure becomes so great that the final excruciation of losing is almost unbearable.

Since the emphasis is on the man instead of his party, personality becomes essential and demagoguery becomes easy and natural as real issues are buried far beneath the things calculated to draw attention. The candidate is lured away from considering and talking about the real issues and this, combined with all the other aspects of the one-party system, make him the easy prey of the special interests. In the absence of a party structure that maintains campaign machinery and raises money regularly, each candidate must raise his own money and this is always the hardest aspect. In this situation, the special-interest lobbyist is like a shark among minnows. He simply puts, or doesn't put, money into campaign funds. It is not pay-off money. It does not go into the politician's pocket. But it is the lifeblood of getting elected in a state in which a state-wide campaign usually costs more than one million dollars and a liberal in Houston reported one hundred thousand dollars spent against him in a race for a mere legislature seat. Later, should the elected official not see eye to eye on an issue about which the special interest cares, he is torn indeed. Will the people remember and reward his courage if he votes in their behalf against the interests? Probably not. They may even agree with the interests. But he can be sure that the interests will remember and that his opponents in all the races of the future will be well supplied with money and support in all forms.

Occasionally a man like Henry Gonzalez of San Antonio's 20th Congressional District, or Bob Eckhardt of Houston's 8th Congressional District, happily makes that choice and tells the interests and the establishment to go to hell. But all the same, I am not sure that these agonized decisions come up so very often. The establishment is, after all, merely the operational form the action culture takes, which means that its powerful solidarity makes for a natural mutuality of interests between politicians, lobbyists, and businessmen.

This is the more so because of a point that is basic in Texas: that money is power and power is money. The two go together, and in Texas it is almost impossible to have one without the other. Money offers a certain power in any community in America, but in other places it also is possible to achieve power—intellectual, political, spiritual—into which money does not seriously enter. In Texas, however, it does not occur to most people to challenge the automatic relationship or to suggest that there are other and nobler ways to influence. Thus the minister talks of God but orients to money, for he is consumed to build a new or bigger or better church and if he is not, his parishioners will get a minister who is; or, having already built, he is consumed by the note at the bank. High society orients unerringly to money; the most distinguished university professor cannot compete with any paving contractor at any country club in Texas. Newspapers are controlled by advertisers who are controlled by banks. Civic leaders, opinion makers, social leaders, the boards of colleges, churches, hospitals, community chests, are business people without fail, operating in an environment in which money is the only scale of success or failure. I know of no voice in Texas that can influence, let alone command, that is not backed with money except, perhaps, the paid administrators of great organizations like universities or hospitals, who are regarded as businessmen once removed, and the occasional maverick politician whose appeal to the people is so great that he can override and ignore the establishment.

While the linkage of power and money is both an imperative of and a consequence of the action culture's outlook, it is also true that this has a quite practical aspect. Every businessman of any size realizes that he can hardly function in the modern economy, let alone make his profits, without the most thoughtful handling of state and federal government with its power to tax, regulate and, particularly, to disburse big contracts.

It is for all of these reasons that most successful politicians are or soon become substantial men. I do not suggest anything so crude as their going on the take (though occasionally it is no more subtle than that) but rather it is that money and power are so intertwined that as a man moves up one ladder, he moves up the other too. Normally, this takes the form of a gentle nurturing by the interests of the political figures who might serve the state well in the future. After all, there is no better way for the establishment to welcome such a man to its midst and bind him to its interests than to help him become a part of it. At the same time, acquiring money is important to the aspiring political figure simply because in a money society a man without money, no matter his position, does not merit the same respect as the man with money. As money is the tool in the action culture, so also it is the rating. It is all very well to be the senior senator from Texas—but to be the senior senator who took off that morning in his own plane from the lighted strip on his own ranch and landed on your ranch to confer, now that is really something. And then the mere possession of money, as anyone knows who has ever discussed a loan with a bank functionary, gives a feeling of superiority that can be overcome only by opposing money. I think that money as such bores most politicians. Their real motivation is power. But in Texas, they need one to achieve the other.

The establishmentarian-politician this system ultimately produces seems fully separated from the very people who most need him and are most at his mercy, the people who live in poverty at the bottom of society. The number of these people in Texas is startling. After a tour of Texas along the Mexican Border (though poverty is not limited to that area) an officer of the Office of Economic Opportunity was quoted as saying, "Texans would gag on their food if they could witness the kind of poverty I saw on that tour. It is shameful and stupid that nearly 700,000 families—29 per cent of the population—should be hopelessly locked in poverty in this prosperous and progressive state. There are human beings existing in the border towns of Texas under conditions as indescribably cruel as can be found anywhere in the world."

These are the people who are being left behind in an ever-widening gap by the furious pace of a society which, like that of the rest of the country, is growing increasingly urbanized and technological. In part, at least, the old drive and opportunity of the action culture grew from the feeling that every man could be an entrepreneur if he worked hard enough. There is still a good deal of that feeling (and I think that the way to success is still more open in Texas than in most places and that this contributes to the heady sense found there) but just the same, in today's patterns of efficiency through increasing corporate size, there are ever fewer entrepreneurs and ever more workers.

This leads to a fundamental disagreement between the action culture and the aspirations of those who live in it, which turns, naturally, on the use of money. There is an increasing feeling that in a maturing society, money should be used to make people's lives better and thus improve the tone and the moral texture—for who prospers when his brother is hungry?—of the whole community. Adequate and well-staffed schools, hospitals and other eleemosynary institutions are important, but the basic way that money improves people's lives is if they have enough of it to live comfortably, through welfare if necessary, through pensions and through decent wages. Out of its building creed, however, the action culture finds it very difficult to accept the concept of diverting money from immediate building. Instinctively it feels that if it is allowed to build enough, everyone will prosper. That is the heart of the reason why, as late as May, 1965, the school board in San Antonio resisted applying to the Office of Economic Opportunity for a badly needed Neighborhood Youth Corps project. It objected to the fact that the Corps would pay the youngsters the then national minimum wage of $1.25 an hour. Board President George Guthrie was quoted as saying that introducing such a wage would wreck San Antonio's economy, adding, "The students would be getting more than their parents."

The establishmentarian-politician who is on the spearpoint of the state's social problems is singularly ill equipped to deal with points of view so violently opposed. For by now, the most significant thing about him is that he is totally and emotionally committed to the establishment. It is not a matter of an eye to his own best interests or of toeing any line. It is hardly even a conscious thing; he is of it and it is of him. That is why he serves it so well: because, finally, he serves it as his own.

It is this commitment that so often reduces good intentions to poor performance. He can see the people's needs, from the poverty-stricken to the average citizen, for it is to them, after all, that he appeals for votes, and he would like to respond to those needs. He likes public recognition at least as well as the next man. But the people's needs soon conflict with the establishment's interests and then his strength of combat ebbs, his conviction fades and though he does not publicly withdraw his support, the measure does not seem to survive in its original and necessary strength. It emerges a pale shadow and is about that useful.

The plain fact is that Texas does not do nearly what it could do and should do for its poor. The action culture, in its modern form, is corrupted; it has exchanged the old verities for new selfishness.

This quality permeates Texas life today and it also affects many people in the middle class who are not poverty-stricken but who do not receive their share of the product of the affluent society. In a culture which ignores the poor, fights labor unions as a matter of policy and finds reasonable the idea that introduction of the minimum wage could shatter the economy of the fourteenth largest city in the United States, it is not likely that the idea of sharing with the workers will appeal. People like mechanics, school teachers, bus drivers, piano tuners, house painters, newspaper reporters, YMCA executives, policemen, clerks, window washers, and all the other simple folk who make the town and the state go are consistently underpaid. Most of them accept it as simply the way of Texas, the penalty for the pleasure of living there.

Hank Brown, a San Antonio plumber with an active social conscience who now is president of the Texas AFL-CIO, talks about the workingman's lot in Texas with rough anger. He is a tall, physically strong-looking man and though he speaks in a slow and sardonic voice, his fist keeps beating the desk. "Let me tell you, we've got the big rich in Texas, but we've sure got the poor poor too. We have 800,000 functional illiterates in this state. We've got a million workers, nearly a third of the work force, making less than the minimum wage set by the federal government. We're the fifth state in the union in industry and we have the most restrictive labor laws in the nation. There are endless rules about unions and striking designed to prevent a strike or weaken it until it doesn't matter. Only 13 per cent of our workers belong to unions and we rank thirty-fourth in per capita income, $400 below the national average. We have a weak industrial safety law and we kill and cripple more workers per capita than any state in the union—but our workmen's compensation payments for injuries ranks forty-fourth among the states. They talk about the big dealers and the big deals. Big deal, hell."

Raw poverty exists in many places in Texas, among Anglo-Americans and Negroes as well, but nowhere is it more sharply etched than in the faces and the lives of the Mexican-Americans who live in South Texas. They are not only an ethnic but a cultural minority, with their own language and customs setting them apart from the Anglo-American majority. Many speak no English. Nearly half the adults are illiterate in any language. Few are trained for anything but agricultural work, which in South Texas, under the impact of mechanized competition elsewhere, pays less than a living wage. At least half the families living in every county in South Texas make less than $3,000, which is the level at which the federal government says real poverty begins. In Laredo, which is often called the poorest city in the nation, some 80 per cent of the 60,000 people are Mexican-Americans, and their median annual income is $2,425. A San Antonio reporter, David Roberts, has written about Cotulla, a little town in the heart of the Brush Country between San Antonio and Laredo. "Total population is 5,972, of whom nearly 4,000 are Mexican-American. Among the latter group, the median family income is $1,585 a year and for those twenty-five years or older, the median school year completed is 1.4. Cotulla reflects poverty from one city limit to the other. Crude, one-room unpainted shacks are spread along the highway. They have the typical leaning look of shanties, no plumbing, corrugated metal roofs. They are crowded together on badly pocked dirt roads (in Cotulla a gravel street is a good street) and yards or other evidence of home landscaping are almost nonexistent. An occasional shrub or planted tree is conspicuous in its loneliness. Most of the men work for menial wages on nearby ranches. Yet, despite low income, the cost of living is high; groceries, for instance, are estimated to cost 10 per cent more than in San Antonio."

In the winter of 1950, I was working for the Brownsville *Herald* in the nearly tropical Lower Rio Grande Valley when a devastating freeze struck. The temperature remained below freezing for five days, killed more than ten million citrus trees and was particularly hard on the poor. One morning I was at the police station when a call came that a child was dying at a certain address. A county nurse was to go and a police officer. I went too, but the others were delayed somehow and I arrived first and alone. The house was just one room, about ten feet by ten. It was in a cluster of like houses, a *corral*, as it was called, which shared a single privy and a water tap which now was frozen. The house had no windows and must have been fetid in the summer, but neither did the opening in front have a door that could be closed against the cold. A few bits of charcoal were burning in a bucket just inside the door, pointlessly, I thought, for it was no warmer inside the house than outside. I walked up carrying a big Speed Graphic camera and both parents came out to greet me. They looked old, but they probably weren't. Suddenly, with real horror, I realized that they had mistaken me for a doctor and my camera for medical equipment. They spoke no English and I no Spanish and in their anxiety mixed with relief that someone had come, there was no way to explain myself. The mother took my hand and led me into the house, stepping carefully around the bucket with its smoldering bits of charcoal. There were several children huddled on the floor. On the bed, wrapped in filthy covers, was a child of a year or two, face flushed, gasping, obviously consumed with the fever of pneumonia. I have thought many times of what I might have done, and today I think I would have done something quite different, but I was very new then and I did the only thing I could think to do: I raised the camera and took the child's picture, the big old flashbulb exploding the darkness for a blinding instant. Then I left, found a phone, urged the police dispatcher to send an ambulance and went back to the paper. When I took the film from the developer and looked at it in the light I saw for the first time that there had been two children in that bed, the other about the same size and also ill. By the time I had dried the film and printed the picture, both children were at the hospital and both were dead.

That was a long time ago and it would be nice to think that now things are different for little children in South Texas, but it really would not be true. In San Antonio, which Texans consider the pearl city of their state, a Headstart program began in 1965 on the city's Mexican-American west side. At one center, Roberts reported, many of the youngsters had never used fork or spoon and at first refused to eat with them. Few of the children had ever used a toothbrush and many were horrified at the idea of a bath. Four doctors who examined 1,000 youngsters in the program found that 15 per cent had never been seen by a doctor, 25 per cent had never had a routine examination and up to 30 per cent had never been immunized against any disease. They reported 52 suspected cases of heart disease, 28 possible cases of kidney disease, 13 positive tuberculosis cases, 11 cases of eye disease, 2 possible diabetics and 18 hernias; 97 children failed the eye test, 297 had severe dental decay, some 200 were chronic bed wetters, indicating emotional trauma.

In mid-1967, describing malnutrition to a panel of visitors who were investigating hunger in America, Dr. Vera Burke of San Antonio's city-county hospital, the Robert B. Green, said, "Often children one year old are brought in weighing less than their birth weight." A San Antonio pediatrician said that he had seen children at the hospital "three, four and five years old and weighing around twenty pounds." So many expectant mothers were anemic, it was reported, that the hospital gives at least one blood transfusion as part of its regular prenatal care. At least a quarter of the babies born there weigh less than five pounds, indicating premature birth or mothers suffering from malnutrition.

There are some 350,000 Mexican-Americans living in San

Antonio and about half of them, or 44,000 families, live on less than $3,000 a year. About 15,000 of these live on less than $2,000 a year and 10,000 on less than $1,000 a year. There are about 107,000 functional illiterates in San Antonio, more than in any other city in the United States. "In one 100-square-block poverty tract," Roberts writes, "80 per cent of the population earns less than $3,000 per family and the median income is only $1,400 a year. Half the school-age children are not enrolled in classes. The average adult has completed only the third or fourth grade. Houses are bunched together in clusters of six or seven. Sometimes a single toilet is shared and sometime a shower stall."

If you drive out on San Antonio's west side you will encounter a section called Linda Vista, which means Beautiful View and is less than an accurate name. Technically, it is outside the city limits, or was when I visited it in 1966, but it still belongs to the city. When you reach Linda Vista if you drive down Mayo Street, slowly so as to spare your axles, you may encounter Narciso Aguillar standing in front of his house and patiently trying to fix his 1950 Ford automobile, as he was the day I met him. I suspect that he is still there and that his life is no better. He was forty-eight and native born (in Austin), a round-faced man with a cheerful smile and manner. His house was made of scrap lumber, twenty feet by twenty with four rooms, and he had added a nine-foot section across the back. Years before a lumber company had erected the house for quick sale and it had passed through many hands since then, often returning to the company for resale. Now its unpainted walls were frayed and its tarpaper roof was held in place with stones. There was a privy behind the house and each week Aguillar poured in a bottle of pine oil and when the hole was full he dug another and moved the privy over it and used the dirt to fill in the old hole. There was no water, except for two barrels standing in front of the house. The covered one was drinking water and the other held washing water. When they were empty a truck came by and filled them for 40 cents each. Aguillar bought the house in 1960 for $2,695, which he was paying out at $28 a month. He did not know the rate of interest or when the mortgage would be retired. He was pleased with the company, for if times were hard and he missed a month, it did not press him.

From time to time he did slip a payment, for there was not much money. The best year he could remember was 1963 when the whole family worked as migrant crop pickers and made a grand total of $2,700. He was not downhearted, however, for things had taken a better turn: his son, seeing the family's needs, had dropped out of high school to work (thus ending his own chances for a future in the action culture) and with what he made, everyone was eating. Aguillar continued to tinker with the old car as he talked. He needed it to get to work, when he had work, since there was no public transportation in this area, but it would not start.

"I had twelve children, all together," he said reflectively, "but four of them died. I don't know why. I was in Morton, Texas, years ago when my little girl got sick. I took her to the hospital and they said she was sick and I already knew that. They didn't say anything more and the next day she died. Then in Corpus Christi once I had another baby got sick, a little girl three or four months old. She had some kind of germ infection, I don't know what, and she died. Not long ago my twins died at the hospital here. Joe and Josie. They were just babies. I don't know what they had, some kind of infection, it turned the insides of their mouths white. They died very quickly. I was sick, then, had the flu and I couldn't work for three weeks and you know, when the head man's down, ever'thing stops. I had to sell my old pickup truck to get us all some food. There wasn't any money, so I had to ask the county to bury my twins, a pauper burial. I didn't like that."

CHAPTER

1

It was a dark night and the white alkaline dirt of the yard, packed as hard and dry as paving, was lighted by a single big bulb set high on a pole, there, said Domingo Arredondo, to discourage the rattlesnakes that slid in from the dry fields in search of moisture. The heat of the day was easing; the temperature had fallen back into the nineties. The light struck the timbers of an old windmill standing over a well long since gone to salt, and threw glaring bars of light and shadow across the pale ground. Arredondo stood with his back to the light as he talked. His face was in darkness, except when he turned and the light struck his hawk-Indian profile. A 1954 Pontiac automobile with a license two years out of date stood in a shed with its hood up. Two 1955 Buick sedans were drawn up before it in a V. Their hoods were up too and young men indistinct in the shadow were running cables from the batteries of the Buicks to the Pontiac in hopes of starting its long-stilled motor. Both Buicks were running. Their carburetors sucked noisily and their old valves and bearings chattered. Smoke came from their tailpipes and blew away on the night wind. Their lights were on to guide the young men's work, but there was a short circuit in one of the cars so that its horn kept blowing unexpectedly, and then the lights on both cars would dim to yellow and the horn's note would crack and run falsetto and the young men would laugh and curse. Children ran in and out of the bars of light, blurs of motion at the corners of the eyes, squealing and laughing, their little feet thudding on the hard dirt. Pale old hogs lay in heaps by the fence and now and then one would heave himself upright and wander into the light bars, snuffling a soft, fluid grunt as he searched for particles of food. And Domingo Arredondo stood with his face in the dark and talked of the way he and his people live.

This is Starr County, on the Mexican Border, rimmed on one side by the Rio Grande and most of the rest by something very near desert. It is the poorest county in Texas and the eighteenth poorest in the United States. Its people are more than 90 per cent Mexican-American and its main and almost only economic activity lies in some 26,000 acres of land irrigated by the river's waters, which are trapped upstream by the Falcon Dam and released as needed. Eight large farms dominate this fertile acreage. They are operated with high efficiency, raising crops nearly the year round, and their owners talk in terms not of farming but of "agribusiness." They raise cotton, many kinds of vegetables and, their most lucrative crop, cantaloupes. The cantaloupes are succulent things, growing round and heavy on vines that lie on the hot sandy soil while river water streams down the furrows. City people find something atavistic and delightful in the idea of food springing from the ground ready to eat as soon as the sun has warmed and sweetened it. But for the people in Starr County who pick the produce of the land, it is not so joyful.

Arredondo is a farm worker. He is a slender, muscular man in his forties, with very little education but considerable wisdom. He lives in a house of about 14 by 16 feet which he built of scrap lumber. It stands in a compound of several buildings, all on a five-acre plot owned by his father-in-law. He has six children living in his little house and he struggles above all else to keep them in school. "That is their only chance. I tell them, 'You do good.' I beat them if they don't do good. Otherwise, they will be like me." A hog snuffled behind him and then the horn blew and Arredondo turned toward it, the harsh light catching the side of his face. "They call us stoop labor," he said, patient, explaining, "because we stoop over all the time in the fields, picking, chopping, cleaning, always with back bent. It is unnatural. You never get used to it. People think you do, they think you don't mind, but your back never learns not to ache. You make 50 cents an hour, 60, 70 sometimes—I've even made 80—it all depends on I don't know exactly what, maybe just what the grower feels like. But now [in 1967] you cannot live on that, even working 10 or 12 hours a day. We buy our food at the supermarket in Rio Grande City, that's where the prices are best and the food is all packaged very nice. They say the prices are higher here than in the big cities. I don't know why. You would think that we who grow food and work with it all the time would have plenty, but we don't. I keep these hogs and sell one once in a while, but that don't bring much. I don't keep a garden. This land ain't good for garden, which maybe is why we were able to get it. Anyway, there's no water. We buy water in town, nickel a barrel, and then you got to haul it home. But mostly it's because the work is so hard. When you come back from the fields you have no strength left for your own land. You come home sick. You would rather rest even than eat. You just come home and fall down. If you could look ahead and see how things were going to get better, don't matter how long it would take, if you could just look ahead, maybe you wouldn't mind so much. But you can't. You can't never get ahead. You can't even live. That is why we made the union and started the strike."

The vegetable pickers' strike in Starr County began as an independent movement. It was backed somewhat by organized labor and eventually affiliated with the grape pickers' movement in California. Arredondo was the president of the local organization. Its aim was wages of $1.25 an hour, but it was not having much luck. Between the Texas Rangers and the hordes of workers who came from Old Mexico to work for even less, the scales even of starvation remaining relative, the strike had been little more than an inconvenience to the Starr County growers.

The old Pontiac's engine coughed, turned over for the first time in two years and then died again. Arredondo, suddenly elated, ran over and exhorted it to try again. Old cars are important, for people have no other way to get to work. Arredondo lives several miles from Rio Grande City where, before the strike, before he was blackballed by every grower in Starr County, he went to meet the crew boss.

"This crew boss, he is a bad fellow, whole thing is bad. He is one of us, you see, but somehow he gets some money, who knows how, and he pays down on a truck and then he becomes a boss. He goes to the grower and he contracts to bring him fifty workers, guaranteed delivery right at the farm on every day there's work to be done. There's always people looking for work. So the boss, he rounds them up and he loads them on the truck, all standing up and jammed together, and takes them to the farm. Then he sees that everybody works. If he don't push them hard enough, maybe the grower won't make no more contract with him. So he works them hard, he drives them, trying to look good to the grower. That makes it easy on the grower. He don't have to see how the people are treated, he don't have to be mean himself to get the work out of them, the boss does that. Then the grower pays the boss and the boss pays the workers after he takes out his cut. If the grower pays maybe 80 cents an hour, the boss keeps 10 or 15 cents of it. Since the strike some growers have gone up to a dollar an hour and even more, and the bosses started taking up to a quarter for themselves. The boss says he gets us the job, he takes us there in his truck, he even supplies water with a piece of ice in it so we can work through the heat of the day. But what it really means is that we are paying so that the grower can have a guaranteed steady labor supply. Because, you see, if you go out there alone and ask for work, the grower won't hire you. The only way you can work is through the crew boss. The boss keeps everyone in line because there are always more workers than jobs, so if you speak up, next day he just don't choose you to go on his truck and then you don't work at all and your family goes hungry. Is all made to suit the grower, but he don't pay for it. We pay for it."

2

Starr County lies a hundred miles inland and is the uppermost part of the Lower Rio Grande Valley. Approaching it from the east, one passes groves of small, dark-leafed orange and grapefruit trees, sometimes lined with rows of towering palms that run for miles, their tufts of fronds like blue-green metal balls glittering and clicking in the wind against a hard blue sky. But all that is left behind upon entering Starr County. It is arid country, its whitish soil covered with mesquite, cactus and scrub grass, and it seems quite unbelievable that its river bottoms could produce so richly when coursed with water. The summer heat is a heavy, constant thing, the temperature soaring daily into the hundreds, leaving the air dry and very clear except on dusty days so that the buildings have a sharp look, as in a good photograph. It presses down, dries the eyes, dehydrates, until even the hardiest people feel it.

Rio Grande City, the county seat, has a curiously shrunken look, like a man whose clothes are too big, as if it was built with more people and more activity in mind and neither materialized. Its streets are often empty, its stores quiet, their keepers somnolent. On beyond is the town of Roma at which the movie *Viva Zapata!* was shot because it looked so much like a Mexican village of fifty years ago, and it still does.

The politics here are simply feudalistic, operated by the New Party and opposed by the Old Party, which are indistinguishable except for faces and names. The county vote is delivered in a bloc, which means the system finds its ready protectors at the state level who see to it that it is left alone to perpetuate its backwardness. The status quo is supreme, for its rulers have things precisely as they want them.

The natural result is poverty, which also is useful in maintaining the status quo. The average family income is about

$1,700, the per worker income about $900, the per capita income about $534. Rio Grande City is not incorporated and so is not a town at all and offers none of a town's services, such as health and sanitation. The county handles all functions of government, and like any feudal system, rewards those who obey and deprives all others. A loyal man can count on leniency if arrested, a welfare berth if needed, even a loan in extremity. A man who challenges can count on just the opposite. It has not been hard to maintain control. It rarely is when work is short, people are hungry and the educational level is below four grades.

The Starr County establishment reacted with predictable outrage to the strike, which was modest enough in its demands and involved relatively few people. But it is interesting that the establishmentarian-politicians who run the state, and who might normally be pleased that people were trying to lift themselves above starvation wages, were equally outraged. I met one who waxed incoherent whenever the subject came up. The point is, of course, that any general and, particularly, sudden uplifting of the Mexican-American in South Texas, of which the Starr County strike might be considered a preliminary move, would be unsettling to the interests of the establishment which in turn are the interests of the action culture itself. Thus it is that a proper establishmentarian could well become unhinged by such a thing as a vegetable pickers' strike.

And in fact, the Texas establishment worked very hard to defeat the strike, at least for a time. But in this respect it is unrealistic indeed, for any fool who walks the ground can see that the people are moving, in Starr County and elsewhere, and that eventually the action culture will have to accommodate them because it cannot stop them.

3

Two women, both slight and pretty, were on the picket line at the gate of La Casita farm. Big signs in Spanish and English forbade entry to the farm, which at 2,700 acres is the largest in Starr County. The road passed through the gate and dropped abruptly to the river's flood plain and ran straight through green fields to a group of low sheds perhaps a mile away, hazy in the heat, and then continued on to the hidden river itself. The women stood under a feathery mesquite tree, which dimmed but did not block the sun. It was hot and quiet, with the rustle of the wind and the soft sounds of their voices. A flag flapped limply from a staff wired to the fence; it showed a black thunderbird on a white circle on a red field with a single sequin for an eye. Signs cried, *Huelga,* meaning strike, and gave the basic aim: *Lo que quieramos es* $1.25 *por hora.*

The women were much alike, something willowy and very feminine in their slender arms and long hands, and at the same time something hard and resilient in their fiber. The older, Mrs. Gregoria Solis, was married and had four children. She was developing the cynical twist of mouth and voice that comes with years of seeing no light ahead. The other, Imelda Peña, was still a girl, seventeen years old, fiery, not yet pressed down.

"I got to the sixth grade in school," Mrs. Solis was saying, "but that didn't mean nothing because I wasn't ever there. My father was a migrant worker, he is picking cotton in California right now, and I have been working in the fields since I was eight years old. Every year my father would patch up his old truck and get it running again. It was stake bed, open in back, and we would drape a canvas over it for cover. He would borrow money from the bank and we would start out in the old truck and go wherever there was picking to be done. We picked everything. We worked all together in the field, my mother too, minding the little ones as she went, and if you stopped to play you got taught better pretty quick. At first my hands would get torn and I would stop and cry, but there wasn't time for that, you had to hurry, because there never was enough money and there were other people waiting to take your job. My father collected the pay for all of us and as soon as we were done in one place we went on to the next, wherever we knew there were crops that were ready, and my father would go and find work for us while we sat under the truck in the shade and waited, and that's all the rest I remember getting. And then there would be another field and we would pick there until dark that day and start again early in the morning. We would move clear across the country, from field to field, and I remember two different years we got to the beet fields in Washington. Then, when it was over, we would come back here and there would be just enough money left to pay the bank, and we would go lean and hungry through the winter. And I would go to school for a month or two, if we happened to think of it, and I would get passed on to the next grade and then in the spring my father would patch up the old truck and we would start again. You can't get nowhere. My father never did. I never did. You know what I want, all I really want? I want all my kids to finish all their school, all they can get, and then go away and get real jobs and never work in the fields."

The La Casita gate stands near a little settlement which also is called La Casita. Its houses are made of a locally produced brick or red cinderblock. They have privies in back and yards of hardpacked alkaline dirt innocent of any grass. On that day the sun baked the little houses and here and there a bush hung languid in the heat. Butterflies and big dragonflies fluttered about the two women, who brushed them aside.

Imelda Peña said, "When I was thirteen I started picking cotton, not far from here. I had an eight-foot canvas sack with a big strap that went over my shoulder. I crawled on my knees, picking out the cotton bolls and putting them in the sack. It dragged on the ground behind me and got heavier and heavier and the strap cut into my shoulder. They paid $1.50 for a hundred pounds and at first it took me nearly all day to make a hundred pounds. The cotton boll grows in a little cup of thorns and to get it you have to reach in among the thorns and when you go quickly you keep stabbing your fingers. Of course you can't wear gloves, you'd never catch the boll with gloves, and the thorns break off in your fingers and under your nails and every evening when the picking was finished you'd sit by a lamp and dig them out with a needle." She held up her slender, pretty hands, looking at them. "Is hard, you know? When we planted onions, we used to have to put the seed on the end of the finger and push it into the ground, and at the end of the day your fingernail had separated from the quick and your whole finger was swollen. We got 45 cents an hour for that. That was three years ago, now they make a hole with a tractor and we drop in the seed."

Mrs. Solis nodded. "It is very hard work. In the winter we work in the lettuce fields here. We chop out the weeds and loosen the dirt. We use short hoes with handles only a foot long. With a short hoe you work fast without damaging the plant. That means you work bent over all day." She crouched in demonstration, knees bent, left hand braced on left thigh, right vigorously chopping only a few inches from the ground, and the strain on her back and the backs of her legs was obvious. "It would be more comfortable to put your knee down on the ground, but that slows you and the crew boss is watching and he yells at you." Suddenly, in raucous, surprising imitation of the crew boss, she shouted, "Hey, you, get to work! Get off your knees. You're not being paid to kneel, you can kneel in church, here you work!" She grinned, her mouth twisted. "But if you stand up straight and put your hands on your back, you are not working. The boss threatens to fire the whole crew at once, fifty people working, and you look around at your friends and you don't do nothing. You bend down and chop. You work ten hours a day and you get 50 cents an hour and when you finish your back and your legs ache so you can't hardly stand up and you feel like you're crippled."

There was a sudden roar, very loud, and an old Stearman biplane, a crop duster with an open cockpit, painted bright yellow, came over the houses and dipped toward the fields. The pilot was wearing goggles and he looked down incuriously at the women as he passed overhead. In a moment a cloud of bug-killing dust streamed from beneath the plane and spread in the propwash. The women hardly noticed the plane. They were talking about cantaloupes, which bring the grower the most money and the picker the most pain.

Imelda Peña waved at a big butterfly that seemed to be thinking of landing on her face. She had an airy look; she must have weighed about a hundred pounds. "You always stoop when you work in the cantaloupe fields," she said. "The vines run along the ground and they must be gathered and put on top of the furrows so the water can run freely between them. You put a foot on each side and stoop over and walk like a duck, putting the vines together with both hands, and you go all the way bent over. The vines are tender and you must handle them carefully so they won't break or damage the melons. Everyone starts his furrow at the same time and you've got to stay in line, if you fall behind the boss yells, and if you hurry up so that you can get to the end and rest, the boss makes you help someone who is slow. He is afraid the big boss will see you resting and think he is not getting enough work from you. When everyone gets to the end of the furrow you can straighten your back and get a drink of water.

"Cantaloupes get very heavy. Before the strike began, I got 50 cents an hour for picking them. One day my little sister, Oralia, she is thirteen, wanted to work too, and they offered her 25 cents an hour because she was so small." A look of infinite scorn flashed across her face and suddenly one realized that dressed and placed in the right situation, she could be a regal woman. "I wouldn't let Oralia work for that—I made her go home. The work is too hard. The fruit gets ripe very quickly when it is ready and sometimes you pick the same field three times in a single day. You go along stooped over, very fast, and you give each fruit a little twist, just right, and if it is ready it comes off in your hand and you put it in your bag. The bag is canvas, it hangs from the shoulder and it has a metal hoop to keep its mouth open. I guess it holds about 35 cantaloupes and they each weigh a couple of pounds or more, so the strap starts to cut into your shoulder. And when you lean forward to try the next cantaloupe the bag swings forward too and you have to brace yourself real quick. Sometimes it throws you right down on the ground. The bag spills and the fruit roll out and the boss yells. You get up very fast and put all the fruit back in the bag and start picking again.

"The bag fills up and then you got to carry it to the truck. You can't drag it, that would bruise the fruit, you have to carry it. You have to balance it just right, too, because it's heavy and you've got to hop over each furrow so that you won't kick the vine and disturb the cantaloupes that aren't ripe yet. Sometimes you hop over ten or fifteen furrows to get to the truck. At the back of the truck there is a long narrow plank and you walk up this, leaning out to balance the bag, and at the top you ease it down and let the fruit spill out and you straighten your shoulders."

4

Mrs. Herlinda Dimas lived in an adobe house on beyond La Casita. She was pretty in a quiet, withdrawn way. She had been working in a Dairy Queen in Lubbock three years before when Pedro Dimas came in for an ice cream, met her, married her and brought her home to his mother's house. He had been a migrant picker then and he continued to work in the fields. They had two babies and when the strike began, Dimas joined it and now there was even less money. The house in which they all lived had two rooms and a lean-to kitchen that the older woman had built with discards from a nearby brick plant. It was hot and airless and there was no touch of color or comfort or grace inside or outside. A mesquite tree stood in the yard like a robber, giving neither shade nor pleasure, and the sun had burned dirt and wood and plastered adobe the same pale gray. A calendar hung on an inside wall. Electricity came into one room and there was a light bulb and an old refrigerator. They cooked on charcoal, used a privy in the back and drew water from a crude rural system that, whenever it worked, produced water directly from the river. Sometimes it would settle out an inch of mud in the bottom of a glass. She had come a long way from the Dairy Queen.

They ate beans and *tortillas* and occasionally vegetables from someone's garden, and yes, they had meat—she hesitated, remembering, and nodded—perhaps every two or three weeks. She rarely left the tiny house, for there was neither transportation nor money for things like movies or beer, and the only other attractive place, cool and lined with green, was the river, and that was on the other side of the great farm that lay on its banks and there was no passing through. She stood by the door, her shoulder finding familiar grooves, her eyes unseeing, waiting for her husband.

The electric washing machine was new. It was a tub and wringer, both in shiny white enamel, with the price, $149.50, still scrawled on the lid in marker ink. They had bought it for a pittance down and a bit more every month and now there was no more money and soon someone would come and take it. But perhaps this did not matter to the girl. Did she enjoy the machine, was it helpful? Her eyes were big and solemn. She nodded, yes—but instantly she added that it did not belong to her, it belonged to her mother-in-law. A few scrawny chickens cackled in the yard, but they belonged to her mother-in-law too. Suddenly one realized that the house also belonged to her mother-in-law and from the tightening of her lips that this too was significant, and that the problem was old as poverty itself and no kinder because of it.

How bright the Dairy Queen, the people, laughter, talk, children biting into the sweet, the big cooling machines throbbing, the young man coming in from the fields to win her—would she stay here where there was only one house in sight and it was empty and her shoulder was learning the grooves in the door? Her face was neutral and all Indian. She glanced out the window. "My husband is building a house," she said. She did not come outside to look. It was to be one room, perhaps 12 by 16 feet, and the uprights were already in place, framed at the top with two-by-fours. Every day the girl had gone to the brick factory and come back with all the rejects she could carry. Pedro had made a hole in the ground and filled it with water and used the mud for mortar. He had raised parts of two walls.

But the house shivered when it was touched. Even the new brick walls swayed. The upright timbers that were to brace the walls and bear the weight of the roof were old and rotten and already they had palsied the whole structure. There were places where a man's fingernail could dig into the heart of the wood.

EPILOGUE

The Texans. Good and bad, cruel and kind, some of them hungry and some of them rich—they are Americans in prototype, outlining in their raw extremes the lives of us all. They are the product of their past and their past is that of all America, if told in louder voices and brighter colors. We are a crude people, Americans, young, strong, arrogant, loud, insensitive, untempered by time and defeat, but yet, not quite cynical, still altruistic in our way, still enthusiastic and hopeful and confident. The Texans come in extremes; and in their extremes they delineate the larger nation, and that is why they are important.

I like Texas, and most people who go there like it. Perhaps it is the overriding sense of opportunity and of action that is so attractive, for that is the kind of people we are. Anyway, motion means possibility, and possibility is hope. There are signs that Texas is maturing. The two ethnic minorities are on the rise. In Starr County, even to strike would have been unthinkable a few years ago. Both Negroes and Mexican-Americans are putting their people in public office in increasing numbers and this is much more widely accepted. The poor in general, and there are as many Anglo-Americans among them as otherwise, are being heard a little more clearly. Even the establishment itself, though white-lipped and angry, is showing signs of yielding a little to the future. You see that, oddly enough, in the inferiority feelings that surface in even the most adamant establishmentarians, as if they know they have a hole in their sock through which a clay heel is showing. There is an anxiety for their image, an unlettered feeling, a little core of apprehension that they may be laughed at and worse, that somehow they are cause for laughter. "You know," a man said to me, worrying about the impending visit of a middlingly important Easterner, "we're so goddam, you know, crude, gauche and all. We don't know what the hell to do—how to entertain this guy, how to treat him."

At the other end of the establishment spectrum is Stanley Marcus, president of Neiman-Marcus, which is considered among the nation's great stores. One of the most powerful men in Dallas, the shining citadel of the action culture, Marcus is that rarity, an enlightened voice from within the establishment. He is articulate, thoughtful, cultured, possessed of a strong social conscience; he has a superb collection of art in and outside of his home on a lane puckishly named Nonesuch, and his library is a big, pleasant room with shelves of books to the ceiling that reflect the range of his interests. In early 1968, Marcus told some two thousand suppliers that the six Neiman-Marcus stores would lean henceforth toward buying from companies which did not discriminate against minority groups in their hiring, and would consider this as important as merchandise quality, service and price. He wrote them bluntly, "We would rather do business with a company which is actively and sincerely pursuing a policy of equal opportunity than to continue to do business with one that is not." He shook up retailers from coast to coast, which says something about America, and as for Texas, the implications for the action culture were revolutionary.

Despite the heritage of ranches, Texas is an urban state today, and as change comes it will focus in the cities. These cities are not beautiful, but they are lively. The thing that strikes visitors first is the physical openness, even within the city, the flat, far horizons at the end of wide streets and the big blue bowl of the sky. And then there is the air conditioning. Erik Jonsson, mayor of Dallas and a power at Texas Instruments, likes to say, "The north will rise again when it learns about air conditioning." I've long suspected that it is no coincidence that the rise of the south accompanies the perfection of commercial air conditioning. After all, it is hard for people who are melting to compete. There was a time, the old story says, when Houston's climate was considered so foul that British diplomatic officers stationed there drew hardship pay. Now air conditioning has conquered climate in automobile, home, office, factory, church and even, in Houston, the ballpark, and it changes the very style of living. Houses have small windows and enclosed porches, clothes are heavier and more formal, people go outside less often and with less pleasure. Far from giving a strictured feeling, however, this only seems to enhance the psychic charge of the cities, which comes from opportunity's vigor and enthusiasm. Sometimes this feeling is almost vulgar, so strong does it get, a kind of sweaty, coarse thing that seizes you and sweeps you along. You feel this in most Texas cities, but nowhere more strongly than in Houston.

Because Houston is an industrial city, it is somewhat unlike the rest of Texas. It is a center for oil equipment and supplies, and it has a vast complex of refineries and chemical plants that use their by-products. Petroleum provides at once the power and the raw materials for the petro-chemical industry, though chemists have been unlocking petroleum compounds so rapidly and developing such useful products that Dillon Anderson, Houston attorney and former special assistant to President Eisenhower, foresees "the time when to burn oil and gas will be like burning Chippendale furniture to warm the room." The chemical industry that starts at Baton Rouge, Louisiana, and sweeps down the Texas coast nearly to Corpus Christi is the biggest in the country and it centers on Houston.

The multiple needs of an industrial society are not quite so encouraging to the elemental qualities of the action culture. A single industry has single needs, and this is particularly true of an extraction industry like oil, but a strong many-sided economy's needs are so diverse as to counterbalance each other and keep any from controlling. Power is more spread out. Industrial labor leaders, for instance, hold power in a way that is parallel rather than subordinate to plant managers. And those managers are more interested in a society that is stable and attractive to their work force than one that is oriented strictly to making money. Robert Eckhardt, United States Congressman from Houston and long a prominent liberal, believes there are more arch conservatives in Houston than in Dallas, but they have less influence. Eckhardt has been running for years in across-the-spectrum districts and has always been able to put together combinations of support despite his anti-establishment views. He has an interesting theory that part of Houston's strength and flexibility grows from the fact that the most powerful people there tend to be lawyers instead of, as in Dallas, bankers. The senior member of four big law firms sit on the boards of most of the bigger businesses in Houston, so that in a sense they constitute a sort of superboard. "Lawyers are philosophic and pragmatic," Eckhardt says. "Businessmen are dogmatists, true believers, ideologists. A philosophic pragmatist works better every time than a dogmatic ideologist."

There is ferment here, as if yeast bubbles just below the asphalt. Construction crews are always working and buildings go soaring up. They are tall and even interesting, but none catches Houston quite so well as the domed stadium which the Harris County voters were kind enough to build for Judge Roy Hofheinz, promoter, entrepreneur, showman, politician and, lately, sportsman. The county financed the $45-million stadium with revenue bonds which were to be retired by the rental the judge pays on his long-term lease. Most Houstonians feel that the judge's imaginative marvel is well worthwhile, since it attracts both fame and money to Houston, and they may be right, though one can't help pondering the decaying slums that stand nearby.

Hofheinz is a big man with a paunch he lets hang slackly

before him. He has a powerful quality of raw energy and he enjoys the part of the excessively crude boômer. He talks in a big, brassy voice, mixing outrageous boasting with little self-deprecatory remarks, and it is easy to see him as a buffoon until one notices his sharp litttle eyes. His office, in the stadium, is almost embarrassing. The fifteen-foot desk is inlaid in marble. Light panels in the ceiling are in the three primary colors, and by working rheostats in concert he can bathe the room in a weird symphony of constantly changing color. The wall behind the desk is of translucent Mexican onyx, and lights behind it can be turned up to catch the stone's fine grain or muted until it merely glows. In a corner are two handsome urns. "These here are Etruscan burial vahses," he said. "I like to say vahses, show's I ain't ignorant. I'm telling you those are Etruscan vahses, else likely you'd pick 'em out as spittoons." Six-foot temple dogs from Thailand sit at each end of the desk, and there is a superb Thai carving on the wall as well as various other Oriental objects. His secretary said brightly, "When the Judge went to Thailand last year he bought twenty-six thousand pounds of Thai antiques and had them shipped home in big crates." She laughed admiringly. "We heard that right after that the Thai government banned the removal of antiques."

That was Hofheinz's buffoon side, betrayed only by the bright little watching eyes, but in his box overlooking the field, the boomer quickly became evident. This was the man who built a fortune out of nothing, made himself a political power and an associate of President Johnson, and finally rammed through his dream stadium where, that night, 25,297 fans sat in air-conditioned comfort, seventy-two degrees, fifty per cent humidity, while a summer rain slashed at the dome outside. It was night and from the outside distance the dome glowed softly, like a flying saucer hovering on the horizon. Inside, the natural grass was slowly dying but the fake grass carpet glowed bright green so far below the Judge's box that the players looked like little capering figures. Hofheinz sat in a yellow-velvet swivel chair with a gold-plated telephone and a gold-plated ceramic catcher's-mitt ashtray and benignly watched his own Astros play the Atlanta Braves in a lackluster game. Then, in the last inning, the Braves hit a run and then another. There was a long hit and two Astro outfielders running for it collided and dropped the ball and two more runs came in. There was another hit, which one of the same outfielders dropped again, letting another run in, and a moment later there was a sixth run. Hofheinz hardly blinked. The crowd was screaming for the head of the hapless outfielder, who, by chance, had been wildly acclaimed as the hero of the game the night before. Someone in the box protested such fickleness and Hofheinz suddenly tilted the velvet chair forward and grated, "They oughta boo him. He messed up. Yesterday don't count for nothing—today is what counts."

As the big cities grow the country population shrinks. Small industry goes out occasionally to a small town, but the gain is more than matched by the loss to mechanical agriculture. By the mid-1960s more than ninety per cent of the cotton crop in South Texas was picked by machine. In the high plains country around Amarillo, they developed a machine to pick tomatoes and then developed a tomato that better suited the machine. "It's not such a hot tomato," a friend told me, "but economically it's by far the best." As a by-product, it sends tomato pickers to the city.

So today's Texan is a city man and in most of his outward aspects, he is not unlike city men everywhere. He is a few pounds overweight, lives in a suburb, spends his weekends working on his lawn and his evenings with his television set, has a regular job and meets regular mortgage payments on his house, car and furniture. But I think that he is a little different, too. It is not that he seizes the opportunity around him so often, for this is very difficult and demands peculiar qualities of ambition and strength. Rather, it is that he is a little more personally independent. He is a little more willing, given provocation, to punch the boss's nose and move on to something new. He does as he damn pleases, and what he damn pleases very often is to conform to what every other Texan is doing, for he is very like them—but now and then it pleases him to do something different and the terms of the action culture are that, on such occasion, he does it. In the aggregate, he leaves his mark on the great cities of Texas.

If the city men are much alike, their cities certainly are not. The difference is clear: Dallas with its slick glitter and its focus on money and business; Fort Worth with its comfortable wide streets and easy manner; El Paso with its desert air, nearer San Diego than Houston; Amarillo on the way to Kansas; and Corpus Christi on the sea, none to be confused with another. But there is still one more, which all Texans seem to accept as the heart city, the place they all like and remember, and that is San Antonio. It represents what Texas once was and, in manner and attitude, what Texas would like to be and sometimes pretends to be but rarely is. It is old, sophisticated, sensible, self-indulgent. Its streets wind to the cartage trails of centuries past and it understands that since life is not forever, one might as well have some fun on the way. Of course it is a big, modern city—but it still is properly viewed in terms of nostalgia.

Some years ago there was a proposal to air-condition the Alamo. *Air-condition the Alamo?* Profane its sacred, so to speak, confines with mechanical pampering? Deny it the warm, scented air and the musical sounds of the street that Jim Bowie and David Crockett knew? Oh, of course, it would be somewhat more comfortable, and it's true that San Antonio has never found fault with comfort. In fact, the city's very beginnings might be said to have grown directly from the comforts of the San Antonio River, which gushed full grown from the ground. Indians had lived here for centuries before the Spaniards founded the first mission in 1718 and thus started the city. The river still wanders gracefully along. At one time the hippo house of the San Antonio Zoo admitted to a barred section of its waters, making it perhaps the only river in the United States in which a hippopotamus lived. The downtown section is marked with little bridges and below them is the river walk at water level shaded by cypress and willow trees, and it is hard to believe that just above one's head a major city bustles about. But just the same, air-condition the Alamo?

By 1778 San Antonio was said to have more than two thousand people, which was two-thirds of everyone in Texas, not counting wild Indians. By then it was a distinctly secular place, an outpost, an oasis for travelers and a garrison. The latter is important, for it became increasingly a military town and it still is today. The Alamo was one of history's most gallant if not most useful battles and afterwards San Antonio remained a staging place for combat with Mexicans and Indians. Eventually Fort Sam Houston, which became the belle of Army posts, was built. At one time the Indian chief, Geronimo, was held captive where peacocks and tame deer now wander. The Rough Riders began here. Lt. Benjamin Foulois made the first military airplane flight here, General Billy Mitchell was court-martialed here—and now, in faint irony, San Antonio is one of the nation's most imposing Air Force centers.

In these years, San Antonio became a comfortable city. The Menger Hotel on Alamo Plaza probably was the finest hostelry between New Orleans and San Francisco at one time; and well before the turn of the century there was an opera house, first-class restaurants and the Buckhorn Saloon, famous all over the world for its extraordinary collection of wild animal horns. Many a man who was heading west, or so says the legend, would give the Buckhorn Saloon as his forwarding address, sure that he would get there eventually. The generations of military men fitted right to San Antonio's patterns. It is only in our time that home-garrisoned military duty has taken on a civil-service tone; in years past the military was a genuine social force in the community, its impact ranging from bordellos to high society (and San Antonio had plenty of both). At the upper end of the scale, it was fine indeed. In the days when young Lt. D. D. Eisenhower was courting Miss Mamie Doud, who was visiting on McCullough Street, there was a distinct and rather gallant manner, albeit provincial, about the social side of the officer corps. There were balls and white uniforms and a great deal of ceremony; and when the officers, in their hard-blocked campaign hats with their corps colors woven in the braid and their English boots and Prince of Wales spurs that jingled when they walked, mounted their big horses and wheeled around the parade ground at Fort Sam, oh, it was something to see.

There was a sense of manner in San Antonio, of form and propriety and therefore of civilization at a time when the country all around it was still somewhat uncivilized. And then, in the way of the soldier home from the war or the pioneer in from the range, there was something lighthearted and comfortable about it, and looking back, one has the sense of endless parties among the palm fronds in the Menger patio, and if this is not quite true, I think it close enough to be meaningful.

This is why San Antonio is different from the rest of Texas. It was established and its attitudes were set in easy, pleasant ways before the action culture really got started. Today it lags behind the other big cities of Texas in the things the action culture holds dear (bank deposits, for instance), and it has neither the polish of Dallas nor the wealthy bustle of Houston, and it probably likes it that way. Of course, it is part of modern Texas too, but one can't escape the feeling that just the same, it considers the action culture somewhat vulgar.

Anyway, the action culture has distinct Anglo-American connotations, and San Antonio is a Latin city. Some forty per cent of its people are Mexican-Americans, toward whom the Anglo-Americans have maintained a rather ambivalent attitude. They have absorbed a good deal of the Latin's easy complaisance and they are delighted with his culture, customs, language, music, food, dress, parties—with nearly everything about him, in fact, except his presence. Always with a few exceptions, Mexican-Americans ranked low on the social scale and were expected to keep their place. That has changed considerably today, in large part because of a big, romanesque man named Henry Gonzalez, who wears plainly in his face his Spanish and Indian ancestry. Gonzalez, who remembers that as late as 1937 the San Antonio Chamber of Commerce issued an official report saying the reason the city suffered so during the Depression was that it had so many Mexicans and that a reasonable solution would be to send them to Mexico, was a juvenile probation officer, which gave him a good chance to see how his people lived. In 1950 he filed for a place in the state legislature. Mexican-Americans just didn't run for office in San Antonio and people (meaning Anglo-Americans) were horrified. Gonzalez was the only Mexican-American name on the whole Democratic primary ballot in Bexar County that year.

"I borrowed two hundred fifty dollars to make the race. I spent one hundred dollars on the filing fee and one hundred fifty dollars on a few placards, a few bumper stickers and fifty thousand little cards and that was it. I remember that at one of the very first political meetings of that season, I came up behind old Maury Maverick, Sr., one of the great names in San Antonio politics, with a tongue like a cactus, and he was saying to somebody, 'Who the hell is this crazy fart Henry Gonzalez?'

"But, you know, I got around. I handed out about forty-nine thousand of those cards. Each one had my picture and the place I was running for, Place Three, and something about good government for all, and on the back there was a little poem, I forget now, but to the same effect. And in giving out those cards, I found that the best campaigning of all is getting out and talking to people. I would go down to Produce Row at five in the morning and I'd give the workers my cards. They would turn them over and over. They couldn't all read, but they saw my picture. And they would say, 'Hey, guy, so you're the one that's running—but for what?' and I'd say Place Three, and they would ask what that meant and sometimes they'd say, 'Yeah, but this legislature, what's all that?' So I'd explain the legislature, I'd give them a little civics lesson there at the market place before the dawn came up. And I could see their pleasure. I was the first politician they had ever met and I learned that most politicians don't politick. 'You're the guy that's running,' they would say, 'you're the guy right here on the card.' One day I met a man and his wife and I gave him a card and he nodded at his wife and said, 'Give her a card, too,' and I learned that you don't overlook anybody. I also learned not to campaign in bars. Everybody wants you to buy him a beer—and nobody has paid his poll tax [then required in Texas].

"Well, I was running against two men. One night there was what they called Candidates' Night at the Woodlawn Shopping Center, where all the candidates appeared and got five minutes to speak. When one of my opponents spoke he attacked the other, and when the other spoke he attacked the first, and neither one of them even mentioned me; it was as if they were in the race by themselves and I didn't exist. A candidate for another place, he wasn't even running against me, spoke just before I did, and pretty soon I heard him saying that an election is like a horse race and you want to know who you're betting on, you want a thoroughbred, a good name. Well, he went on, everybody knew his name, he was from an old family that had come to San Antonio right after the Alamo fell. 'My name is well known,' he kept saying. And I got mad. I was the only Mexican-American running and I thought that was what he was getting at. So I ignored my opponents and I went after this guy. I said that we don't have ancestor worship here, that is not the American way, and I said, 'But since he wants to make an issue of it and talk about how long his family has been here, I'd just like to say that when Columbus sailed the ocean blue back in fourteen hundred and ninety-two, half of my ancestors were with him—and the other half were waiting here to greet him!' "

It was quite a race. When the votes were counted Gonzalez was in the runoff and this time his surviving opponent paid a great deal of attention to him and managed to defeat him. But just the same, Gonzalez had kicked the door wide open. He continued to run for office and today he is the impregnable U.S. Congressman from San Antonio's district and it is quite common for Mexican-Americans to run for office in San Antonio and otherwise assert themselves.

Latin attitudes have not changed so much, however, as to negate the old interest in a little gaiety, and San Antonians continue to boast that while they may not know much, they do know how to throw a good party. They prove this every April with their fiesta, which is by far the best such celebration in Texas and attracts people from all over the state. It is not related to Lent or to religion, having started in commemoration of the Battle of San Jacinto in which, to put it bluntly, the Texans whipped the Mexicans. Since San Antonio is now fascinated with things Mexican and prates constantly about international goodwill, it no longer talks much about San Jacinto but concentrates instead on everybody having fun. And that is just what they do.

The fiesta runs through more than a week of activities. There are several elaborate parades, including one at night by the light of torches and another on the river so that the floats really float while the crowd stands on the river walk and watches them go by. There is a band concert in which all the school bands join and it is surprisingly stirring to hear a thousand horns at once backed by a hundred drums. There is a high-society aspect, somewhat the equivalent of debutante presentations elsewhere, in which the city's eligible maidens are presented as members of a fantasy court. In a pretty little theater on the river, the stage on one side of the water and the seats on a grassy bank on the other, an elaborate spoof of this presentation is given with gusto and skill so that those who find debutantes interesting and those who don't may be equally pleased. Woven in and out of the ceremonies, activities, and fun are round after round of private parties all over the city.

The biggest and the best party of all, however, is public. It is given for four nights in *La Villita*, which means the little village, and is a remarkably well-done re-creation of an original block of old San Antonio. It is about three blocks from the Alamo and it is a gentle place with narrow streets, shaded patios and friendly little adobe houses. It is owned by the city and inhabited the year around by artists and artisans who often work in its courtyards, and if it is perhaps slightly self-conscious, it still is soothing to the spirit and it lacks entirely

228

the determined cuteness of some commercial evocations of the past.

For the four nights of "A Night in Old San Antonio" La Villita loses its placid sense of antiquity and boils to the motion of a genuine old-fashioned fiesta. Thousands upon thousands of people crowd into its narrow streets and walk, laughing, shouting, dancing, jostling, listening to the endless music and watching the endless shows, eating the bewildering array of foods and following them with draughts of beer. Every ethnic area involved in San Antonio's rather diverse heritage is there. Of course, Mexico predominates. There are guitarists and flamenco dancers and women who sing in marvelous brassy voices of the *dolor* in their *corazons*. There are stands serving up every sort of Mexican food, *tacos* and *anticuchos* and *jalapeñas* guaranteed to give *dolor* of the stomach. But there also is an Irish Flats where the beer is green and the tenor is good, and a Chinese village with egg rolls and German places serving heaps of sauerkraut while a brass band marches around. There are Czech cookies and French pastries and New Orleans coffee and doughnuts, and ham with honey and biscuits, and cotton candy. There are real flowers to buy for your lady and *piñatas* and balloons and a chance to drop a pretty girl into a tub of water if your aim is accurate and you are so inclined, and if you do not look alive, Henry Gonzalez will lure you onto a stage and test your knowledge of the Spanish language, thus embarrassing you before the crowd. Fast-draw specialists using .45 thumbbusters loaded with blanks act out their deadly pantomimes and Western bands play and *mariachis* stroll the streets with guitars and songs of love and in the Juarez Plaza a little girl dances the flamenco on and on, her heels drumming on the shiny red tiles. And the people come—women with seats too big jammed into jeans too tight, new airmen with their heads still shaved, deputy sheriffs with huge gold-butted *pistolas*, a man in a clown's suit and a clown's face, a general officer surrounded by a covey of colonels, a little boy on his father's shoulder trying to decide if he should cry, men with faces mottled by the sun and men with black suit coats hung on a thumb over their shoulders, ranch hands with bellies hanging over buckles won at rodeos and high-school girls with pert round bottoms who feel so knowledgeable and are so innocent, lovers who go hand in hand and eye in eye, and cowboys and hardware salesmen and university professors and housewives, and wandering through them all, nearly floating in his sense of contentment, a rotund man in leather shorts who carries a hundred pretzels speared on a fencing foil and will give you one for a nickel.

Time is set awry and the clock is out of true, and if by some odd chance Col. Crockett should come marching back to San Antonio at the head of his Tennessee boys, surely this is where he would come to stand belly to the bar and roar for a drink. Air-condition the Alamo? Good Lord, yes. Why not? And so they did.

The reason that San Antonio's fiesta delights the spirit is that the people put it together for fun, because they wanted to, because they find meaning in it beyond the dictates of the action culture, beyond making money or gathering prestige or asserting power. It is their dream and they find it very satisfying. Occasionally, for there are not many of these in the world, other dreamers of special dreams turn up; and it is in their nature that having dreamed, they go out and do something about it.

There is Dr. Michael DeBakey at the Texas Medical Center in Houston, a slender man of high energy and intensity who is one of the great pioneers in cardiovascular surgery and has saved a great many lives with his synthetic artery. He, and others on his surgical team, dreamed for years of an artificial heart that would relieve at least some of the natural heart's burden in that dangerous period after surgery or an attack. The heart has extraordinary recuperative powers; given even some help, its chances for full recovery would be magnified. DeBakey developed a wondrous little machine, a small affair of plastic and fiber with a membrane inside that goes rhythmically back and forth, back and forth; plugged into the human heart, it fills with the patient's blood and sends it coursing along, stroke by stroke, while his own heart mends. One of these days, DeBakey is sure, there will be a full artificial heart.

Down in the Lower Rio Grande Valley years ago, there was a man named Frank Ferree whom the Mexicans called "El Samaritano." He stood six feet four inches and he was nearly fifty years old when he came to the Valley in the early 1940s: he had been a sect preacher in California and a farmer in Colorado and Wisconsin and a logger and a cowboy. He was a thin, shambling man even then with stirred conscience, and he looked about him at the way the Mexicans lived on both sides of the river. They wore rags and were on the edge of starvation. Women's milk dried and babies cried and wasted and people were covered with sores. Children's eyes were glued shut with disease; once he found a child's finger grown into her palm. Ferree began to collect medicine, including the then new penicillin, and put it in a knapsack and began walking among the people and treating them. Soon he was doing this full-time, living on his seventy-dollar World War I pension. His own clothes turned to rags. His shoes collapsed and he began wearing Mexican thong sandals. He walked for many miles, on both sides of the river, and the people began to know him and watch for him. Gradually the prosperous people in the valley recognized him too: doctors and surgeons donated their services, canneries gave him damaged cans, bakeries offered day-old bread. Someone gave him an old bus, and filling stations gave him fuel. He opened clinics in Mexican border towns and would appear with the old bus groaning with food and medicine. He was a one-man relief agency and as the word about him spread food began arriving by the tons and finally in carload lots. He had no family and no pleasures save this single one of helping people. Late at night he would get back to the little house he owned and open a can of food; Ronnie Dugger once counted six opened cans of beans in the house, each with a spoon, each obviously an unfinished meal. How many lives did he save, how many children cured, families kept together? Over the years, the figure might be hundreds, or it might be thousands. He was a strange, evangelical figure and he stuttered sometimes and his thoughts tumbled out in jerks, but he knew what it all meant. Years ago, Ferree told Dugger: "I have found, I believe, this is my belief, this is my belief, that the only thing you can take with you when you leave this earth is the good you have done here, the good you have done here on earth—that's the only thing you will go away with."

In 1956, Dr. Harry Huntt Ransom, who had started at the University of Texas twenty-one years earlier as a grader of papers in the English Department and by this time was Dean of Arts and Sciences and therefore dealing directly with the Board of Regents, made two unusual requests. He asked to take over the University's rare books and then he asked for $25,000 to buy more of them. Never before had more than $7,500 a year been spent on these special collections of rare books, manuscripts, original research and documents of all sorts that are the foundation of serious scholarship. But Ransom, who is quiet, intelligent and persuasive, got the money. Then, having received an inch, he took a mile and then another mile and then quite a few more. When he became chancellor of the University in 1961, there was no holding him. He built the special collection furiously, at the rate of two to three million dollars a year in purchases and gifts. One Regent still refers to him as the "chancellor of second-hand books," but the humanities collection is among the top five in the United States and its resources focused specifically on the twentieth century probably are not equaled elsewhere in the world. The university has the best Texana collection anywhere, the best Mexican collection outside of Mexico, one of the great Latin-American collections. The New York publisher, Alfred Knopf, gave it his library. Elias Tobenkin, though he had never been to Texas, gave the library his Russian and modern-politics collection and endowed its maintenance. It has an immense collection of George Bernard Shaw and another of D. H. Lawrence and countless pieces of the work of other authors and whole sections devoted to such diverse things as the history of science with special attention to radiation from the Curies to Oak Ridge, the history of the book, of graphic arts, of printing, theater, dramatic arts, cinema, the history of philosophy—and collections of presidential papers and data. The University also will be the site of the library housing President Johnson's papers. Clark Kerr, former president of the University of California, no small collector itself, has been quoted as saying, "Each time we hear about a new library find in some odd corner of the world, it turns out Harry Ransom already has Texas bookplates pasted over it."

"You see," Ransom explains in his soft, polite voice, "we felt that research was just as important in the humanities as in the sciences. As we've built laboratories in the sciences we've built the humanities laboratory and I'd say we've spent about equally. After all, it's as important to have research facilities for history students as for biology students, for literature studies as for engineering." But his interests were not limited to basic research books. When he decided the closed stacks of the main library inhibited undergraduate reading, he built a handsome new undergraduate library, stocked its open shelves with two hundred thousand of the most read books, kept it open from eight in the morning to two the next morning and approximately doubled the students' library use. He housed some of the special collections in the new building, which uses stone and glass in a pleasing way, and arranged for paintings on the walls and sculpture in the gardens. "Cheap, too," he said, with a pleased little look, the perfect administrator, "we built it for $18.74 a square foot." But the youngsters have the real measure of Ransom's interest. They call the new library "Harry's Place."

Out in the little oil town of Odessa one night, I talked to a woman of middling size and middling age who had yellow ringlets and eyes that glowed like blue lights behind the crystal chips of her glasses. The West Texas wind fluttered the ruffles on her blue chiffon dress and people went by, nodding and smiling, proud of her and no longer questioning her good sense, and passed into the strange theater she had caused to be built on the desert. Her face was made of arcs and circles and smiles and enthusiasm and she combined without the slightest oddity a little girl manner and a will of iron.

"You know what I tell my students?" she said. "Some people ask for peanuts and they get peanuts. And if you ask for the stars, you can have stars."

Stars for Marjorie Morris. How else to explain in such an improbable place a theater which was as faithful a copy as possible of that old Globe in London where William Shakespeare's plays were first presented. That old Globe burned for the last time in 1613 and neither plans nor even sketches of it survive today. Yet it must not have been dissimilar from this building in Odessa, called the Globe of the Great Southwest, which was opening for the first time with a rousing version of *Julius Caesar* by a company brought out from the Dallas Theater Center. The theater was filling with people who were well and simply dressed, sun-darkened as so many in the desert are, but obviously city people who were interested but not awed.

When they were seated a television crew asked a section of the audience to applaud and then stand, simulating an ovation they might give the players when the play was done. They did so, smiling, clapping, enjoying themselves, and after the cameraman nodded and lowered his machine and the man with him had waved them back into their seats, the rest of the audience burst into applause of its own for their nice performance for the camera. In high good humor a number of them rose again and bowed gracefully to the applause and Mrs. Morris cried with a smile, "See what fun Shakespeare can be?"

Then the play began, strong theater that captured the audience. The wind outside came across the empty country and blew against the building. Odessa is the supply center for the oil fields that dot the whole Permian Basin. Its population went from 8,500 to 85,000 in two decades and now it is an engaging, clean-looking town with wide streets. The buildings are almost all so new that everything has a fresh, prosperous look with attention to architecture and detail. Even the highway, which is lined with truck depots, tool houses, pipe yards and supply yards, seems neat and clean. But it is a working town; it is, as the banker told Carl Hearn, a beer town, not a spudnut town. It does not seem like a center of culture.

That never bothered Mrs. Morris. She was a high-school and then a college teacher in Odessa, infecting her students with her own great love of Shakespeare. She does stress, as she puts it, *"only* the good, the true, the beautiful," which makes it necessary to excise some of Shakespeare's gamier portions. Nevertheless, he did plenty of clean plays, enough to keep any theater busy, and one day in 1948 the idea of building a replica of his theater struck. She took what was at best an impractical dream to an Odessa architect named J. Ellsworth Powell, a catlike man with a hunger, one suspects, for something more meaningful than the big homes he was building all over the state. He took up the study and spent years integrating the facts into a hard building plan. It would be octagonal, with 14-inch walls of plastered cinder block and hand-adzed beams, functional and creamy, supporting a peaked roof made of cedar shakes with a cupola on top. The audience would sit in a steep horseshoe around a stage that was exactly the size of the original and had the heaven and hell of the Elizabethan theater. Every one of the 418 seats would be within 45 feet of the stage. It turned into a first-class theater building and it was all Powell's. But its spirit belonged to Marjorie Morris, for she had to make it possible.

It would cost $175,000, even with donated and discounted materials, and she set out to raise the money. The Houston Foundation gave her $30,000, and there was a gift of $5,000 and two of $1,000, and the rest came in nickels and dimes and hundred-dollar checks. They started building but Powell would not let them go into debt. As they got a bit more money they built a bit more building, and each bit was painful.

"People looked at me and said, 'She's crazy.' They said, 'How can you get money for something like this?' And many of them looked me right in the eye and said, 'I don't care for Shakespeare,' can you imagine? I went to their houses. I went in dust storms and when the sun was blazing and during northers when the sleet burned my face. And some of them slammed doors in my face and some of them said things that would make me drive away and stop the car by the side of the road and cry until I thought my heart was broken."

An attorney said, "That woman is crazy. She comes and knocks on your door when you're ready to go to bed and offers to put your name on a plaque on the door of the theater if you'll give a hundred dollars. She reads Shakespeare and skips the nasty words. You might as well have Atlantic City without the water as to have a Shakespeare theater here where nobody has ever heard of Shakespeare but about twenty people and twelve of them thought he was a football player for Notre Dame."

Mrs. Morris said, brightly, smiling, "But I forgave them. Just the same, those years weren't easy. I had my doubts too. I would get depressed. And then after we started the building, after I had taken people's money and spent it, what if we couldn't complete it? Why, that would be like fraud. We had gone too far to stop. I went to my pastor [of the First Baptist Church] and he said, 'Well, at a time like this the proper thing to do is to ask our Maker what his feelings are on it.' And right then we both got down on our knees in his office and asked for guidance and after that I never had any questions about what I was going to do. I stood up straight because I felt God was on my side."

When the play was done the audience applauded and broke up into knots of people walking out, talking and looking happy. Presently they were gone and then the players left and the ushers and finally Mrs. Morris locked the door and went home. The stars stood bright as crystal lanterns in the dry air and shone on this strange eight-sided building from Elizabethan England huddling stone—solid and permanent on the streets of a shiny little desert town. And the wind blew on, as it does in West Texas, without any possibility of end.

INDEX

A Note About the Author

David Nevin's first sight of Texas came in 1927 at the age of two weeks, when he rode a wicker basket in a Pullman car to San Antonio, where his army officer father was stationed. The association was continued by his wartime service in the Pacific theater on the USS *Texas*. After sailing the Caribbean and the Pacific in the merchant service, he studied at Texas Technological College and Louisiana State University, then spent eleven years on various Texas newspapers: the *Brownsville Herald,* the *Dallas Times Herald,* and the *San Antonio Light.* Mr. Nevin free-lanced for a couple of years before joining *Life* Magazine as a member of the Miami bureau. He later came to their New York office as an Associate Editor, and has recently been promoted to Staff Writer.

DATE DUE